1916

PORTRAITS AND LIVES

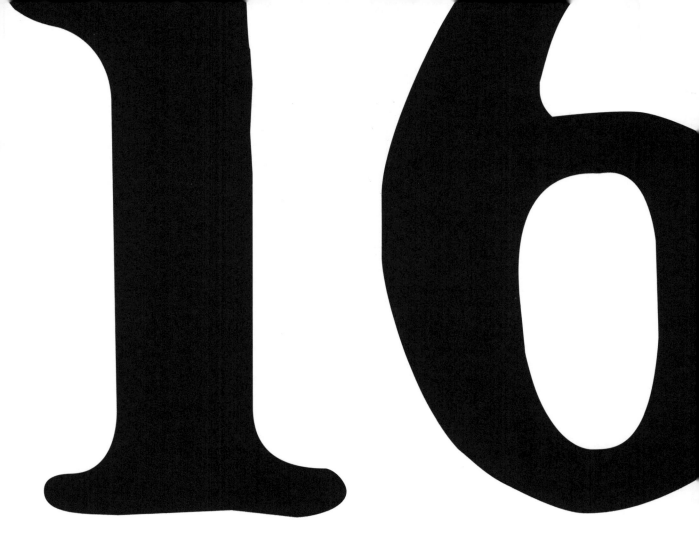

16

PORTRAITS AND LIVES

Edited by Lawrence William White and James Quinn
Introduction and Afterword by Patrick Maume
Illustrated by David Rooney

1916: Portraits and Lives

First published 2015

Royal Irish Academy, 19 Dawson Street, Dublin 2
www.ria.ie

ISBN 978-1-908996-38-1

British Library Cataloguing in Publication Data. A CIP catalogue
record for this book is available from the British Library.

Editor: Helena King
Design and production: Fidelma Slattery
Index: Julitta Clancy

Printed in Italy by Printer Trento

This publication has received support from

10 9 8 7 6 5 4 3 2 1

The forty-two portraits in this volume were commissioned by the Office of
Public Works and the Royal Irish Academy. These original artworks, which
mark the centenary of the 1916 rising, have been acquired for
the Irish State Art Collection.

The biographies in this book are selected from the Royal Irish Academy's
Dictionary of Irish Biography, a comprehensive, scholarly biographical
reference work for Ireland, treating the lives of persons from the earliest
times to the present day, and encompassing every sphere of human activity.
New lives are added twice every year to the online version, which now
comprises some 9,400 articles covering over 10,000 lives. Access to the
online version is available, free of charge, to all schools in Ireland.

CONTENTS

Editors' Note

This volume is a selection of forty articles from the Royal Irish Academy's *Dictionary of Irish Biography* (*DIB*) dealing with forty-two men and women whose careers, in one way or another, were deeply involved with the Easter rising of 1916.

In rendering this selection, we have drawn from the vast diversity of lives covered in the *DIB* generally to compose a broadly inclusive picture of the 1916 rising, representing the spectrum of personalities and perspectives that were involved in the event. Our selection reflects the diverse backgrounds and careers, and the competing political perspectives, of the personalities involved, and the varying natures of their involvement.

The *DIB* includes articles on hundreds of persons whose lives were affected by the Easter rising, including many who fought in the rising as republican insurgents. From this large quantity of articles, we have selected the lives of thirty men and women to represent the perspective of the republican revolutionaries. Twenty-one of these are men who died in 1916 as a consequence of their participation in the rising. They include the seven signatories of the proclamation of the Republic; the nine other men who, along with the signatories, were executed for their parts in the rising; four men who were killed in action (including Richard Kent, who is treated in the article on his executed brother, Thomas); and one insurgent who was murdered upon being taken prisoner.

The Easter rising was remarkable for the number of women participants among the insurgents. We have selected nine of these women who were involved as soldiers or in supporting capacities (one of whom, Julia Grenan, is included in the article on her long-time associate Elizabeth O'Farrell). All were connected to the Irish Citizen Army, a reflection of the feminist ethos of that body and its top leadership. The nine women all survived the rising, and the articles describe the contributions of their later lives, in some cases pursuing notable careers in politics and civil society.

Most of the republican soldiers of 1916 represented in the *DIB* survived the rising and contributed in multifarious ways to the life of the Irish nation in the years that followed. Our selection for this volume does not include the *DIB* articles on such prominent figures as Éamon de Valera, W. T. Cosgrave, Michael Collins and Seán Lemass, some of whom played only minor parts in the rising, and for all of whom the rising constituted a relatively brief episode near the commencement of their respective public careers. Consequently, including their lengthy *DIB* entries would have added considerable material to this volume that was not directly relevant to the events of Easter week. The aforementioned figures and other survivors of Easter week are treated in an Afterword, which briefly describes the roles they played in the rising and discusses the impact of their participation in the rising on their subsequent careers.

The republican insurgents represented only a minority segment of Irish nationalist opinion at the time. We have selected the lives of three nationalist leaders who opposed the Easter rising. John Redmond as leader of the Irish parliamentary party was the foremost mainstream Irish politician of his generation. The Easter rising was as much a blow against his political philosophy and strategy as it was against the British state, and his career provides the essential political backdrop against which the rising took place. The events of 1916 rendered his achievement of an Irish home rule act largely irrelevant and heralded the demise of the political party that had dominated Irish nationalism for the previous half-century. Bulmer Hobson, from his base in the Irish Republican Brotherhood, and Eoin MacNeill, as commander-in-chief of the Irish Volunteers, were both intimate with the conspirators who plotted and executed the rising, but opposed their plans and attempted to prevent the rising, a choice that had a significant bearing on their subsequent careers and historical reputations. Also selected is one murdered non-belligerent nationalist, the pacifist radical Francis Sheehy-Skeffington, the most notable civilian fatality of Easter week.

The regime against which the insurgents rose is represented by six lives. These include the three senior figures in the administration of Ireland in 1916: the lord lieutenant, Viscount Wimborne (Ivor Guest), the crown's representative in Ireland; the chief secretary, Augustine Birrell, the British cabinet minister responsible for Ireland; and the under-secretary, Matthew Nathan, the top-ranking civil servant in the Irish administration. The British army that suppressed the rising is represented by John Maxwell, the general appointed commander-in-chief in Ireland as the rising transpired, who in its aftermath oversaw the restoration of order, the courts martial and executions; and by the Irish-born John Bowen-Colthurst, the controversial officer whose brutal murders of five unarmed prisoners (including two of our subjects) did much to sway public opinion against the government. The local civic authorities are represented by another Irish-born figure, Walter Edgeworth-Johnstone, commissioner of the Dublin Metropolitan Police.

Over the past century, a vast historiography has recounted, assessed, interpreted and debated the 1916 rising. Our selection includes articles on two historians who made considerable contributions to the scholarly debate. Desmond Ryan was, as a young man, a participant in the rising, and as a historian revised his own early uncritically nationalist interpretation to one informed by a socialist republican perspective, while pioneering the historical approach of recounting the events of the rising from the perspectives of a myriad of individual participants. Francis Shaw (the only person included who was not a direct participant in the rising, being only nine years old at the time) became posthumously one of the most provocatively challenging voices of the revisionist debates of the 1960s–70s by critiquing the entire ideological underpinning of the insurgency and of the tradition of physical-force separatism from which it emerged, as expressed in the writings of Patrick Pearse, the 1916 leader most lauded by separatist apologists. Both Ryan and Shaw, from their differing perspectives, incorporated a biographical element in their historiography, asserting their respective arguments by positively reassessing the roles of selected participants in the events of 1916: Ryan reasserting the socialist internationalism of James Connolly in the face of the latter's subsumption into nationalist martyrology; Shaw rehabilitating the patriotism of Redmond and MacNeill against their vilification in nationalist apologia as traitors to the national cause.

The inclusion of these two historians, with their differing revisionist perspectives, reminds us, the editors, as we hope it will remind our readers, that the study of history is an incessant scholarly process, involving disinterested research and continual reassessment, in which there are no final answers, only ever-tentative hypotheses, and new or renewed questions.

JAMES QUINN AND LAWRENCE WILLIAM WHITE
DUBLIN, FEBRUARY 2015

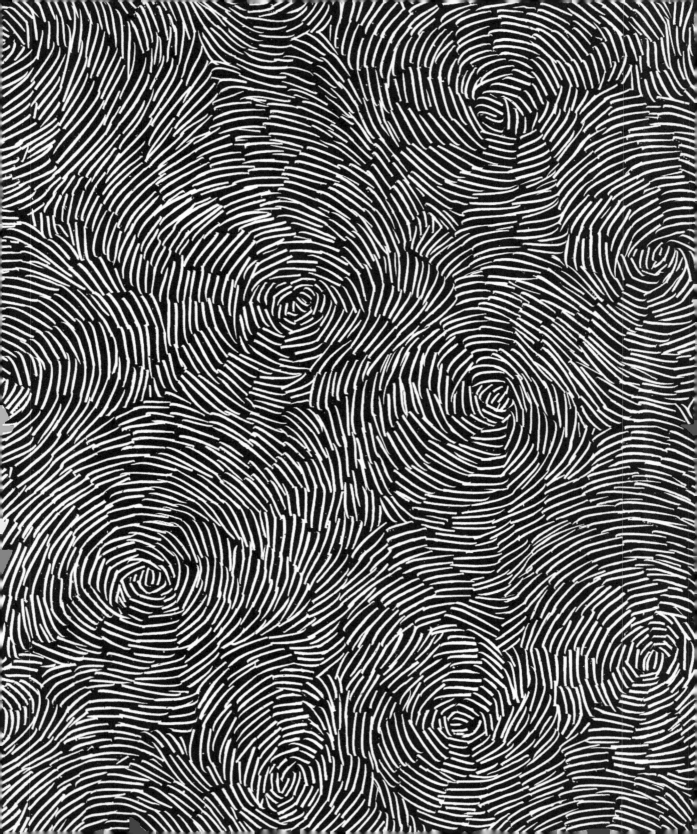

Artist's note

When the Royal Irish Academy invited me to illustrate these lives, I had no idea how complex my relationship with the subject matter was. Working on the first portraits, I soon discovered I harboured prejudice towards my subject.

My formative teenage years were spent in Eyrecourt, Co. Galway, at the height of the Troubles. My father, at that time a Garda Sergeant, is from Fermanagh. He crossed the border to join the guards, and met my mother, the daughter of a 'Dev-opposing' Tuam shopkeeper. I was reared with an aversion, frequently voiced, to the continuation of the armed struggle in the 'spirit of 1916'. So much so that even as an adult, the mere sight of a photograph of Pádraig Pearse would bring those negative feelings to the fore. As I worked my way through the 42 figures for this book, I had to examine this prejudice.

Working on the portraits of the men and women of 1916, I began to feel a growing empathy for the subjects. I was surprised to find that I was often touched by the selflessness, the willingness to sacrifice for a greater good and the idealism personified in so many of them. It was a time when the kind of men and women I know—artists, musicians and writers—were so motivated to act for an ideal that their own lives were comparatively unimportant. It also struck me that this was a time when military idealism and notions of honourable death in battle were common. Advice from a friend to read James Stephens's *The Insurrection in Dublin* at an early stage gave great first-hand account colour to the project, as did being able to dip into the Bureau of Military History's online witness statements.

My interest in film has always influenced how I work. The way I frame, compose and, most importantly, light a picture is a direct result of a love for cinema. The material I use is scraperboard, an engraving technique in which black ink is scraped away to reveal a white chalk-board beneath. My preference for this technique followed from an interest I developed in linocut printing while studying at the National College of Art and Design. After I graduated, I used the technique for decades, as a freelance illustrator for the *Irish Times* and *Hotpress*, reflecting weekly the tumultuous changes in Irish society.

Over the years my work has featured here and abroad in many publications and projects. However, as a book illustrator for The Folio Society in London, my use of the scraperboard technique became more refined and better suited to illustrate historical novels or classic texts. This resulted in recent years in more history or heritage-related projects. In 2010 the BBC commissioned 92 engravings for the five-part television series 'The Story of Ireland'. This work opened up a new vein for me, which I have been happily mining ever since, with projects as diverse as the Titanic Experience Belfast, King John's Castle, Limerick, the Lindisfarne Gospels at Durham Cathedral and the Stonehenge visitor centre.

Scraperboard seems particularly suited to history subjects; the process of revealing is in the technique itself. The figures, built up from thin, white cut lines, emerge from the black-ink darkness. As I scrape away with my surgical scalpel, the sense of bringing the past back to life is often present. I do prepare a pencil drawing initially, which I trace on to the board, but there is still a revelation in the completion of the artwork. Almost always, there is a surprise in store, as the figure emerges with some unintended idiosyncratic detail or expression that a chance flourish of the blade has created. In such moments it is tempting to feel there is an element of the conduit rather than the creator in the process. Most of the engraving work is carried out at night. Once I have absorbed enough reference material on a figure it is often a case of removing my analytical presence—getting out of the way, letting the image almost materialise.

The process of researching and creating these portraits has been a most enriching and illuminating one, and has allowed me to ask, and answer, some difficult questions. It has been a wonderful journey for me, and I hope my work does some justice to the extraordinary lives we have illustrated.

Throughout the project I had wonderful help at every turn from managing editor Ruth Hegarty, Helena King and all the RIA staff connected with the project. The expert advice offered by James Quinn and Lawrence White, in particular, often steered me towards solutions that I could not have foreseen. The OPW and the Per Cent for Art scheme made the commissioning of the portraits possible.

Finally, my heartfelt thanks to the enduring patience and support of my partner Susanne, and to the RIA book designer Fidelma Slattery, whose initial idea it was to get me involved in the project.

DAVID ROONEY
MAY 2015

The 1916 rising changed the face of Irish history

1916: EULOGISTS AND CRITICS

The Easter rising of 1916 occupies a peculiar place in Irish historical understanding. It is still regarded as the foundational event of the Irish state, its sites and leading figures easily recognisable: the General Post Office and the proclamation of the Irish Republic; Pearse and his rhetoric; Connolly the socialist, facing the firing squad in Kilmainham jail strapped in a chair; Countess Markievicz in military uniform; Yeats's verse elegies; the rise of a Sinn Féin party and a new army of Volunteers to renew the struggle under the leadership of the rising's veterans. Simply by occurring, the 1916 rising changed the face of Irish history, and nothing which happened afterwards could alter that.

For decades thereafter Irish politics were dominated by those who had been 'out' in 1916 or in the later struggle, and who laid claim to the mantle of 1916. Until the changes of the 1960s marked a new watershed, 'modern' Ireland was seen as beginning in 1916 in contrast to the *ancien régime* that preceded the first world war. This concept was symbolised by a 1953 *Irish Weekly Independent* series on the legacy of the rising; the heading of each article juxtaposed pictures of the GPO in flames and of Michael Scott's new modernist Busáras building, with the implication that the second derived directly from the first. The contrast was emphasised by the living memory of the old order and by the presence of dwindling numbers of ex-unionists: some having cherished for a decade or two the illusion that the new state would break down and the union be restored, or lamenting that the decline of the British empire had been heralded by Irish appeasement and surrender; others claiming that the stability of the new order rested on foundations provided by constructive unionism and on the expertise of those who had rallied to the new state of affairs after 1922.

The first Dáil Éireann at its initial meeting in January 1919 formally declared itself the successor to the republican provisional government of 1916. In the first week of the civil war, as Free Staters and anti-treatyites fought for control of Dublin, the latter pasted up posters in the capital declaring: 'EASTER WEEK REPEATS ITSELF'. Éamon de Valera prided himself on his status as 'last surviving commandant of 1916' (a claim that could be disputed by some such as Tom Hunter, W. J. Brennan-Whitmore and Sean McLoughlin, who had held the rank but were not garrison commandants); official Fianna Fáil histories such as Dorothy Macardle's *The Irish Republic* (1937) presented 'Dev' as the consistent embodiment of the programme of 1916, temporarily knocked off track by the apostate treatyites but brought to triumphant fulfilment by successive Fianna Fáil governments. Those of his political opponents who, like W. T. Cosgrave and Richard Mulcahy, had fought in 1916, asserted their own claim to the legacy of Easter Week and maintained that the fulfilment of the freedom sought by the rising had been made possible by the achievements of the 1922–32 Cumann na nGaedheal governments. Labour for its part proclaimed itself the party of a highly sanitised (until the 1960s) James Connolly.

Schoolchildren were taught to revere Patrick Pearse as a Christ-figure and to study his writings, which presented nationalism as equivalent to Catholic Christianity in its gospels, its martyrology, its unbroken orthodox tradition from which heretics (such as O'Connell, Sadleir and Keogh, and the nefarious John Redmond) were periodically ejected. Pearse's own writings were duly added to the canon and his name inscribed in the martyrology, and one biographer famously predicted his canonisation.

A less official but nonetheless influential tradition, represented by figures such as P. S. O'Hegarty, Pearse's former pupil Desmond Ryan, and Kathleen Clarke (whose husband and brother had both been executed for their roles in the rising), maintained that Pearse was simply a frontman for a more enduring presence: that the Irish Republican Brotherhood had been the longstanding embodiment of the national will to freedom and, through Clarke, Mac Diarmada, and others, the driving force behind the rising. It had, after all, been the funeral of the IRB veteran Jeremiah O'Donovan Rossa that served as the major dress rehearsal for the rising and the occasion for Pearse's laying claim on behalf of the future rebels to the 'Fenian dead'.

A more embattled subculture of socialist or Marxist republicanism saw James Connolly (presented in somewhat less expurgated form than in the attempts of Catholic commentators such as Aodh de Blacam and Fr Lambert McKenna to reconcile his views with Catholic social theory) as the central figure of a rising whose hopes remained unfulfilled, and would only be attained by the creation of a socialist republic. A smaller group, characterised most notably by the playwright Sean O'Casey, suggested that Connolly was actually to blame for the non-fulfilment; by allying with the separatists he had allowed his radical agenda to be subordinated to middle-class nationalism, and in throwing away his life and those of other Citizen Army members he had deprived the labour movement of its most determined leaders.

These were not the only groups who saw the rising as uncompleted. There were republicans, including 1916 veterans such as the commentator Brian O'Higgins (who had actually been in the GPO, where his principal role—as a respectable and notably pious married man—was to act as chaperone to the female members of the garrison and bear witness that their reputations were uncompromised), who held that the post-1922 state marked an unmitigated defeat of the rising's agenda. Few would have agreed with O'Higgins's uncompromising declaration that 1940s Ireland was if anything less free and more anglicised than it had been before 1916; that de Valera as taoiseach and Douglas Hyde as president differed only in title from their precursors, the chief secretaries and lords lieutenant; and that Charlie Kerins and other IRA men executed for killing gardaí were no different from Volunteers who shot policemen during the rising, and their executions no different from those of the 1916 leaders. Nevertheless, his re-tellings of Irish history in his *Wolfe Tone Annual* were recognisably akin to Pearse's canon of the separatist faith, and were sufficiently akin to the wider nationalist image of Irish history for the *Annual* to become a consistent bestseller even though many of its readers did not share O'Higgins's politics.

Others argued that there was indeed a parallel between hardline republicans and the 1916 rebels, but drew a different conclusion from the parallel. From Stephen Gwynn's *John Redmond's last years* (1919) onwards, a tradition of Redmondite apologetics contended that the Irish parliamentary party had been on the verge of attaining home rule by peaceful means when they were stabbed in the back by irresponsible fanatics; that the deaths of Tom Kettle and Willie Redmond on the battlefield, and of John Redmond, weakened by grief at his bereavement and political defeat, on the operating table, were true martyrdom for Ireland's sake rendered all the more bitter by the vituperation of an ungrateful nation. After electoral defeat in 1918, some Redmondites joined moderate unionists in campaigning for dominion status for Ireland (which the Irish party had endorsed in its 1918 election manifesto) and were later able to claim the 1922 Anglo–Irish treaty as vindication.

While civil war republicans compared pro-treatyites to the Redmondites as politicians who had entered into negotiations with the ancient enemy and betrayed the sacrifices and achievements of the fighting men for the sake of self-advancement, surviving Redmondites pointed out that 1916 had set a precedent for the republicans' defiance of majority opinion on the grounds that a future majority would give them a retrospective mandate. Subsequent Irish governments tacitly agreed, by their silences if not their words, that there was some substance in this argument. The involvement in the Cosgrave government of increasing numbers of middle-class Catholic professionals who might loosely be described as Redmondite (and the absorption into Fine Gael of most of the remaining neo-Redmondite elements in Irish politics) meant that Redmondites could claim some degree of credit for the creation of the new state. Since Redmondite apologists complained of British as well as separatist betrayal, it was possible to incorporate elements of the Redmondite historical image into a worldview tracing its pedigree back to the Easter rising. The portrayal of an idealistic and statesmanlike Redmond let down by untrustworthy British statesmen, and of Redmondites such as Kettle who served in the British army as sincere, and even heroic, but misguided, has been taken up so often by later republican apologists that it is a shock to rediscover the ferocity and extent of contemporary separatist invective denouncing Redmond as a conscious traitor who was deliberately selling Ireland and sending her to destruction, Kettle as a drunken place-hunter, and Irish soldiers as mercenaries recruited from the lowest criminal elements to fight an unjust war of aggression. It is this invective which is echoed in Pearse's denunciation in *Ghosts* of the Irish party as lost souls already so far removed from anything human that their self-justifications can only be discerned as meaningless noise by upholders of the true national faith.

By the 1960s most Redmondites and ex-unionists had died off, and the survivors of the generation that participated in 1916 were themselves passing from the public stage amidst mixed assessments of their legacy. Recent studies of the 1966 commemoration of the fiftieth anniversary of the rising have shown the extent to which it reflected the desire of the survivors definitively to assert their place in history, and of the government of Seán Lemass to claim continuity with what had gone before and present itself as fulfilling the aspirations of the rebels. Certainly the government's economic achievements represented a step towards the economic development and national confidence that nationalists had predicted would be one of the results of independence—even though they had been achieved by abandoning the economic and cultural protectionism which the bulk of the revolutionary generation had presented as indispensable means to that end, and indeed an end in its own right. This disparity was noted by a variety of sources; while leftist republicans expressed scepticism that Pearse and Connolly would have seen capitalist Lemassian Ireland as the fulfilment of their aspirations, the failure of the 1956–62 IRA border campaign contributed to some tentative reassessment of the tradition. (It was also the case that in a more consumerist Ireland Pearse's exhortations to self-sacrifice, admiration for the Connemara peasantry, and unchallengeable faith against all odds sounded less like religious truisms and more like fetishisation of suffering, poverty and defeat.)

The reconciliation of past and present was symbolised by Seán Ó Riada's triumphal score to George Morrison's 1959 documentary film *Mise Éire*, and by the RTÉ 'docudrama' *Insurrection* (1966), which depicted the Easter rising as if it were a contemporary news event being covered by RTÉ reporters.

The 1960s, however, also saw the emergence into public view of another critique of the rising which had been expressed in scattered publications by some of the associates of Eoin MacNeill, the great Celtic scholar and leader of the Irish Volunteers, who had been kept in ignorance of the plans of his subordinates and who had tried to stop the rising and succeeded in disrupting its original mobilisation plans. In the Pearse legend, MacNeill had been cast as a futile and somewhat ridiculous figure, a view reinforced by his subsequent political career; after supporting the treaty, he had mishandled his membership of the Boundary Commission and ended his political career as a scapegoat for its failure. In a series of publications encouraged by MacNeill's son-in-law Michael Tierney (former president of UCD), the historian F. X. Martin presented MacNeill's case more directly than it had been before, publishing two memoranda which MacNeill had produced before and after the rising to set out the moral and strategic rationale for his actions; these emphasised the element of deceit and personal betrayal in the treatment of MacNeill by the leaders of the insurrection. (MacNeill had regarded Pearse as a friend for almost twenty years, which was why he accepted assurances which Pearse himself later admitted were deliberate falsehoods.)

A synthesis of the Redmondite and MacNeillite critiques, which also drew on the research of León Ó Broin into the Dublin Castle administration, was offered by the Celtic scholar Fr Francis Shaw in an article written for a 1916 commemorative issue of the Jesuit journal *Studies*, but refused publication as inappropriate for the occasion. Fr Shaw argued that the nineteenth-century separatist tradition had never been more than a minority tendency that owed more to continental republicanism than to the deeply Catholic instincts of the Irish majority; that Pearse's contention, that this form of republicanism was the 'New Testament of Irish nationality' fulfilling an 'Old Testament' represented by the mediaeval Gaelic tradition, could not be sustained by anyone versed in classical Gaelic literature; that the insurrection had been a reckless and self-indulgent action, glorified in Christian language but based on an egoistic and fundamentally pagan honour code similar to that invoked by later European fascist movements; that Ó Broin's studies of Chief Secretary Augustine Birrell and Under-Secretary Sir Matthew Nathan showed that, far from being the embodiments of an ongoing tyranny (as presented in the rhetoric of Pearse and his eulogists), they were well disposed towards Irish nationalism and actively working with Redmond to prepare for the implementation of home rule; that Redmond, having brought home rule to the brink of success by working with the British, could not have reasonably refused to support the Allied cause in 1914; and that MacNeill's strategy—of maintaining the Irish Volunteers as a deterrent force in being, and gathering popular support while planning to lead general resistance to any attempt forcibly to suppress Ireland—was in fact vindicated by the successful popular resistance to the attempted imposition of conscription in 1918, while the premature insurrection of 1916 was irrelevant and counter-productive since it might easily have brought about the complete suppression of the independence movement.

In the tradition of censored Jesuits, Shaw circulated his article widely among acquaintances, and in 1972, after his death, it was published as a possible contribution to the resolution of the Northern Ireland troubles. The first academic biography of Pearse, *The triumph of failure* (1977) by Ruth Dudley Edwards, completed the demolition of the Pearsean saint-cult by presenting a figure who combined genuine ability and sensitivity with a reckless tendency to drift off into fantasy irrespective of the consequences for others (including his debtors).

The Northern Ireland troubles, and fear that they might spill over into the Republic and destabilise it, produced a new official ambivalence about the legacy of 1916. Were the republican paramilitaries—as they claimed to be, and as some surviving relatives of the dead of 1916, such as Nora Connolly O'Brien and Sighle Humphreys, were prepared to proclaim them—the true heirs of 1916 (Bobby Sands as the new Pearse or Connolly, with successive taoisigh cast as Redmond), and if so should that legacy be repudiated? There was a widespread view in academia that 1916 needed to be questioned and reassessed, and a widespread official reluctance to commemorate it in the terms prevalent before 1969.

This was not, of course, the only view of the matter; outside the 'green' leftist and paramilitary subcultures there remained a strong popular view that 1916 was something to be celebrated. This, however, was less than fully articulated—partly because it was associated with the 'sneaking regarder' attitude of feeling a degree of sympathy for northern republicanism without being willing to embrace the full implications of supporting it, partly because defenders of the favourable view of the Easter rising were unable to attain the critical distance from it needed for a coherent defence. This group often resorted to such tactics as suggesting that those who criticised the rising were British agents or that their view was so obviously perverse as to be outside the bounds of legitimate discourse, amounting to a deathly embrace of an anti-national and anti-human consumer capitalism.

The Northern Ireland peace process of the late 1990s and early 2000s, and the 'Celtic tiger' boom of the same era, brought another reassessment. Northern republicanism came to be normalised to some extent, and its derivation from the contemporary problems and frustrations of northern nationalists rather than from the heritage of the early twentieth century was emphasised. A revived culture of official commemoration partly represented the desire of the southern political establishment (particularly the successive Fianna Fáil-led governments) to dispute with Sinn Féin (now a growing political presence in the Republic) the legacy of the independence struggle. It also reflected a growing national self-confidence related to economic take-off. One element in the reassessment of nationalist orthodoxy, in the 1970s and 1980s as in the 1950s, had been a sense that the southern state had failed economically; as in the Lemass boom of the 1960s, the 'Celtic tiger' brought a new sense of national assertiveness.

The post-2008 crash brought electoral gains for leftist and republican protest parties; the splinter group Éirígí (founded shortly before the ninetieth anniversary of the Easter rising in 2006) produced a 'Proclamation of the Nama Republic', a parody of the 1916 proclamation, in which the supposed signatories—leading politicians and businessmen heavily implicated in the crash—placed themselves under 'the protection of the Most High God, Whose blessing we invoke upon our bank accounts', while proclaiming that 'the ownership of Ireland by private banks is indefeasible. It can only be defeated by the extinction of the Irish people, which is now well in hand.' Other commentators made sarcastic remarks about the contrast between the 1916 proclamation's reference to the Germans as 'our gallant allies in Europe' and the fiscal stringency imposed on Ireland and other debtor nations within the European Union at the behest of the German government. Complaints about the deflationary effect of currency union with a stronger economy ironically mirrored the complaints by older nationalists about the effect upon Ireland of the union with Britain (before independence) and the link with sterling (after independence).

Despite this, what was striking about the protests against economic austerity measures was the absence of any coherent alternative social policy such as both nationalists and socialists in 1916 claimed to possess. The culture which gave Pearse's sacrificial rhetoric much of its force has dissipated with secularisation. Connolly's brand of nationalist Marxism has been attacked as well as defended from within the Marxist tradition, and that tradition itself has lost much of its power after the fall of the Soviet bloc. Many present-day evocations of the Easter rising tend to glorify it as a rebellion against authority per se, without much attention to what the men and women of 1916 were rebelling against. Perhaps 1916 has at last passed into history, its rhetoric surviving like the smile of Lewis Carroll's Cheshire Cat when the rest of that animal has disappeared; perhaps, as Alvin Jackson suggests, we have finally come to 'the end of Irish history'; or, perhaps some new brand of protest politics will reinvent 1916 in its own image.

The genesis of the Easter rising in Victorian and Edwardian Ireland: the liberal state, its hypocrisies and its enemies

In one sense the Easter rising is a victim of its own success. The subsequent creation and survival of an independent Irish state, and its mixed record, makes it difficult to understand the mindset of those who believed—with hope or fear—that Irish self-government might never be achieved, and that its achievement might bring utopia or disaster. One advantage of the biographical approach is that—by tracking the subject throughout his or her life, rather than concentrating on the highpoints of the career—it gives a fuller sense of where attitudes came from. The remainder of this essay will argue that in order to understand the 1916 rising it is necessary to look back beyond the immediate political context of that year to the world of late Victorian and Edwardian Ireland within which the participants' attitudes were formed.

Irish unionism

Let us begin with a group often overlooked in discussions of 1916: the Irish unionists. This group was not coterminous with the Ulster unionists, nor were the southern unionists the powerless rump imagined in retrospect. If there was an Irish revolution in the sense of a social transformation, it is arguable that it took place over two generations and began not in 1912 or 1916 but in 1879. The eclipse of the classically infused official 'high culture' centred on Trinity College Dublin—the defence of which against nationalist populists and Catholic 'ignorantines' underlay much of the unionists' sense that they represented a superior civilisation—and the triumph of a literary revival which can be seen (with some distortion) as in essence popular and nationalist, disguises the fact that the 1890s cultural revival was originally presented as a means of healing the gap between classical-elitist and popular-nationalist culture-worlds which had divided the nation during the conflicts of the 1880s.

The term 'constitutional nationalist' has become so conventional as a description for the home rulers that its origins as a deliberate oxymoron are forgotten; it was coined as a challenge to a widespread view that such a thing was impossible. The union was part of the constitution; to try to overturn it, by this view, automatically placed one outside the realm of political legitimacy, whether or not a majority supported the union. Such a view rested on a mixture of old and new attitudes. The old drew on residual ideas of Protestant ascendancy and aristocratic right to govern; the new on concepts of political economy and technocracy. This view was also reinforced for many unionists by the events of the recent land war. It is easy in retrospect to underrate the extent of agrarian violence in the early 1880s (the 1916 proclamation noticeably does not include the land war among the six armed assertions of the Irish right to self-governance in the previous 300 years), but it was experienced by many unionists as a trauma almost equivalent to a civil war. The winter of 1881–2, before Parnell's break with militancy and the harsh crackdown associated with Earl Spencer's viceroyalty, was recalled with particular dread. Much unionist literature of the third home rule bill era (1912–14) looks back to the agrarian violence of the Land League era (assisted by the fact that the home rulers continued to engage in episodes of agrarian agitation as and when it suited their purposes).

Irish unionists may have been a minority, but they dominated business, the professions and the administration (because of their superior talent and education, said their apologists; because of patronage rings and manipulation of Dublin Castle, said their critics), and they had (or hoped they had) the support of a Britain confident of its imperial right to rule and unwilling to make concessions to Irish nationalism which would call into question the existence of the wider empire. They also had the support of a large minority, centred in north-eastern Ulster, which enabled them to argue that Ireland was not a homogeneous unit and that only the continuance of the union could preserve it from disintegration. The mobilisation of the Ulster unionists against the third home rule bill could be seen as reiterating the claim asserted by unionists at the time of the first two home rule bills that no nationalist government, even with majority support, could be established over their opposition. This view underestimated the depth of nationalist discontent, the implications of the emergence of an increasingly Ulstercentric and Protestant-populist leadership in the north, and the tension between technocratic or ascendancy justifications of minority rule and the liberal political ethos of the right (at least for white Europeans) to self-government. An armed mobilisation by Ulster unionists to assert the right of the minority to rule the majority was one thing, however much support it might receive from those in Britain who could be seen as defending the interest of the classes against the masses; mobilisation as a local majority demanding self-determination was another thing.

BRITISH LIBERALISM

This oversimplified matters, for the distinction between popular opinion and the public interest as perceived by an administrative elite was not a feature of conservative/unionist politics alone. However much publicists like Richard Barry O'Brien might argue that Gladstonian home rule was the logical fulfilment of liberal principles and the continuation of earlier Irish reforms enacted by Liberal party governments, however often the memory of Gladstone was invoked, one of the embarrassments facing the home rule party was that many of its theoretical allies among the British Liberals despised it just as much as the Conservatives did. During the nineteenth century, Whig/Liberal governments had been as willing to rule Ireland under emergency coercion legislation (cited by nationalists as evidence that Ireland was not really free under the union) as Conservative governments had. Gladstone's motives for taking up home rule as his last great moral crusade and committing the Liberal party to its realisation are the subject of considerable debate, and his action certainly meant that home rule could never thereafter be dismissed quite so thoroughly as when a British political consensus against it existed, but in many respects the breakdown of the consensus was more apparent than real, and many of Gladstone's lieutenants who accepted home rule did so with the greatest reluctance and as a matter of expediency. Parnell lied when he claimed during the debates on his deposition as leader of the Irish party that Gladstone had privately told him that he intended to pass a very restrictive form of home rule, but Gladstone's style of politics—which combined a call for a mandate on the great principle with insistence that the details of the measure must be left to his discretion when in power—was bound to disappoint the high nationalist expectations he had evoked, even without the Parnell split and the defeat of Gladstone's home rule bills.

The statements of Gladstone's successor, Lord Rosebery, strongly implied that Gladstonian home rule was being abandoned altogether. Although Rosebery resigned as Liberal leader soon after losing power, for some years he remained a rallying point for 'Liberal imperialists', a right-wing faction who believed that the Liberals must avoid becoming a protest party of 'faddists' (advocates of single-issue causes) and show the public that the party could be trusted to wield imperial power—not least by watering down home rule. The most prominent of Rosebery's protégés was H. H. Asquith, and if popular historical accounts of the third home rule bill era often forget Asquith's Liberal imperialist background, nationalists at the time certainly did not. As home secretary in Gladstone's last government, Asquith had blocked any suggestion that imprisoned Irish-American dynamiters should have their sentences commuted, and he criticised his Tory successor for taking a more lenient view. (Among those affected was Tom Clarke.)

The shortcomings of the 1892–5 Liberal governments were subjected to scathing criticism by John Redmond, then routinely portrayed by the Parnellite press as the dashing young representative of the new generation which had taken the torch from Parnell's failing grasp and whose vigour exposed the exhaustion of the 'effeminated frauds' who led the squabbling anti-Parnellite factions. Many of the criticisms which Griffith and other dissident nationalists levied against the insufficiencies of the third home rule bill were expressed through extracts from John Redmond's criticisms of its 1892–3 predecessor. One of the issues on which the Parnellites attacked the Liberals was amnesty for the dynamiters; in 1912, writing as a committed political enemy of Redmond and as leader of a new generation of IRB plotters, Clarke still made a point in his prison memoirs of acknowledging Redmond's work for his release.

Tensions between home rulers and the Liberals were further increased by the Boer war. While Liberals divided over its justification—with Liberal imperialists supporting the Conservative government, 'pro-Boers' complaining that the war could have been avoided and was being mismanaged, and a centrist group around the leader trying to hold the balance—few if any mainstream British politicians were 'pro-Boers' in the sense that the majority of Irish nationalists were; that is, positively hoping that the Boers would win and celebrating British defeats. Such tensions were also aggravated by a last upsurge of British political Protestantism in the 1890s and 1900s. An evangelical mini-revival led to clashes between Protestant street preachers and Catholic crowds in British and Irish cities, attempts to prosecute British Catholic clergy for such offences as holding eucharistic processions, and the revival of the issue of state subsidies for denominational education (supported by Conservatives and opposed by Liberals, especially the nonconformists who had been particularly susceptible to the Gladstonian moralist plea for home rule). Some Irish ultra-Protestants reacted to these developments by suggesting that the Liberals might be more reliably Protestant than a Conservative party corrupted by anglican ritualism.

The 1906 revival of the Liberals in response to Tory mishandling of the Boer war, the nonconformist resistance to the 1902 education act, and the massive division in unionist support caused by Joseph Chamberlain's attempt to replace free trade with protectionism, did not materially alter this situation. The Liberals neutralised the potentially divisive Irish issue by pledging themselves not to introduce a full home rule measure in the coming parliament. An attempt at a lesser measure of devolution (the 1907 Irish Council bill) was rejected by nationalists—despite some initial interest from the Irish party leadership—on the grounds that it might become a final settlement rather than an instalment. The arrival of Augustine Birrell as chief secretary after his sponsorship, as president of the Board of Education, of an education bill limiting denominational education (which was killed by the house of lords) did not improve matters.

In time, Birrell improved relations with the Irish party by pursuing a policy of appeasement towards them and making himself their ambassador at cabinet level. With the loss of the Liberal majority in January 1910, the passage of the 'people's budget' and the parliament act through Redmondite support, and the introduction of the third home rule bill in 1912, it seemed that the old Gladstonian image of an alliance between the 'British democracy' and the Irish people had returned. This was deceptive; the Liberals might accept home rule as inevitable but they would not be constrained by nationalist opinion in deciding the terms on which a settlement would be reached, and it was tacitly understood that at the strategic moment a compromise would be offered to the unionists (based on partition).

The knowledge that this was the case, seeping out into the public domain by various sources and combined with the ambiguous history of post-Gladstonian Liberal–Irish nationalist relations, explains why Arthur Griffith could argue that when the time to implement home rule came, the secret Liberal–Conservative 'continuity coalition' would manifest itself to wreck the measure, and why Eoin MacNeill believed all his life that Asquith had never intended to implement home rule but was secretly in league with the Ulster unionist leadership and wished to use their agitation as a pretext to abandon the bill. The idea that the Liberals and the Conservatives formed a secret 'continuity coalition' hostile to Irish nationalism was reinforced by the fact that a significant body of British radical backbenchers, irritated by Liberal imperialist dominance at cabinet level, protested long and loud that the Asquith government was abandoning Liberal principles in such areas as foreign policy and relying on tacit Tory support to uphold it against the true believers on its own side of the house. These malcontents were John Dillon's natural allies at Westminster.

IRISH 'WHIGGERY'

Between the unionists and the home rulers in Irish politics was a mass of middle-class Catholic and liberal Protestant opinion which may be called 'whig', which regarded official nationalists as disreputable, dictatorial and incompetent, and in turn was regarded by them as self-seeking and snobbish. 'Whig' was used to describe the Liberals and 'nominal home rulers' displaced by Isaac Butt and Charles Stewart Parnell in the 1870s and early 1880s, with the young T. M. Healy claiming that Pontius Pilate was the first whig. The term was also used by the Parnellites of the 1890s to describe the anti-Parnellites, whom they claimed had sacrificed Parnell, the evicted tenants, the dynamite prisoners, the hope of home rule, and the principle of independent opposition to the lure of Gladstone and the possibility of securing government appointments for their supporters under a Liberal administration. After the reunion of the Irish parliamentary party in 1900, the separatists in turn claimed to represent the Parnellite tradition as against Redmondite 'whiggery", with the added elaboration that Parnell's fate showed that independent opposition could never be carried on successfully at Westminster and required abstentionism and the creation of an unofficial parliament in Ireland.

'Whiggery' was a fluid label. It covered localist and patronage-seeking politicians operating under the Irish party umbrella, some self-consciously high-minded individuals who identified as nationalists or liberals while avoiding submission to the Irish party, and seekers after legal or judicial office. But the term was particularly associated with a type of clericalist Catholic upper-class and upper-middle-class mindset, also found among sections of the Catholic hierarchy and the religious orders running the major Catholic secondary schools. This form of 'whiggery' sought to create a Catholic professional class who would guard the church's interests—especially denominational education—by establishing a presence in the professions and in the administrative system. The tension between this project, with its implicit acceptance of the status quo and its elitist bias, and the more populist nationalist tactic of independent opposition—better suited to periods of intense short-term agitation than to the long haul in which the forces of localism and patronage politics were likely to reassert themselves—was a recurring trait of Irish politics under the union. For nationalists, it was symbolised by the adventurers led by Sadleir and Keogh in the 1850s who had professed clericalist politics to get government office, then revealed themselves as fraudsters and opportunists whose commitment to Catholicism was no more substantial than their other principles. Parnellites claimed that the Catholic bishops had brought down Parnell because they wished to replace a strong centralised nationalist movement with a weaker political leadership susceptible to their influence and forwarding their patronage demands. Others, such as James Connolly's Marxist mentor John Leslie, even claimed the bishops wished to jettison nationalism altogether and turn the Irish party into something like the German Catholic Centre Party. The Healyism of the 1890s (persisting in attenuated form after 1900) can be seen as a form of Catholic 'whiggery'. The term was also applied after 1900 to D. P. Moran's Catholic, cultural-nationalist weekly, the *Leader*, and to William Martin Murphy's *Irish Independent*.

'Whiggery' in this sense was a fluid and incoherent political phenomenon, shifting with the balance of political power. There does seem to have been a Dublin middle-class vote (mainly Catholic but including some liberal Protestants) which could be won for unionism in the 1890s but moved back towards nationalism in the run-up to the 1906 election—partly from opportunism, partly through discontent with the more rebarbative aspects of unionism. There is obviously some substance to Arthur Griffith's view that D. P. Moran's brand of nationalism (centred on culture rather than politics, campaigning for more Catholics in the administration, arguing that the best way to get home rule was to accept the permanence of the British connection) was a new form of 'whiggery', but much of Moran's Irish-Irelander rhetoric was directed against the 'west British' professional products of Catholic colleges to whom the label was more conventionally implied; Moran's complaint that such people benefited from the exertions of earlier generations of nationalists (scorned by earlier respectable whigs), while themselves sneering at present-day nationalist agitators, was the essence of the nationalist critique of 'whiggery'.

For many Irish Irelanders and separatists, and also for many mainstream nationalists, the enemy was embodied in 'Rathmines', the middle-class suburb south of the Grand Canal which maintained a separate local authority (as did neighbouring Pembroke) controlled by a ratepayers' group including both unionists and lukewarm nationalists. Rathmines's spokesmen resisted demands for annexation by Dublin Corporation by claiming that they did not want to be subjected to the irresponsible populism of a corporation whose mismanagement was responsible for the city's social problems and extortionate rates (a view with unionist undertones, given that the corporation was controlled by nationalists). The corporation's defenders retorted that many of the inhabitants of Rathmines worked in the city and made use of its services while declining to pay their fair share of the cost of providing those services.

Irish Irelanders also identified Rathmines (and its constituent district of Rathgar) with genteel pretensions and anxious imitation of British manners, accompanied by contempt for all things distinctively Irish as vulgar and déclassé. (In a satirical article listing the supposed 'commandments of the respectable', Patrick Pearse includes among them: 'Thou shalt not carry a brown paper parcel lest thou shock Rathgar'—that is, you are not to demean yourself by behaving like one of those vulgar people who have to carry their groceries home themselves instead of having them delivered by the shop's employees, for whom such servile tasks should be reserved.) Irish-Ireland romanticisation of the peasantry derived from such factors as nostalgia for lost personal origins, a search for authenticity, and an apologetic desire to defend Irish Catholics and nationalists as a whole against accusations of savagery and backwardness, but it also reflected a sense that suburban life was excessively detached from the lives and labours of those who sustained it, and a sense that true patriotism needed to unite all classes in a common concern. Joseph Plunkett was radicalised by a variety of factors, including experiencing anti-Irish hostility at an English Catholic public school (where he acquired the cadet training which made him the Easter rising's military planner), and the contrast between the poverty he witnessed in Connemara and in the Dublin slums and the self-indulgent displays of fashion and social climbing associated with his mother.

THE HOME RULE TRADITION

In the years before 1916 the most prominent claim to embody the nation as a whole was made by the Irish parliamentary party and its associated movements. This group tends to be remembered as more conservative and more 'respectable' than was in fact the case. The standard image of conservative Redmondism is to a considerable extent a retrospective construct, in which the rump (some of whom would have been 'whigs' in the sense discussed above) that remained after the defection in 1918 of the majority of nationalists to Sinn Féin is presented as representing the pre-1914 party, and Redmond's political hegemony between 1910 and 1916 is assumed to have been the normal state of affairs under his leadership. This may reflect Redmond's own beliefs and aspirations—he continuously tried to project an image of himself as a grave and moderate statesman capable of handling the responsibilities of government—but it did not reflect the full political culture of the Irish parliamentary party as it existed prior to 1916 (and to a considerable extent prior to 1910). Until the balance of power at Westminster and the introduction of the home rule bill gave him something of the charisma formerly enjoyed by Parnell, Redmond was a chairman rather than a chief, his prime concern being to hold the party together. He sat atop an uneasy coalition of local political machines, held together by sporadic agitations aimed at mobilising support or keeping particular interest groups—agricultural labourers, town tenants, smallholders seeking land division—in line behind the party leadership. These agitations often involved defiance of the law, intimidation, and a degree of violence. In order to gain and hold support, the party had to be what would later be termed a 'slightly constitutional party'. It was reunited in 1900 by the western-based land campaign of the United Irish League, whose limitations as much as its achievements led to the negotiation of the 1903 Wyndham land act. In 1908 it responded to the breakdown of its negotiations over relations with the Liberals by launching the 'ranch war' aimed at securing the division of grazing land among smallholders and landless labourers. The growth of Joseph Devlin's Ancient Order of Hibernians as a mass-membership organisation from 1909 combined politics, social recreation, religious profession, strong-arm tactics, and more-or-less dubious machine politics. These agitations often had decidedly sordid elements, involving local politicians using boycotts against business rivals, and anti-grazier agitators being revealed as holding grazing land themselves. At local and national level the movement was characterised by factional disputes, often based around personalities or extended families, and often going back to the realigning elections of the 1880s and early 1890s, in which the new generation were too young to have participated. Both Patrick Pearse and D. P. Moran commented on the contrast between the heroic images of the Irish party leaders they had absorbed while growing up amid the great agitations of the 1880s, and the disillusionment experienced by their more mature observation of the politics of the 1890s and 1900s.

The concept of rival traditions of constitutional and physical-force nationalism, the former deriving from Grattan through O'Connell and

Parnell, the latter from Wolfe Tone through Young Ireland and the Fenians, was certainly employed at the time, but draws much too neat a contrast because it plays down the extent to which both were forms of nationalism—that is, they primarily defined themselves against the opponents of nationalism rather than against each other, and they often overlapped. Many of the Irish party's older activists had been Fenians, and much of their understanding of what it was to be Irish derived from the vast body of popular nationalist literature deriving from the Young Ireland tradition (including the Sullivan brothers, who put a noticeably more Catholic gloss on it than had been the case with the original Young Irelanders). Peter Hart and Joost Augusteijn, when interviewing war of independence veterans, discovered that they predominantly derived their sense of nationality from such material rather than from the contemporary separatist press of the Gaelic revival.

The writings of John Mitchel, the most radical of the Young Irelanders, enjoyed an immense circulation in nationalist Ireland because they offered an explanation for the poverty, humiliation and condescension experienced by much of the Irish population. As young men, the Irish party leaders had themselves responded to this strain in Mitchel; John Dillon had actually been present at Mitchel's deathbed, Willie Redmond attributed his conversion to nationalism to Mitchel's writings, the remorselessly uninhibited parliamentary skirmisher T. M. Healy had taken Mitchel as one of the models for his invective. The Irish party leaders could claim that Mitchel responded to conditions which they had overcome, but he was a double-edged sword. For Mitchel, Irish history remained frozen at the moment of his exile; the Famine had never really ceased, Ireland's endemic poverty being its continuation, and liberalism—especially the British variety—would never be anything but a murderous humbug. Since Ireland remained a poor country, and the tensions among British liberalism, Irish Catholicism, and Irish nationalism in general, were endemic, this view had enough plausibility to keep the Mitchel legacy alive through publicists such as Arthur Griffith (see below). Pearse's last manifestoes, employing a style of Mitchelian rhetoric to which is added a strain of Gaelic revivalism and religiosity reflecting Pearse's own sensibility, argue that the 'apostolic tradition' of Irish nationalism, definitively expressed in the 'four gospels' of Tone, Davis, Lalor and Mitchel, is expressly separatist, that every compromise with that tradition has been recognised as a heresy by the next generation and rejected (echoing the Catholic belief that the church enjoys divine guidance, the nation substituting here for the church), and that the Redmondites, in their support for the British war effort, had committed the unforgivable sin against the Holy Ghost: their expressed views were such unspeakable blasphemy that the faithful could not even comprehend their words as anything more than inhuman gibberish. One reason why this was so explosive was that the Irish party—and its supporters—also recognised the authority of the canon which condemned them as heretics.

In some respects the post-1906 Irish party faced the same sort of criticisms as post-independence Irish governments. Some of the lesser writers associated with the literary revival produced works whose theme suggested that victory in the land war had been anti-climactic, with the defeat of the landlords revealing a socially repressive and economically inefficient society, out of which the most enterprising emigrated. (Examples of this view are Padraic Colum's play *The land* (1905) and Daniel Corkery's *Fohnam the sculptor* (1939), which features a king so preoccupied with devising a great memorial to his historic victory over his kingdom's traditional enemy that he fails to notice that his poverty-stricken people are emigrating in droves to that enemy's country.) Arthur Griffith repeatedly claimed that while the Irish party leadership took credit for victory in the land war—a victory which, in his opinion, had been won by the activists on the ground while the parliamentarians postured and intrigued at Westminster—the continuing outflow of emigration showed that the country was bleeding to death. Only a truly independent Irish government could stem the outflow (a point cited against Griffith's self-proclaimed heirs in Cumann na nGaedheal by their opponents in the 1920s). Only protective tariffs, which could never be implemented under home rule, could produce the economic development necessary to end emigration (a proposition tested to destruction under Fianna Fáil governments after 1932).

As with the unionists and the parliamentary nationalists, the separatist subculture had been deeply marked by the experience of the early 1880s, when hopes of using the land movement as recruiting ground and launching pad for a mass separatist movement were defeated by the political skills of Parnell, the unexpected willingness of Gladstone's administration to make concessions to the Irish tenantry at the expense of the Irish landlords, and the ruthlessly effective deployment of coercion legislation, supported by the dark arts of the spy, informer and agent provocateur, against the separatist movement. The sheer ruthlessness (including downright illegality) of this process has only been fully revealed in recent years by writers such as Owen McGee and Christy Campbell. The fragmentation, driven both by personal rivalries and by the mutual suspicions engendered by the spymasters and their agents, did much to reinforce the warnings of clerics, Mitchelite nationalists, and parliamentarians against the demoralising effects of secret societies. By the 1890s the IRB in both Ireland and America was a divided and demoralised rump; but in the same period a separatist revival began, driven first by the emergence of new openly separatist groups and newspapers out of the decay of Parnellism, then by the reunion of the Clan na Gael in 1900 (which provided Irish-based separatists with a valuable source of financial and other support), and finally by the emergence of a new generation of younger leaders (including Seán Mac Diarmada) who displaced the IRB veterans in Ireland, and who looked back over the defeats of the 1880s to a romanticised (though not entirely false) image of Fenian heroism in the 1860s. The significance of this development was concealed from Dublin Castle by the decay of their counter-subversive organisation, partly through the retirement of veterans, partly through economising ordered by Under-Secretary Sir Antony MacDonnell after the Wyndham land act to show that reform, by pacifying Ireland, made possible savings in official expenditure.

A key figure in this separatist revival was Arthur Griffith, whose conservatism has been exaggerated by a view which reads his career backwards from his support for the treaty settlement of 1921. Griffith's papers formed an important gateway through which younger men were recruited to separatism. His pre-1914 political journalism was based around the tactics of never acknowledging any good in his adversaries—in a style familiar to impossibilist left-wing groups today, except that where these appeal to Marxism, Griffith appealed to radical nationalism—and a classical republican analysis based on corruption versus patriotism. Griffith raged that Dublin Castle and its hangers-on, the degraded lumpenproletariat who joined exhibitions of loyalty, and the Catholic upper-middle classes—particularly the Irish party and its protégés—did well out of official patronage at the expense of the honest poor who would be the first concern of a native government. This was an historically oriented nationalism (and incidentally one which was much more direct in its arguments that Irishness was not exclusively Catholic, and independence was in the best interests of Protestants as well as Catholics, than some newer strains), for Griffith's message was that, despite the changes which had taken place since Mitchel's death, his message was still valid. Gladstone and the post-Gladstonian Liberals were just as hypocritical and malevolent as the Whigs who had toyed with O'Connell; the Famine had never really ended, with Irish poverty—including the notorious Dublin slums—and emigration (the latter being equated with death, since emigrants were lost to Ireland) en couraged through deliberate British policy. In short, it may be suggested that in rhetorical terms Griffith laid the egg which Pearse hatched, and that Pearse's description of the Old and New Testaments of Irish nationality added a patina of religiosity to a genealogy laid down by Griffith.

In 1910 the IRB separatists established their own monthly front-paper, *Irish Freedom*, with Mac Diarmada as manager, after deciding that Griffith was too much in love with his own bright idea of a Hungarian-style dual monarchy; but Griffith remained a significant ally. It was this group which, in response to the militarisation of Irish society by the creation of the Ulster Volunteers, undertook in late 1913 the creation of the Irish Volunteers with Eoin MacNeill as their willing frontman, capitalising on a widespread sense that if the unionists had an armed wing so too should nationalists. At first the Irish party tried to resist this development (since it reinforced unionist warnings that a home-rule Ireland might raise unofficial military forces, and also raised

the prospect of clashes in Ulster between the two groups of Volunteers), but it was forced to join in by the extent of popular support for the new movement (which MacNeill was already presenting as an independent force, above politics—including the Irish party). Redmond managed to assert nominal control of the new movement, but the separatist group continued their operations without reference to him. The 'Curragh mutiny' of March 1914 increased political pressure for a partition compromise, and the rival gun-runnings of summer 1914 reinforced the sense that the liberal state was more responsive to force than it pretended, and the answer was for nationalists to wield force of their own. (As Pearse put it, 'the Orangeman with a gun is a great deal less ridiculous than the nationalist who can only wield a pun'—the latter possibly being a reference to Kettle, whose polished Chestertonian style and use of ironic humour were intended to drive home the message that the Irish party knew what they were doing, and that his listeners could be sure that the unionists, once their bluff was called, would submit rather than make good their threats.)

OTHER INFLUENCES

In the 1880s, under Parnell's leadership, the Irish party had succeeded in establishing dominance over nationalist civil society. As its hegemony was shattered in the Parnell split, and never fully reconstituted, groups which had previously been marginalised asserted their independent existence.

For much of the nineteenth century the Irish trade union movement had been dominated by craft unions of skilled workers and (outside Ulster) by a nationalist analysis which maintained that Irish workers and employers shared a common interest in the growth of Irish industry. (It is perhaps an indication of the limitations of this outlook that William Martin Murphy—whose cultivation of good relations with the skilled printers of the Dublin Typographical Provident Society was key to his ability to keep producing his newspapers during the 1913–14 lockout— was widely regarded in the 1890s as a friend of labour.) Unions of agricultural labourers appeared from the 1870s but were generally subsumed into the Irish party's support coalition as junior partners in land agitation. Small groups of socialists (such as Connolly's late-1890s Irish Socialist Republican Party) could be found in Dublin and Belfast but had little political leverage. From the late 1880s, 'new unionism', which attempted to organise unskilled workers into mass-membership general unions, spread in Britain, and the figure most associated with its arrival in Ireland is James Larkin. The Dublin labour disputes of 1911–14 displayed the strength both of his union in appealing to the Dublin poor (the ability of the ITGWU to survive the lockout for much longer than had been expected was highly impressive), and of the forces which combined for its defeat. It also showed up the weaknesses of the Irish party (its Dublin MPs were mostly decrepit or conservative), and while Larkin's supporters denounced the party for doing nothing to prevent the victimisation of the workers and the use of the police force to repress them, Murphy accused the party of equivocation out of hostility to his paper, and complained that the Asquith government had been unwilling to repress the strikers with sufficient force for fear of losing votes in Britain. The strike also showed the support of a significant body of the intelligentsia for the strikers (though Griffith, adhering to the older nationalist concept of labour relations, denounced Larkin as a saboteur).

The literary and Gaelic revivals were linked to the presence of significant numbers of educated and under-employed young people looking for meaning in existence and often finding it in new forms of nationalism and cultural expression. It is from this milieu that several of the signatories of the 1916 proclamation emerged.

One aspect of the growth of an educated Catholic intelligentsia was the expansion of the women's suffrage movement; pioneered decades earlier by Protestants and unionists, it now attracted growing numbers of middle-class Catholic professional women. (There was also significant female involvement in the republican movement, often overlapping with suffragism. In discussing the military involvement of certain women activists, such as Constance Markievicz, it may be worth bearing in mind that military service was presented as essential to citizenship not just by nationalists but by significant sections of British public opinion, and that one of the major arguments advanced by anti-suffragists was that women would not become soldiers and were thereby unqualified to assess questions of war and peace. The willingness of militant suffragists to suffer imprisonment and risk their lives can be seen as a symbolic riposte to this view.) Although the Irish party contained a minority of suffragists it also contained a significant number of opponents (including both Redmond and Dillon), and its decision to block suffragist legislation at Westminster for fear it would obstruct the passage of the home rule bill (and destabilise a government led by the fiercely anti-suffragist Asquith) roused considerable criticism from suffragists. It is significant that the 1916 proclamation included a specific commitment to women's suffrage.

Although it has been much less systematically explored than the Gaelic revival, it seems clear that from the late 1890s there was a revival of Catholic fervour and activism in Ireland. In part this was the fruit of the clerical, educational and devotional infrastructures developed during the nineteenth century. Part of this revival was the fear, expressed in particular by members of certain religious orders, and reinforced by the willingness of large numbers of Irish Catholics to defy clerical advice and support Parnell in the split, that Irish popular Catholicism rested on external devotional observances which for all their emotional fervour might prove shallow-rooted in face of the forces of infidelity spreading across the Irish sea. (The presence of atheist or agnostic intellectuals in Dublin—Sheehy-Skeffington being a very public example, and the agnostic Thomas MacDonagh a less conspicuous one—and the appearance of small socialist groups were other signs of danger.) The Catholic response combined mobilisation against the threat of English mass media (particularly popular newspapers—some of which, embarrassingly, employed members of the Irish party as journalists and provided platforms for their attempts to convince the British public that home rule was the natural outgrowth of radical politics), which foreshadowed post-independence censorship, and an intensification of forms of devotionalism which could develop a deeper interior spirituality: Marian, Ignatian, or drawing on the French Salesian tradition. Those clerics who took up the Gaelic revival appear to have seen the Gaelic tradition both as a barrier against English Protestant, unbelieving, and socialist influences, and as the repository of a deeper ancestral spirituality; Pearse's self-identification with Christ owed something to continental Catholic spirituality, with its invitation to the devotee to visualise and identify with Christ's sufferings on the cross, and to examine one's conscience to see how lukewarmness and unbelief contributed to those sufferings.

The retrospective view, the contrast between the world of mid 1914 and the scale of the destruction that followed, makes it seem that the first world war erupted out of a clear blue sky. In fact, the possibility of a European war aligning Britain, France and Russia against Germany had been realised for some years. Kathleen Clarke claimed that her husband's eventual return to Ireland from America in 1907 was partly prompted by Clan na Gael's awareness that such a war might break out in the near future. (The force of this prophecy is somewhat reduced by the fact that during an 1896 Anglo–American diplomatic crisis, and to a lesser extent during the 1898 Spanish–American war, Irish-based separatists looked forward to war between Britain and America; and during and immediately after the centenary of the 1798 rising many nationalists revived old hopes of a new war between Britain and Ireland's traditional ally France arising out of colonial rivalries. Griffith, for example, regularly eulogised French republicanism as superior to British liberalism, both in its ethos of active citizenship and in its state-led economic development, until the Anglo–French entente of 1904, when he abruptly decided that these virtues were in fact embodied in the German *Kaiserreich*.)

In 1910 the play 'An Englishman's home' by Guy du Maurier, depicting complacent citizens neglecting calls for military preparedness until they are rudely awakened by a German invasion, was staged in Dublin. It was disrupted by an organised group of separatists (including the future 1916 rebel Margaret Skinnider) who booed its expressions of British patriotism and roundly cheered the invading Germans. This prompted a debate in D. P. Moran's *Leader*, with one contributor arguing that in the event of a successful invasion, the Germans might prove much more oppressive than the British, and might even introduce a new plantation of German colonists. A Germanophile opponent who pointed out that if the Germans attempted such a thing they would be met with cattle-driving more intensive than the ranch war, received the rejoinder that everyone knew a Tory government would have suppressed the ranch war immediately, and the Germans would presumably have even fewer inhibitions in such matters. The idea of a new plantation of German colonists derived from awareness of developments in the eastern borderlands of Germany, where German nationalists organised agrarian colonies in an attempt to secure demographic dominance over the Catholic Poles; it would resurface in wartime British and Redmondite propaganda aimed at Irish farmers.

Similarly, Francis Sheehy-Skeffington's anti-war activities were not simply a reflection of his pacifism but also reflected a fear—shared by some British radicals and many German socialists—that the result of an Allied victory would be to entrench and expand the reactionary and tyrannical power of Russian tsarism at the expense of the comparatively advanced Germans. (It is not clear how far Connolly's writings to a similar effect—highlighted by recent commentators—represent an opportunistic effort aimed at assisting an alliance between his socialists and the nationalists of the Irish Volunteers, who had been influenced by Arthur Griffith's long-standing eulogies of imperial Germany as freer, more advanced, and more socially just than Britain. It is certain that the unaffiliated Sheehy-Skeffington—who had denounced Griffith for producing apologetics for German militarism—was expressing his sincere opinion.)

The 1916 rising cannot be fully understood without the context of the first world war. This is one of the most significant elisions in Fr Shaw's attempt to combine the Redmondite and MacNeillite critiques of the rising. Having argued that in view of the imminence of home rule, Redmond had no option but to support the British war effort, and that his moral commitment to the Allied cause was essentially correct, Shaw then laments that the Volunteers were split by Redmond's uncharacteristically foolish decision to support recruitment for overseas service, and that this could have been prevented if MacNeill's approach had been followed. But if Redmond's support for the Allied war effort was justified both on moral grounds and because of the imminence of home rule, sending Irish recruits to the front was a natural and unavoidable corollary, and Shaw's defence of Redmond logically entails the view that MacNeill was wrong and should have supported Redmond.

There were two central problems with Redmond's policy. One was that he regarded himself as the equivalent of a dominion prime minister, committing Ireland to war as an independent ally. The fact that he and his lieutenants held private consultations about the implementation of home rule reinforced this impression, but in fact he was regarded by the government simply as a party leader holding no elective office, and hence with no direct control over the administration. The second problem was that Redmond, on behalf of nationalist Ireland, had taken on an open-ended liability which proved much greater than had been expected, both in financial terms (rising war taxes revived over-taxation as an issue for separatist propaganda) and in blood. Redmond's policy, implemented with full consistency, implied acceptance of conscription for Ireland as part of the common war effort, whose requirements were placing further pressure on the liberal state. Conscription, seen as an expression of continental despotism (though advocated before the war by a section of the Tory right) was introduced in Britain in 1916. In the January 1916 parliamentary debate on conscription, Redmond explicitly stated that he opposed conscription for Ireland only because he believed it would do more harm than good, and he would support conscription in Ireland if it became necessary for the war effort; this speech was recycled by the British government in 1918 after Redmond's death to justify its attempt to impose conscription on Ireland.

During 1915 the pressure on Redmond increased. Redmond and his closest allies within the Irish party joined in a recruiting campaign aimed specifically at the farming population. (For example, Kettle produced an open letter, 'To the man on the land in Ireland', appealing for recruits.) This produced limited results, and can hardly have helped their standing with their rural support base (opposition already being fairly strong in towns). The formation of a coalition government in May 1915 added to the strain on Redmond. Although some Conservative journals noted the increasing activity of the Irish Volunteers, the Conservatives generally tended to accept Birrell's assurances that all was well and to stay out of the Irish situation. It could not be guaranteed, however, that this would continue indefinitely.

One area where Redmondite influence over the administration was exerted with ambiguous results was in limiting Dublin Castle's repression of the separatists. After an initial crackdown on separatist newspapers (the most prominent victims being Griffith's *Sinn Féin*, *Irish Freedom* and the *Irish Worker*), a new 'mosquito press' appeared to carry on their work. Some Irish Volunteer organisers and anti-recruiting activists were prosecuted (with mixed results), but no attempt was made to suppress the whole movement. By the standards of later wartime governments (not least de Valera's in 1939–45) it is quite extraordinary that in 1915–16 separatist newspapers were allowed to proclaim that the much-maligned Germans had been forced to defend themselves against a malevolent Britain seeking to recapture lost trade by force of arms (with the assistance of French freemasons and the tyrannical Russians); that they were nonetheless winning the war by sheer force of material and moral superiority; that Sir Roger Casement (known to be in Berlin) represented the true sentiments of the Irish people more accurately than the British hirelings of the Redmondite party and press; and that the sooner Germany invaded Ireland the better. It was even more extraordinary that the Irish Volunteers were allowed to parade and drill publicly (even to take over the policing of Dublin for the day, as they did for the funeral of Jeremiah O'Donovan Rossa (1 August 1915)), so that nobody paid much attention to their behaviour on Easter Monday until they actually seized the GPO. One wonders whether an actual Redmondite home-rule government would have been quite so patient. Nevertheless, the Redmondites had little room for manoeuvre, since the nationalist public saw such measures as were taken in terms of what had gone before—namely, the long history of emergency coercion legislation against Irish nationalists, and the separatist narrative that state professions of liberal principles had always been hypocritical and its true repressive face was now emerging.

It was widely expected that the war would end in 1916. For months before the Somme offensive of summer 1916, the *Irish Independent* predicted that the arrival of 'Kitchener's armies' at the front would be followed by a great offensive in which the French and British, in combination with a revived Russian army, would strike the decisive blow against the Central Powers. The rumours known to have circulated among separatists before and in the early stages of the rising, that Britain was about to sue for peace and that only by striking now could Irish nationalists secure representation at the peace negotiations, were part of the same pattern (albeit with the implication that the Germans would win, at least on points). In this sense the Easter rising was part of a general pattern, whereby the year 1916 made it clear that the war would continue indefinitely and that a speedy victory and resumption of the pre-war pattern were unattainable.

Shortly after the 1916 rising, Aodh de Blacam, a Sinn Féin activist who had converted to Catholicism after a fundamentalist Protestant upbringing, wrote a novel (*Holy Romans* (1920)) in which the rising is presented as an apocalyptic judgement on a cruel and corrupt old order; St John the Divine, traditional author of the final book of the New Testament which describes the Second Coming, appears as a minor character gazing approvingly on the rebels. The new heaven and the new earth prophesied by the different strands of nationalism may have proved something of a disappointment, but the 1916 rebellion, and the events that followed it, were unquestionably a product of—and a judgement on—the old.

PATRICK MAUME
Dictionary of Irish Biography

CHRONOLOGY

of the

1916 RISING

and associated events

1907

NOVEMBER
Thomas J. Clarke returns to Ireland from America and helps to invigorate the IRB

1909

16 AUGUST
Constance Markievicz and Bulmer Hobson found Na Fianna Éireann

10 DECEMBER
H. H. Asquith, the Liberal prime minister, promises 'self-government' for Ireland

---

1910

JANUARY
UK general election: Liberal party fails to win an overall majority and requires the support of John Redmond's 70-strong Irish Parliamentary Party to govern

26 JULY
James Connolly returns to Ireland from America

DECEMBER
Another UK general election; Liberals still the largest party with Irish Parliamentary Party holding the balance of power

---

1912

9 APRIL
At a unionist demonstration at Balmoral, near Belfast, Andrew Bonar Law, leader of the Conservative party, pledges the support of British unionists to Ulster unionist resistance to home rule

11 APRIL
Asquith introduces home rule bill in house of commons

28 SEPTEMBER
Unionists throughout Ulster sign the Solemn League and Covenant to resist home rule

---

1913

16 JANUARY
Third reading of home rule bill carried in house of commons

30 JANUARY
Home rule bill defeated in house of lords

31 JANUARY
Ulster Volunteer Force founded

15 JULY
After passing in the commons, home rule bill again defeated in the lords

26 AUGUST
Tram workers of James Larkin's ITGWU go on strike—a general lockout of union members follows

19 NOVEMBER
Irish Citizen Army founded by trade unionists in Dublin

25 NOVEMBER
Irish Volunteers formed at meeting in Dublin, presided over by Eoin MacNeill

---

1914

20 MARCH
'Curragh mutiny'—General Hubert Gough and most of his officers in the 3rd Cavalry Brigade announce their unwillingness to enforce home rule on Ulster

2 APRIL
Cumann na mBan founded as women's auxiliary to Irish Volunteers

24–5 APRIL
UVF gun-running: large quantity of rifles landed at Larne, Donaghadee and Bangor

25 MAY

Home rule bill passes through commons for third time

28 JUNE

Assassination of Archduke Franz Ferdinand and his wife by a Slav nationalist in Sarajevo, Bosnia

10 JULY

Ulster unionist provisional government meets in Belfast

21–4 JULY

Government, nationalists and unionists fail to reach agreement on the status of Ulster at Buckingham Palace conference

26 JULY

Rifles for Irish Volunteers landed at Howth; British troops who failed to disarm Volunteers fire on a crowd at Bachelor's Walk, Dublin, killing four and wounding thirty

1 AUGUST

More rifles for Irish Volunteers landed at Kilcoole, Co. Wicklow

4 AUGUST

UK declares war on Germany after German invasion of Belgium

9 SEPTEMBER

At a conference in Dublin, militant nationalists (mostly IRB) discuss mounting an insurrection during the war

18 SEPTEMBER

Government of Ireland act, 1914, suspends the introduction of home rule for the duration of the war

20 SEPTEMBER

At Woodenbridge, Co. Wicklow, John Redmond encourages Irish Volunteers to join the British army

24 SEPTEMBER

Eoin MacNeill and other Volunteer leaders repudiate Redmond's leadership; Volunteers split, the majority forming Redmond's 'National Volunteers'

OCTOBER

Volunteer minority, still calling themselves the Irish Volunteers, re-organise with Eoin MacNeill as chief of staff, Patrick Pearse as director of military organisation, Joseph Mary Plunkett as director of military operations, and Thomas MacDonagh as director of training

Sir Roger Casement travels to Berlin to seek German help for an Irish insurrection against British rule

1915

MAY

IRB creates a military committee of Pearse, Plunkett and Éamonn Ceannt to begin planning for an armed insurrection

1 AUGUST

Pearse gives stirring graveside oration at the funeral of Jeremiah O'Donovan Rossa warning that 'Ireland unfree shall never be at peace'

DECEMBER

IRB military council of Clarke, Seán Mac Diarmada, Pearse, Plunkett and Ceannt formed

1916

JANUARY
IRB supreme council gives approval for armed insurrection

19–22 JANUARY
James Connolly confers with IRB military council and is co-opted into their plans (Thomas MacDonagh co-opted in April)

3 APRIL
Pearse issues orders to Volunteers throughout Ireland for manoeuvres beginning on Easter Sunday (23 April)

20 APRIL
A trawler, the *Aud*, arrives in Tralee Bay with German arms for the Irish Volunteers and is arrested by a British patrol ship

21 APRIL
Sir Roger Casement lands from a German submarine at Banna Strand, Co. Kerry, and is arrested

22 APRIL
Eoin MacNeill, of the Irish Volunteers, learns of planned insurrection and countermands orders for Easter Sunday manoeuvres

23 APRIL
Military council meets at Liberty Hall and decides to go ahead with insurrection on Easter Monday (24 April); a revolutionary proclamation is signed by the seven members of the council

24 APRIL
GPO and several other buildings in Dublin seized by Irish Volunteers and Citizen Army

An attack on Dublin Castle by a Citizen Army unit is repulsed; the unit briefly holds City Hall until overwhelmed later that day

25 APRIL
British army reinforcements arrive in Dublin and surround insurgent positions; martial law declared in Dublin

Citizen Army force in St Stephen's Green comes under heavy fire and withdraws to College of Surgeons

26 APRIL
Liberty Hall destroyed and GPO damaged by British shelling

Francis Sheehy-Skeffington and two other prisoners summarily executed at Portobello barracks on orders of Captain J. C. Bowen-Colthurst

Wexford Volunteers take over Enniscorthy

Heavy fighting as British troops advance on insurgent positions around the Four Courts and the South Dublin Union

Unable to hold the Mendicity Institute on Usher's Island, the small Volunteer garrison under Seán Heuston surrenders

26–7 APRIL
British army reinforcements advancing on Mount Street bridge suffer heavy casualties at the hands of Volunteers from Éamon de Valera's 3rd battalion

28 APRIL

Volunteers in north County Dublin under Thomas Ashe and Richard Mulcahy seize Ashbourne RIC barracks and ambush an RIC patrol sent to re-take it

GPO on fire; insurgents evacuate building and set up their headquarters in 16 Moore Street

29 APRIL

Pearse and Connolly agree to unconditional surrender, and send orders to other insurgent posts to do likewise

30 APRIL

Final surrenders of rebel commandants in Dublin end the rising; 64 insurgents, 132 crown forces and about 230 civilians killed

2–9 MAY

Courts martial of 187 leading insurgents; 88 sentenced to death, with 73 commuted to various terms of imprisonment. Over 400 insurgents sent to Britain to be interned; over 3,000 other suspects also arrested, of whom about half are interned

2 MAY

Gun battle ensues between Kent family and RIC at Bawnard House, Castlelyons, near Fermoy, Co. Cork, when Kents resist arrest

3 MAY

Executions of Pearse, Clarke and MacDonagh

4–12 MAY

Executions of remaining insurgents; Connolly and Mac Diarmada the last to be shot

3 AUGUST

Found guilty of treason, Roger Casement is hanged in Pentonville jail, London

22 DECEMBER

Release from Frongoch camp and Reading jail of remaining untried Irish political prisoners; convicted insurgents remain imprisoned

17–18 MAY
'German plot' arrests of
Sinn Féin leaders

11 NOVEMBER
Great War ends

14–28 DECEMBER
General election: Sinn Féin
wins 73 of 105 Irish seats

25 SEPTEMBER
Thomas Ashe dies in Mountjoy
jail after forced feeding

26 OCTOBER
De Valera elected president
of Sinn Féin

1917

16 JUNE
Remaining 120 Irish prisoners,
including Eoin MacNeill, de Valera
and Markievicz, released from
British jails

1918

18 APRIL
A broad front of Irish nationalists
oppose conscription at Mansion
House conference

1919

21 JANUARY
First meeting of Dáil Éireann
at Mansion House, Dublin,
declares independence

Irish Volunteer attack on RIC at Soloheadbeg, Co. Tipperary kills two policemen and marks the beginning of the war of independence

1920

23 DECEMBER
Government of Ireland Act, 1920, provides for two subordinate Irish parliaments, one for six Ulster counties, the other for the remainder of the country

1921

22 JUNE
George V opens Northern Ireland parliament in Belfast

9 JULY
Truce ends Irish war of independence

6 DECEMBER
Anglo–Irish treaty signed by British government and Sinn Féin delegates in London

1922

7 JANUARY
Dáil Éireann approves Anglo–Irish treaty by 64 votes to 57

14 JANUARY
Irish Free State provisional government elected by pro-treaty representatives; Michael Collins elected chairman

28 JUNE
Free State troops attack anti-treaty forces in Four Courts, beginning the civil war

20 JULY
Limerick and Waterford taken by Free State troops (Cork taken 11 August)

12 AUGUST
Arthur Griffith, president of Dáil Éireann, dies of cerebral haemorrhage

22 AUGUST
Michael Collins killed in ambush at Béal na Bláth, Co. Cork

17 NOVEMBER
First of 77 executions of anti-treatyites by Free State government (last on 2 May 1923)

6 DECEMBER
Formal establishment of Irish Free State with W. T. Cosgrave as president of the executive council

1923

24 MAY
De Valera orders anti-treatyites to cease armed operations, ending the civil war

BIOGRAPHIES

Augustine Birrell

1850–1933

Augustine Birrell, chief secretary for Ireland, was born 19 January 1850 near Liverpool, son of Charles Birrell, Baptist minister, and Harriet Jane Birrell (née Grey), of Edinburgh. A legacy enabled him to study law at Trinity Hall, Cambridge, graduating BA (1872). He was called to the bar at the Inner Temple (1875) and took silk in 1895. He was Quain professor of law at University College, London (1896–9). His talents were, however, as much literary as legal, and while developing a strong practice at the bar he also became a noted essayist and bibliophile.

Birrell was elected as MP for West Fife (1889), but when he switched constituencies in the 1900 general election he failed to take a seat in Manchester. He had more luck in the Liberal landslide of 1906, taking North Bristol. He was immediately appointed to the cabinet of Henry Campbell-Bannerman as the Liberals set out on a path of radical social reform. Birrell's first post was president of the board of education. There he won plaudits from all sides for his management of an education bill intended to provide fairer treatment for nonconformist schools. Supporters and opponents alike appreciated the eloquence, sensitivity, courtesy, and finesse with which he sought to produce a successful compromise; what in retrospect was perhaps as significant, however, was that the measure failed when it was rejected by the house of lords.

Birrell became chief secretary for Ireland in January 1907, succeeding James Bryce. His legislative initiatives must be seen in the wider context of the unprecedented radicalism and dynamism of the Liberal government from 1906 to 1911. This had a spill-over effect in Ireland, in terms both of UK-wide reforms such as the children's act and the introduction of the old age pension. It also created a climate in which specifically Irish reforms became possible.

Birrell inherited two major schemes of reform which Bryce had been persuaded to embrace by his powerful under-secretary, Sir Antony MacDonnell. MacDonnell believed that the heat could be taken out of the home rule issue through practical, disinterested administrative reform, embodied in an 'Irish Council' bill; Birrell's political instincts suggested that this was a non-starter, and he made little effort to push it through the commons. He also discounted MacDonnell's advice to court the Irish centre ground, instead setting out to maintain the closest possible relations with the nationalist leaders John Redmond and John Dillon.

Birrell inherited a recommendation, backed by MacDonnell, that the five Irish colleges—TCD, UCD, and the three Queen's colleges at Belfast, Cork and Galway—should come within a federal university. This would have met Catholic and nonconformist grievances about university education within a non-denominational framework. Birrell initially attempted to achieve such a federal system; but, faced with strong religious reservations all round, he compromised, overseeing the creation of the NUI and QUB, accommodating respectively largely Catholic and nonconformist interests, to stand beside TCD. This largely segregated university system endured unchanged till 1968 (when the New University of Ulster was established in Northern Ireland) and 1989 (when Dublin City University and the University of Limerick were created), a very Irish solution to an Irish problem.

From 1907 Birrell was confronted with renewed agrarian agitation because of the slowing pace of land reform in the west of Ireland, arising largely from a shortage of funds. He was harshly criticised by Conservatives for his unwillingness to use coercion to quell unrest, but his constructive approach was vindicated. He showed resolution and guile in securing cross-party support for the funds and powers of compulsory purchase necessary to clear the log jam in the 1909 land act, despite the reservations of many landlords and the reflexive hostility of the Treasury to any further expenditure on the Irish land question.

Birrell was unequivocally in favour of home rule. Until the constitutional crisis over the 1909 'people's budget' culminated in the removal of the house of lords' power of veto over legislation through the parliament act, there appeared no prospect of introducing self-government for Ireland. In tandem with this, the two general elections of 1910 saw the Irish nationalists emerge as a key factor in the commons, holding the balance between the Liberals and the Conservatives. The nationalists demanded and got a home rule bill, which Birrell brought to the commons in 1912. It met nationalist but not Ulster unionist demands, and it set in train a sequence of events that might well have culminated in civil war in Ireland in the summer of 1914, had the Kaiser not also been on the move. In the face of furious Ulster unionist resistance to home rule, including the formation of the Ulster Volunteer Force, Birrell and his officials in Dublin Castle adopted an understandably cautious approach. The home rule crisis was of such a magnitude that only a united cabinet could address it. In those circumstances Birrell took the view that the Irish authorities should not take any steps that might inflame Ulster. There were also technical legal reasons why action against the importation and carrying of arms might fail, although these could have been remedied by legislation. The result was what amounted to a policy of drift, where Ulster unionism was allowed to build up a private army, encouraging the creation of a matching nationalist volunteer movement in November 1913, without let or hindrance.

In Ireland itself other forces were also at work. The charismatic trade union leader James Larkin led a bitter transport strike in Dublin in 1913. This was met with a sharpness of repression at odds with Birrell's general style of governance. Birrell had never taken much interest in questions of law and order or in the activities of the police forces, leaving these matters to officials in Dublin Castle, but he had overall responsibility. To an extent, official excesses during the 1913 disturbances—including what appeared a vindictive and disproportionate prosecution of Larkin—may reflect Birrell's progressive disengagement with Ireland: his second wife was desperately ill with a brain tumour, and he had already attempted to resign on more than one occasion. The legislative battle for home rule had been won, and solution of the outstanding intractable question of Ulster would be the responsibility of the cabinet as a whole.

In April 1914 the Ulster Volunteers successfully smuggled and distributed 20,000 rifles at Larne. This gun-running operation took place under the eyes of the Irish authorities, who did nothing. In July, when the Irish Volunteers attempted a similar coup on a smaller scale at Howth near Dublin, there was a disastrous attempt to interfere. Some weapons were seized by the police, only to be returned because of doubts about their legal powers, but the bulk of the arms were spirited away. Events culminated in the deaths of three onlookers, shot by troops during a minor riot at Bachelor's Walk in central Dublin. The episode underlined the danger of over-zealous law enforcement; it also threw up familiar problems arising from outdated legislation on firearms and public order. The Bachelor's Walk fiasco can only have reinforced a tendency not to act precipitately against armed groups.

Birrell had one stroke of good fortune in 1914. He acquired a very able under-secretary for Ireland in Sir Matthew Nathan, a former Royal Engineer. The great question, once war broke out and the bulk of the unionist and nationalist volunteers enlisted in the army, was what to do about the rump of advanced nationalists who remained as the Irish Volunteers and the Irish Citizen Army. These continued to prepare for armed conflict, parading and practising under the eyes of the authorities. The balance that had to be struck was between ensuring that no outbreak took place, and not inflaming public opinion by repression of a movement which most Irish nationalists appeared to regard as an irrelevance. Redmond and Dillon were anxious that Ireland be governed with caution and toleration: it was important not to damage recruitment to the armed services, and to prevent any disruption in the war economy. Neither Birrell nor Nathan was aware that a circle of conspirators within the Irish Volunteers had already made arrangements for German help for a rebellion, a matter that became known to naval intelligence through decodings of German diplomatic cables between Washington and Berlin in 1915–16; had the extent and limits of London's foreknowledge been passed on to Dublin Castle and assessed in parallel with what the police knew, it is likely that action to thwart the conspiracy would have followed.

Nevertheless, the increasing boldness of the Irish Volunteers, culminating in their mock attack on Dublin Castle in March 1916, should surely have prompted firm action by the Irish administration. As it was, the outbreak of the Easter rising took Dublin Castle by surprise.

Had Birrell retired as he wished in 1913 or 1914, his political obituaries would undoubtedly have been kinder. His first six years in Ireland saw a succession of notable innovations, some the product of the rising tide of social legislation enacted by the Liberals, others specifically Irish and his responsibility. His misjudgement in tolerating the seditious activities of the Irish Volunteers after 1914 cannot be separated from the earlier home rule crisis and the government's unwillingness to prevent the arming of Ulster, but there is no doubt that he failed to appreciate the enhanced threat posed by even a relatively small group of committed militants in the changed circumstances of war.

Birrell willingly accepted political responsibility for the rising, and bore without complaint the attacks made on him by many who had flouted the spirit of the law and the constitution themselves only a few years earlier. Sir Henry Wilson maintained that Birrell should be tried for dereliction of duty and shot if convicted; yet the same officer had supported the militarisation of Ulster resistance to home rule from 1911. Birrell wrote ruefully of his time in Ireland in a posthumously published memoir, *Things past redress* (London, 1937). He was conferred with an honorary degree by the NUI in 1929 (though bad weather prevented his attending the ceremony). He lived in comfortable retirement in London, surrounded by books, till his death on 20 November 1933 at the age of 83.

He married first (1878) Margaret Mirrielees, who died the following year. He married secondly (1888) Eleanor (née Locker; d. 1915), widow of the Hon. Lionel Tennyson; they had two sons.

Eunan O'Halpin

Sources

Who was who, iii: *1929–1940*; León Ó Broin, *Dublin Castle and the 1916 rising* (1966); León Ó Broin, *The chief secretary: Augustine Birrell and Ireland, 1907–16* (1969); Patricia Jalland, *The Liberals and Ireland, 1911–1914* (1980); Eunan O'Halpin, *The decline of the union: British government in Ireland, 1892–1920* (1987)

Winifred
Carney

1887–1943

Winifred ('Winnie') Carney, trade unionist, feminist, and republican, was born Maria Winifred Carney on 4 December 1887 at Fisher's Hill, Bangor, Co. Down, youngest child among three sons and three daughters of Alfred Carney, commercial traveller, and Sarah Carney (née Cassidy; d. 1933). Her father was a Protestant and her mother a Catholic; the children were reared as Catholics. After her birth her parents moved to Belfast and separated during her childhood. Her father went to London and little more was heard from him; her mother supported the family by running a sweetshop on the Falls Road. Winifred was educated at the CBS in Donegall Street, Belfast, where she became a junior teacher. Independently minded, she later worked as a clerk in a solicitor's office, having qualified as shorthand typist from Hughes's Commercial Academy. In her early twenties she became involved in the Gaelic League and the suffragist and socialist movements. She had a wide range of cultural interests in literature, art and music, had a good voice, and played the piano well.

In 1912 she took over from her friend Marie Johnson as secretary of the Irish Textile Workers' Union based at 50 York Street, Belfast, which functioned as the women's section of the Irish Transport and General Workers' Union (ITGWU) and was led by James Connolly. Her pay was low and irregular, but she and her colleague Ellen Grimley worked with

great enthusiasm to improve the wages and conditions of the mill girls, and Carney managed the time-consuming and tedious insurance section of the union. During the 1913 lockout she was active in fund-raising and relief efforts for the Dublin workers. Many of those connected with the ITGWU were drawn into the republican movement and she was present at the founding of Cumann na mBan in Wynn's Hotel, Dublin (2 April 1914). A close friend of Connolly, she joined the Irish Citizen Army (she was a crack shot with a rifle), and became his personal secretary. She appears to have been completely in his confidence and in full agreement with his revolutionary aims. On 14 April 1916 he summoned her to Dublin to assist in the final preparations for the Easter rising, and for the next week she typed dispatches and mobilisation orders in Liberty Hall. She was the only woman in the column that seized the GPO on Easter Monday, 24 April (although several others arrived later). During the rising she acted as Connolly's secretary and, even after most of the women had been evacuated from the GPO, she refused to leave and replied sharply to Patrick Pearse when he suggested she should. She stayed with Connolly in the makeshift headquarters at 16 Moore Street, typing dispatches and dressing his wound, and attending to the other wounded men. After the surrender (29 April) she was interned, first in Mountjoy and from July in Aylesbury prison, and was released 24 December 1916.

In autumn 1917 she was Belfast delegate to the Cumann na mBan convention, and was appointed president of the Belfast branch. In 1918 she was briefly imprisoned in Armagh and Lewes prisons. She stood for Sinn Féin in Belfast's Victoria division in the general election of 1918 (the only woman candidate in Ireland apart from Constance Markievicz), advocating a workers' republic, but she polled badly, winning only 4 per cent of the votes. Afterwards she was very critical of the support she had received from Sinn Féin. In 1919 she was transferred to the Dublin head office of the ITGWU, but did not get on well with colleagues such as Joe McGrath and William O'Brien, and returned to Belfast after a few months. She was Belfast secretary of the Irish Republican Prisoners' Dependants Fund (1920–22). She became a member of the revived Socialist Party of Ireland in 1920 and attended the annual convention of the Independent Labour Party in Glasgow in April 1920.

Never deviating in her hope for the establishment of Connolly's workers' republic, she opposed the Anglo–Irish treaty, and sheltered republicans such as Markievicz and Austin Stack in her home at 2a Carlisle Circus, Belfast. On 25 July 1922 she was arrested by the RUC and held in custody for eighteen days after 'seditious papers' were discovered in her home. She refused to recognise the court and was fined £2. Critical of partition and the social conservatism of Irish governments after independence, she remained in Belfast, concentrating on helping the local labour movement. She refused to accept a pension for her part in 1916, relenting only weeks before her death. In 1924 she joined the Court Ward branch of the Northern Ireland Labour Party (NILP) and was active in the party's radical wing promoting republican socialism. In discussions with colleagues she always praised Connolly and defended the 1916 rising, but was modest about her own part in it and never revealed what she knew of its planning; she also shared Connolly's distrust of James Larkin. Some regarded her as rather austere and sharp-tongued, but close friends spoke of her kindness and charm, and praised her strong personal and political loyalties. She continued to work for the ITGWU in Belfast and Dublin until September 1928, when she married George McBride. McBride (1898–1988), a Protestant, was a textile engineer, staunch socialist, and NILP member, who had joined the UVF in 1913 and fought in the British army (1914–18). They lived at 3 Whitewell Parade, Whitehouse, Belfast, and, despite their disagreements about Irish nationalism, their marriage was very happy; they had no children. In about 1934 Carney joined the small Belfast Socialist Party, but her health was deteriorating and she took little active part in politics. She died 21 November 1943 in Belfast and was buried in Milltown cemetery, Belfast.

James Quinn

Sources

GRO (Dublin); Cathal O'Shannon, 'Winifred Carney—a link with Easter week', *Torch* (Dublin), 27 November, 4 December 1943; Desmond Ryan, *The rising: the complete story of Easter week* (1949); Margaret Ward, *Unmanageable revolutionaries* (1983); Michael Foy and Brian Barton, *The Easter rising* (1999); Helga Woggon, *Silent radical, Winifred Carney 1887–1943: a reconstruction of her autobiography* (2000); Diane Urquart, *Women in Ulster politics, 1890–1940* (2000); Sinéad McCoole, *No ordinary women: Irish female activists in the revolutionary years 1900–1923* (2003)

Roger Casement

1864–1916

Roger David Casement, humanitarian and Irish nationalist, was born 1 September 1864 in Sandycove, near Dublin, youngest child among one daughter and three sons of Roger Casement, retired army officer, and Anne Casement (née Jephson). He was brought up as a member of the Church of Ireland, although his Catholic mother arranged for her children to be baptised secretly in her own faith. After her death (1873) the family moved to Co. Antrim, where Roger was educated in the Ballymena diocesan school. When his father died (1877) the children were left in straitened circumstances and became wards in chancery. Roger was cared for by relatives in Antrim and Liverpool. As an adolescent he admired and identified with Irish rebels of the past, and he remained a romantic idealist all his life.

AFRICA

At the age of 15 Casement began work as a clerk in the Elder Dempster shipping company, and four years later this led to a post as purser on one of the company's ships bound for West Africa. From 1884 to 1891 he lived in the Congo, which became a personal colony of the Belgian king, Leopold II. His occupations included those of surveyor, explorer and (briefly) assistant in a Baptist missionary station. From 1892 to 1895 he was employed as a surveyor and customs official in the Niger Coast protectorate, after which—because of his extensive African experience—he was absorbed into the British consular service. Joseph Conrad was impressed by him when they met in the Congo, remarking that 'he could tell you things! Things I have tried to forget, things I never did know' (Reid, 14).

Casement was a tall, handsome man of considerable charm. During his time in Africa he was efficient and energetic, he was 'brave, diplomatic and usefully observant' (Sawyer, 26), but he was also frequently bored, irritable and depressed. He suffered from malaria, jaundice and other illnesses, and throughout adult life was often debilitated. He veered rapidly from enthusiasm to anger and despair, showing signs of bipolar disorder. He hated routine and disliked most of the places where he lived. Early in his career he was an imperialist, believing that colonialism was a force for enlightenment and that it eliminated abuses such as slavery. He supported the British war in South Africa at least partly because of the Boers' maltreatment of the black population. (In later years he became a harsh critic of British policy towards the Boers.) He could be snobbish, and at times displayed some of the racist views characteristic of the period, but he liked Africans and they reciprocated his affection. He was a warm-hearted man who sided psychologically with the underdog or the oppressed. On two separate occasions the consular service provided him, improbably, with a challenging role in which he could display his initiative, independence and courage.

After serving in Luanda and Lourenço Marques (later Maputo), Casement went back to the Congo as British consul. The turning point in his career came in 1903 when he was ordered to investigate reports of atrocities carried out by Leopold's agents. He rented a steamboat and travelled to remote areas of the Upper Congo, remarking that he was ceasing to be a consul; he had become a criminal investigator (Ó Siocháin and O'Sullivan, 37). In the course of his journey he encountered plentiful evidence that the collection of rubber was associated with forced labour, extortionate taxes, mutilation, murder and depopulation; he observed colonialism in its most brutal form.

In February 1904 Casement's report on the Congo was published as a sixty-page government white paper. It was well structured, solidly factual, and detached in tone—in contrast to the intemperate and emotional style that characterised much of his correspondence. It was a formidable indictment of a system based on oppression and cruelty. He was aggrieved when the Foreign Office watered down his original version, describing the final result as 'cooked and garbled' (Inglis, 86), and felt that he was inadequately supported against Leopold's counter-attack. Nonetheless, his findings were confirmed by an international commission appointed by the king, and his report was one of several pressures that led the Belgian government to take over the administration of the Congo in 1908. His achievements were recognised by his inclusion in Edward VII's birthday honours list, but this gave him no satisfaction; he never opened the parcel containing the insignia of his award. More significantly, they also led him to establish a close working relationship with E. D. Morel and other critics of colonial abuses.

SOUTH AMERICA

Partly for reasons of ill health, Casement interrupted his consular career in 1904–6 to spend eighteen months in Ireland and Britain, and for most of this time he was seconded without pay. In Ireland, as abroad, he was peripatetic; he had no home or base, and he stayed in lodgings, hotels and the houses of friends. He became a committed Irish nationalist who supported the ideals of 'Irish Ireland', and in particular the revival of the Irish language. He excused his continuing membership of the consular service, which he loathed, by the fact that he could (and often did) give away much of his salary. While he was parsimonious in small matters he was always extravagantly generous in his financial assistance to individuals or groups that won his sympathy—such as wayward members of his family, Morel's Congo Reform Association, and an Irish-speaking community in Co. Galway.

He was a difficult subordinate and the foreign office was reluctant to reemploy him, but in 1906 he rejoined the consular service and took up the first of a series of postings in Brazil. These culminated in his appointment as consul-general in Rio de Janeiro. Although he continued to be efficient in the conduct of his duties, he became increasingly frustrated, and disliked the Brazilian people. During this 'exile' his commitment to Irish causes deepened. But he was aroused by a new challenge: he was directed to investigate reports of atrocities in the region of the Putumayo, a remote tributary of the Amazon. In its collection of rubber the Peruvian

Amazon Co. was accused of exploiting not merely local Amerindians, but also some British subjects from Barbados. This new task seemed to replicate his experiences in the Congo.

In August 1910 Casement joined a commission of inquiry established by the company. Once more he was a diligent and persevering investigator, interviewing victims and witnesses, keeping detailed records, and taking photographs. He discovered that many of the indigenous population of the Putumayo were treated as slaves, and that practices such as flogging, rape, starvation, mutilation and murder were commonplace. He wrote a second report for the Foreign Office, which he completed in March 1911, and then returned for another visit to the Amazon. His report attracted widespread publicity and praise when it was eventually published, but in practice it did little to improve the conditions of the inhabitants of the Putumayo. Ultimately they were saved not by the intervention of foreign consuls and governments but by the collapse of the market for wild rubber.

Casement had become a dissident within the consular service and (despite his graceful acknowledgment) was embarrassed by the award of a knighthood. He became even more committed to Irish causes and advocated a fully independent Ireland—which he believed could be achieved with German assistance. In August 1913 he retired at last from the Foreign Office. Until then he was better known abroad than at home, having spent more than thirty years in Britain, Africa and South America; only now, aged almost 49, did he begin to play a significant role in Irish affairs.

NATIONALIST AND REBEL

At first Casement tried to win over Ulster Protestants to Irish nationalism, and his predictable failure threw him into one of his many fits of depression (although to the end of his life he persisted in his belief that unionists and nationalists could join forces). But the formation of the Irish Volunteers in November 1913 provided him with a new role and a new crusade. He became a member of their provisional committee and travelled around the country, organised paramilitary units, made speeches, and relished what he described as intrigue and gross sedition. He believed that not merely would the creation of a Volunteer force strengthen the hand of Irish nationalists, but it would also provide the Irish people with much-needed discipline.

Casement took the initiative in the Volunteers' most spectacular exploit, the Howth gun-running of July 1914. In contrast to the inactivity displayed by most members of the IRB, he and a small number of friends decided to follow the example of the Ulster Volunteers and to import guns from continental Europe. Together with Erskine Childers, Alice Stopford Green, Bulmer Hobson, and a few others, he organised the purchase of 1,500 rifles and ammunition in Belgium and their transportation to Ireland. Some of these weapons were used two years later in the Easter rising.

Casement was always impatient and impetuous, and by the time that the arms were delivered to Howth he had already arrived in the US with the aim of raising funds for the Volunteers. The success of the gun-running made him a hero among Irish-Americans, but the outbreak of the first world war a week later soon distracted attention from Irish affairs. The results of his campaign were disappointing. He wrote an incautious letter to the *Irish Independent* in which he claimed that Ireland's real enemy was Britain and not Germany, thereby ruling out his return to Ireland. Instead he travelled to Berlin in October 1914 as the envoy of Irish-American leaders. He persuaded the German government to declare that if its forces landed in Ireland they would do so as liberators. Later he had a friendly interview with Chancellor Bethmann Hollweg—but he was already accustomed to the company of the powerful, having met King Leopold in Brussels and President Taft in Washington. His actions disconcerted the British authorities, and he was flattered by reports that a substantial sum of money would be paid in return for information leading to his capture.

Otherwise the eighteen months he spent in Germany were a failure. He tried to induce captured Irish prisoners of war to change sides and to join an 'Irish brigade' which would support the Central Powers by liberating Ireland—or, alternatively, Egypt. His methods were clumsy and the response was disillusioning: he secured only fifty-six recruits from a total of about 2,300 prisoners. Casement's communications with friends and allies in Ireland, Britain and the US were equally inept. He encouraged the Germans to assist an Irish rebellion but he became dismayed by what he saw as their inadequate commitment, describing their plans (almost prophetically) as 'practically three men in a boat to invade a kingdom' (Reid, 335). He denounced them with the same fervour with which he had earlier abused Belgians, Brazilians, Americans, Irish unionists, home rulers, and various others. His health was wretched, and he was often lonely and depressed.

Casement believed that an Irish insurrection would be crushed unless it received substantial assistance from Germany, and when it became clear that adequate help would not be forthcoming he decided to travel to Ireland and try to prevent the planned rebellion from taking place. The Germans obligingly sent him there by submarine, and it was intended that he would arrive on Good Friday, at the same time as a ship carrying a modest supply of arms. The two vessels failed to rendezvous in Tralee Bay, but Casement, accompanied by Robert Monteith and Daniel Bailey, set off for the shore in a dinghy. It capsized, and Casement landed on Banna Strand in north Kerry, ill, drenched and exhausted. He hid and waited for his companions to return with assistance, but was soon captured. He persevered with his original intentions, and while under arrest he tried to send a message to Dublin, warning that the rebellion should be aborted. He was brought to London, and during his interrogation in Scotland Yard on Easter Sunday asked to be allowed to communicate with the rebel leaders to persuade them to call off the insurrection. This was not permitted.

After the suppression of the Easter rising Casement was tried for treason in the Old Bailey in June 1916. The case against him was based on a statute of 1351 which, in translation from the original Norman French, defined treason as 'levying war against the king or being adherent to the king's enemies in his realm, giving them aid and comfort in the realm or elsewhere'. He was accused of having tried to recruit Irish prisoners of war to form an Irish brigade which would fight the British, and of having participated in a German expedition to Ireland. His counsel, A. M. Sullivan, argued that any treason of which he was guilty had taken place *outside* the realm, but this plea was not allowed. Sullivan also failed in his more reasonable effort to link Casement's actions with the plans for rebellion made by the Ulster Volunteers—in which they had been supported by F. E. Smith, who was now attorney general and counsel for the prosecution. Neither side mentioned the fact that Casement had landed in Ireland in an effort to prevent the rising. The prosecution remained silent because such evidence would complicate its case for treason, and the defence because Casement did not wish to repudiate the rebels. In any case, he was obviously guilty of treason while in Germany.

Among the witnesses were some of the prisoners of war whose loyalty he had tried to subvert and who had (foolishly or cynically) been returned by the Germans as part of a prisoner exchange.

After a trial lasting four days the jury took less than an hour to declare Casement guilty. Following an old Irish tradition he made an eloquent speech from the dock. He ridiculed the 1351 statute, claimed that he should be judged only by an Irish jury (particularly since he had landed in Ireland rather than in Britain), praised the Ulster Volunteers, and argued that Irishmen should fight for their freedom at home rather than abroad. An appeal against his sentence was rejected, and Casement was hanged on 3 August 1916, a day after he had been received into the Catholic church. He was buried in Pentonville jail, and his remains were returned to Ireland only in 1965. After an elaborate state funeral they were reburied in Glasnevin cemetery.

THE DIARIES

Even before Casement's trial British officials circulated portions of diaries, supposedly written by him, in which the author described homosexual encounters with young men and adolescents. They contained numerous accounts of partners' physical details and of payments made. Their circulation to journalists and to influential figures in Ireland, Britain and the US was designed to blacken his reputation and to undermine any movement for clemency. In the probable event of his execution they would also help to prevent his being viewed as a martyr. The tactic succeeded in the first of these objectives. At a time when homosexual tastes and practices were widely loathed, several among those who were shown the diaries chose not to involve themselves in the appeal for a reprieve.

Over many decades some of Casement's supporters claimed that the diaries were forged. There were strong arguments in favour of such a view: none of his friends and acquaintances suspected he was a homosexual; accounts of the diaries' discovery were inconsistent; the 'black' or compromising diaries related to the years in which he made his two river journeys, when his movements were uniquely well recorded; and some of the entries for 1911 indicate rash behaviour at a time when Casement was under constant surveillance by his enemies.

On the other hand it was argued that the diaries were preserved carefully by the British government (although access to them was denied until 1959), and that this would have been self-defeating if they were forgeries; F. E. Smith clearly believed they were genuine and offered them to Casement's counsel for inspection—an offer which was wisely declined; the diaries contained inconsistencies (such as criticism of homosexuality) which seemed to weaken their impact, and which a forger might sensibly have avoided; the sheer volume of material was superfluous, increasing the risk of incriminating errors; and any forgery had to be carried out in a hurry, since there had been no need to produce the diaries until Casement was captured a mere five weeks before his trial.

Eventually in 2002 scientific examination vindicated their authenticity to general (although not universal) satisfaction. But in contrast to the long-standing disagreement over whether the diaries were genuine, the unscrupulous use that was made of them in 1916—to smear the reputation of a condemned man and thereby help ensure the failure of his appeal against his death sentence—has met with nothing but embarrassment and distaste.

The diaries have provoked understandable controversy, but this cannot obscure Casement's importance. He was a humanitarian who fought with bravery and determination against the enslavement of indigenous peoples in the Congo and Amazonia. He was the principal organiser of the Howth gun-running, without which the Easter rising might not have taken place. Despite his attempts to prevent what he believed would be a doomed insurrection, he was also the last victim of the executions that followed the Easter rising, and thereby became a nationalist martyr.

Michael Laffan

Sources

Brian Inglis, *Roger Casement* (1973); B. L. Reid, *The lives of Roger Casement* (1976); Roger Sawyer, *Casement, the flawed hero* (1984); Reinhard R. Doerries, *Prelude to the Easter rising: Roger Casement in imperial Germany* (2000); W. J. McCormack, *Roger Casement in death* (2002); Angus Mitchell (ed.), *Sir Roger Casement's heart of darkness: the 1911 documents* (2003); Seamas Ó Siocháin and Michael O'Sullivan (ed.), *The eyes of another race: Roger Casement's Congo report and 1903 diary* (2003); Mary E. Daly (ed.), *Roger Casement in Irish and world history* (2005)

Éamonn Ceannt

1881–1916

Éamonn Ceannt, revolutionary and Irish Irelander, was born Edward Thomas Kent on 21 September 1881 in Ballymoe, Glenamaddy, Co. Galway, sixth among seven children (six boys and a girl) of James Kent (1841–1912), RIC constable originally of Co. Tipperary, and his wife Johanna (née Galwey) (d. 1895) of Co. Cork. In 1883 James Kent was transferred to Ardee, Co. Louth, where Edward attended the De La Salle national school. He was a shy and studious boy, who enjoyed fishing, bird-watching and long walks in the countryside. After five years in Ardee, the family moved to Drogheda, where Edward attended the CBS in Sunday's Gate. James Kent retired from the RIC in 1892 and settled his family in Dublin, at 232 Clonliffe Road, Drumcondra. Edward went to O'Connell CBS, North Richmond Street, where he was a diligent student, and a keen rugby player and hurler. He did particularly well in his final exams in 1898 and became a clerk in the city treasurer's office of Dublin Corporation.

The centenary commemorations for the 1798 rebellion sparked his interest in cultural nationalism, and he began to study Irish, being tutored by his father, who was a native speaker. In September 1899 he joined the Gaelic League and adopted the Irish form of his name (although he was still often known as Kent). He was soon fluent in Irish and teaching classes himself, and was elected to the league's governing body in 1909; he fought

a successful three-year battle with the authorities to insist that his son's birth should be registered in Irish. He enjoyed learning languages and in his youth often spent time at Dublin port talking to foreign sailors; besides Irish, he spoke French and German reasonably well. His dedication to Gaelic culture led him to become an accomplished uilleann piper: he spent his holidays travelling throughout Gaeltacht regions collecting old airs and won many prizes at the annual feiseanna for his piping (he also played the flute, tin-whistle and violin). In 1900 he and Edward Martyn founded the Dublin Pipers' Club (Cumann na bPíobairí) of which Ceannt was honorary secretary for many years. On 7 June 1905 he married at St James's church, James's Street, Dublin, Áine Ní Bhraonáin, a student from his Irish classes. They lived at 2 Dolphin's Terrace, South Circular Road, Dublin, and had one son, Ronan (1906–74).

A devout Catholic, in September 1908 Ceannt travelled to Rome with a group of Irish athletes and musicians who were members of the Catholic Young Men's Society to celebrate the jubilee of Pope Pius X and, dressed in a colourful traditional piper's costume (now in the National Museum), played the pipes in a private audience with the pope. During the trip he insisted on conversing with his colleagues only in Irish. He joined Sinn Féin in 1907, and was elected to its national council. He was a regular at separatist demonstrations and organised protests against the visit of George V in 1911. In 1913 he proposed a motion to the Sinn Féin national council that Irishmen should learn the use of arms; he himself had already joined a rifle club and become a crack shot. An effective speaker, Ceannt spoke regularly on political and cultural topics to various nationalist organisations. He was one of the main contributors to *An Barr Buadh* (March to May 1912), Patrick Pearse's short-lived militant Irish-language journal, and also wrote articles and songs for *An Claidheamh Soluis*, the *Irish Nation, Sinn Féin,* and the *Volunteer Gazette*, in both Irish and English. Widely read, he had a good knowledge of the social theories of Marx and Engels and was more sympathetic to socialist policies than most of his Sinn Féin colleagues; he was chairman of the Dublin Municipal Officers' Association and during the 1913 lockout he defended Dublin workers against the criticisms of Arthur Griffith.

Recognising an uncompromising militant, Seán Mac Diarmada recruited him into the IRB in 1911, and Ceannt assisted with the production of the IRB newspaper, *Irish Freedom*. He was urged by Mac Diarmada to become a founder member of the Irish Volunteers in November 1913, and with Mac Diarmada and Pearse, all key members of the IRB, was elected to the Volunteer committee. As captain of A company, 4th Dublin battalion of the Volunteers, he participated in the landing of rifles at Howth on 26 July and at Kilcoole, Co. Wicklow, on 1 August 1914. He was a leading organiser of the conference of separatists held (9 September 1914) in the Gaelic League library at 25 Parnell Square, Dublin, which decided in principle to use the opportunity of the European war to mount an insurrection in Ireland. He voted against John Redmond's nominees to the Volunteer executive (16 June 1914) and, after the Volunteer split (24 September 1914), became a leading member of the Irish Volunteer executive, serving as director of communications and commandant of the 4th Dublin battalion. In 1915 he became a member of the IRB supreme council, and in May 1915 Ceannt, Pearse, and Joseph Plunkett, all regarded as dedicated insurrectionists, were the first appointees to an IRB military committee that became the military council that planned the Easter rising. Ceannt was involved in various subterfuges to keep moderate Volunteer leaders in the dark, such as sending the director of recruiting, Seán Fitzgibbon, to Kerry to supervise an arms landing in the days before the rising.

At a meeting on 18 April 1916 Ceannt was one of the seven signatories of the republican proclamation and during Easter week (24–30 April) his under-strength battalion held the South Dublin Union and its outposts. The Union, close to several British army barracks and controlling one of the main approaches to the city, saw some of the insurrection's bloodiest fighting. Ceannt proved to be an effective and courageous commander who led from the front in several fierce close-quarter actions in the Union's lanes and corridors. His spirit, and that of his vice-commandant, Cathal Brugha, inspired the small garrison of forty-two Volunteers to mount a tenacious defence of their post and hold off repeated attacks from vastly superior British forces. During the fighting he regularly led his men in saying the rosary. Prepared to fight to the death, he was dismayed to receive Pearse's order to surrender, and reluctantly ordered his men to lay down their arms. When court-martialled at Richmond Barracks (3–4 May), he showed considerable composure and did his best to cast doubt on the prosecution charges, apparently trying to secure an acquittal on technical grounds. Condemned to death, he was executed on 8 May 1916 by firing squad in Kilmainham jail, Dublin, and was buried at Arbour Hill prison cemetery. In his final letter from prison, he regretted surrendering and advised republicans 'never to treat with the enemy, never to surrender at his mercy, but to fight to a finish'. He believed that 'in the years to come Ireland will honour those who risked all for *her* honour at Easter in 1916' (MacLochlainn, 136).

Ceannt was regarded by many contemporaries as a rather dour and taciturn figure. Not renowned as a poet, political theorist, or arch-conspirator, he is probably the least celebrated of the proclamation's seven signatories. However, his courage, dedication and determination were much respected by fellow separatists. Committed to achieving Irish independence through force of arms, he was impatient with the flamboyant oratory of colleagues such as Pearse. He believed that the rising had a real chance of success and told his wife beforehand that 'if we last a month the British will come to terms' (Ryan, 98). Tall, with a stiff military bearing, he was, according to Seán Fitzgibbon, 'more naturally a physical force man than any of the other leaders' (cited in MacDonagh, 512).

A portrait of Ceannt by P. H. Marrinan is held at Ceannt Barracks, the Curragh, Co. Kildare. Ceannt Fort in Kilmainham commemorates his defence of the South Dublin Union and the main railway station in Galway was named after him in 1966. His brother William, a colour sergeant with the Royal Dublin Fusiliers, was killed in action in France in 1917.

James Quinn

Sources

GRO; 'Events of Easter week', *Catholic Bulletin*, vi (1916), 395–6; 'Fighting in the South Dublin Union area', *Catholic Bulletin*, viii (1918), 153–6, 205–20, 257–60, 309–12; *Leader*, 28 April 1945; 20 April 1946; Donagh MacDonagh, 'Eamonn Ceannt', *An Cosantóir* (October 1946), 509–16; Desmond Ryan, *The rising: the complete story of Easter week* (1949); Michael J. Lennon, 'The Easter rising from the inside', six parts, *Irish Times*, 18–23 April 1949; Martin Shannon, *Sixteen roads to Golgotha* (1966), 5–15; Florence O'Donoghue, 'Ceannt, Devoy, O'Rahilly and the military plan', F. X. Martin (ed.), *Leaders and men of the Easter rising Dublin 1916* (1967); Martin Daly [Stephen McKenna], *Memories of the dead* (n.d.); Piaras F. MacLochlainn, *Last words: letters and statements of the leaders executed after the rising at Easter 1916* (1971); *Beathaisnéis*, iv (1994); Michael Foy and Brian Barton, *The Easter rising* (1999); Brian Barton, *From behind a closed door: secret court martial records of the 1916 Easter rising* (2002); William Henry, *Supreme sacrifice: the story of Éamonn Ceannt* (2005) (portraits)

Thomas Clarke

1858–1916

Thomas James ('Tom') Clarke, revolutionary, was born 11 March 1858 in Hurst Castle, Isle of Wight, eldest child among two sons and two daughters of James Clarke (b. 1830) of Carrigallen, Co. Leitrim, bombardier in the Royal Artillery, and Mary Clarke (née Palmer) of Clogheen, Co. Tipperary. His father was an Anglican and his mother a Catholic, and Thomas was baptised a Catholic. In April 1859 James Clarke was posted to South Africa and took his family. In 1867 he was sent to Dungannon, Co. Tyrone, and quit the army on 26 December 1868 with the rank of sergeant. Thomas was educated in St Patrick's national school, Dungannon, where he became a monitor; he always considered Dungannon his home town. Sympathetic to nationalist politics, he was impressed by the visit in 1878 to Dungannon of John Daly, a national organiser for the IRB, and later joined the organisation, becoming first district secretary of the Dungannon IRB.

PRISON AND NEW YORK, 1880–1907

Sought by police after firing buckshot at them during a riot in Dungannon, in August 1880 he emigrated to New York, where he was employed as a hotel porter. He joined Clan na Gael, attended the bomb-making classes of Dr Thomas Gallagher (1851–1925), and in March 1883 went on a bombing mission to England. Spotted in London carrying a suspiciously heavy black bag, he was arrested 5 April 1883 with Gallagher in possession of explosives. On 11 June 1883 he was convicted of treason felony and sentenced to penal servitude for life. Held in Millbank, Chatham, and Portland prisons, he used his alias, 'Henry Hammond Wilson', throughout his imprisonment. The regime imposed on treason felons in Chatham (where he served most of his sentence) was particularly severe: in addition to hard labour, little exercise, and enforced silence among prisoners, there were harassments such as interruption of sleep and frequent punishments for infringing prison rules. Under this pressure several Fenian prisoners, including Gallagher, went insane. However, Clarke's reason remained unimpaired, thanks to his own mental resilience and the support of his fellow inmates John Daly and James Francis Egan, also convicted on dynamiting charges. The three worked out ingenious ways of communicating together and forged strong and lasting friendships. Clarke's account of his imprisonment was published in *Irish Freedom* in 1912 and as *Glimpses of an Irish felon's prison life* (1922). After repeated requests from the Amnesty Association, he was released 29 September 1898. Fifteen years in prison had left their mark: he was socially awkward and prematurely aged, slightly stooped, with a gaunt and sunken face. He was, however, as zealous a Fenian as ever and never forgot nor forgave the harsh treatment that he and his comrades had suffered. Fêted in Dublin and Dungannon, he received the freedom of the city in Limerick (2 March 1899), where John Daly had become mayor.

He settled with his mother and sister in Kilmainham, Dublin, but found it difficult to find work and emigrated to America in 1900. In New York he was employed as a metalworker and also as a clerk for Clan na Gael, acting as private secretary to John Devoy. Here he was joined by John Daly's niece Kathleen whom he had met in Limerick; they were married 16 July 1901 in New York (Major John MacBride was the best man) and had three sons. In September 1903 Clarke helped launch the *Gaelic American*, on which he worked as assistant editor to Devoy. He became a naturalised US citizen on 2 November 1905. During these years he was active in several Irish-American organisations and in promoting Irish cultural events. In 1905, with his wife suffering from ill health, he resigned from the *Gaelic American*, and bought a small market garden farm at Manorville, Long Island; afterwards, gardening was his only hobby.

CONSPIRACY, 1907–16

Anxious to renew his Fenian activities, in November 1907 he returned to Ireland, and in February 1908 rented a tobacconist's and newsagent's shop at 55 Amiens Street, Dublin; in 1909 he bought another shop at 75a Parnell Street, and in 1910 moved shop from 55 to 77 Amiens Street; he also took a house at 10 Richmond Avenue, Fairview. He arrived back in Ireland at a time when younger IRB members were attempting to breathe new life into a largely moribund organisation. Because of his sufferings and dedication to Fenian ideals he was revered by young IRB radicals, who regarded him as the embodiment of militant Fenianism, and he was co-opted on to the IRB supreme council and appointed treasurer. He helped young militants gain control of the organisation and befriended several of them, especially Seán Mac Diarmada, who became his right-hand man; he assisted Mac Diarmada's appointment as IRB national organiser in 1908. Much of the IRB's business was transacted through front organisations, particularly the Dublin Central Wolfe Tone Clubs Committee, founded in 1910 and presided over by Clarke, and his shop in Parnell Street became the hub of IRB activity in the city. In July 1911 he organised a pilgrimage to the grave of Wolfe Tone in Bodenstown to counter the visit of George V to Dublin, and during the visit displayed a large poster outside his shop, proclaiming 'Damn your concessions, England, we want our country!'

Active in almost all aspects of the nationalist movement, Clarke joined the Gaelic League. Although he spoke little Irish, he saw the League as a useful vehicle for separatist ideals, and attempted to manipulate its appointments. With similar intentions he joined Sinn Féin. Griffith admired him and asked him to stand as Sinn Féin candidate for Dublin corporation but Clarke was dismissive of electoral politics and his response was 'none of that for me' (Le Roux, 84). He regarded Sinn Féin

as 'all right as far as it goes, but it doesn't go far enough' (*Glimpses*, 8). He sympathised with the working class and supported trade unionism, but deplored Irish trade unions' dependence on English unions, and regarded labour agitation as a minor sectional struggle compared with the great national struggle for independence.

With IRB militants Denis McCullough, Bulmer Hobson, and Mac Diarmada, he published the republican journal *Irish Freedom* from 15 November 1910 and kept it going until its suppression in December 1914. Although sharply critical of the Irish parliamentary party and its pursuit of home rule, Clarke was overjoyed at the way in which the home rule crisis polarised Irish politics: colleagues remembered him rubbing his hands with glee whenever he spoke of the UVF. Always on the lookout for dedicated activists, he invited Patrick Pearse to give the oration at the Wolfe Tone commemoration at Bodenstown in June 1913 and facilitated his entry into the IRB in November 1913, overriding the reservations of those who suspected Pearse of personal ambition and political unreliability. Operating behind the scenes, Clarke helped found the Irish Volunteers in November 1913, and strongly opposed accepting the nominees of John Redmond on to the Volunteer executive in June 1914—an issue on which he broke bitterly with Hobson, accusing him of being a Castle spy. Clarke and Mac Diarmada were the main figures behind the coup of 24 September 1914, when anti-Redmondites seized the Volunteer headquarters at 41 Dawson Street, and issued a manifesto repudiating Redmond's leadership. They were delighted with the ensuing split, which increased their control over a militant rump of Volunteers.

On 9 September 1914 Clarke presided at a conference of separatists, mostly IRB men, which decided in principle to use the opportunity of European war to mount an insurrection. Clarke, as treasurer, and Mac Diarmada, as secretary, were the key figures on the IRB supreme council—McCullough's presidency was essentially nominal. They were fervent advocates of revolutionary action and increasingly bypassed the supreme council. To prepare for insurrection they established in May 1915 a military committee (later council) which became the real power in the IRB and which they themselves joined in September 1915. During his long imprisonment Clarke had brooded on the inadequacies of previous Fenian conspiracies; now that he was in control, he insisted on rigorous planning and absolute secrecy. He hid his intentions from almost all his IRB colleagues and responded to their suspicions with evasion, indignation and, on occasion, lies. Anxious to control all aspects of the physical-force movement, Clarke was president of the O'Donovan Rossa funeral committee and it was at his instigation that Pearse gave the famous graveside oration (1 August 1915). When Pearse asked how far he could go, Clarke replied 'Make it as hot as hell, throw discretion to the winds' (Le Roux, 156). The funeral, well orchestrated and marshalled, attracted a huge crowd and was a great propaganda coup for the IRB, strongly associating the Volunteers with the Fenian tradition.

As a close friend of Devoy, Clarke was an essential link between the IRB in Dublin and Clan na Gael in New York. Wary of the negotiations of Roger Casement with the German government, in October 1915 he sent Robert Monteith to Germany to assist and monitor his activities. By December 1915 the military council had decided to rise at Easter 1916 and Clarke worked feverishly with Devoy to arrange the landing of German arms in Ireland. He also planned many of the details of the Dublin rising but his preparations were interrupted in January 1916 when he was accidentally shot in the right arm by Seán McGarry; Clarke never regained use of the arm. Although he generally shunned the limelight, his reputation and position at the centre of a web of separatist committees could not fail to attract the attention of Dublin Castle, which regarded him as the brains behind republican revolutionary activity in Ireland. DMP detectives rented a room opposite his Parnell Street shop to observe his movements, and the government was preparing to arrest him just days before the outbreak of insurrection. At a meeting on 18 April 1916, the other leaders insisted that he be first to sign the revolutionary proclamation since he had done more than anyone else to bring about the rising.

Clarke denounced the countermanding orders of 22–3 April from Eoin MacNeill as treachery, and was determined to press on as originally planned. Presiding at a military council meeting in Liberty Hall on Easter Sunday (23 April 1916), he alone advocated a rising that evening and only reluctantly agreed to a day's postponement. He served in the GPO during Easter week (24–9 April), and although he held no official position or military rank he presided at military council meetings and, after James Connolly was badly wounded (27 April), played a major part in directing military operations. After fleeing the blazing GPO to a makeshift headquarters at 16 Moore Street, Clarke was the only leader who insisted on fighting on to the end, but was overruled, and he broke down sobbing when Pearse decided to surrender. Many Volunteers were incensed by Clarke's treatment on the Rotunda hospital steps after the surrender, when he was verbally abused and roughly stripped by a British army officer, Captain P. S. Lea-Wilson (who, as an RIC officer, was shot dead in Gorey in 1920). During the search Clarke was greatly taken aback when a DMP detective read from his police file a detailed account of his entire career, from his conduct in prison, to his time in America, to his recent IRB activities. Court-martialled in Richmond barracks (2 May), Clarke made no attempt to defend himself and was sentenced to death. Allowed to see his wife, he told her that 'between this and freedom Ireland will go through hell, but she will never lie down again until she has attained full freedom' (Kathleen Clarke, 95); he also told her he was glad he would be shot, his greatest dread being that he would be imprisoned again. He was shot in the first round of executions at Kilmainham jail (3 May 1916), and buried at Arbour Hill prison cemetery.

ASSESSMENT

Clarke was probably the most single-minded of all the 1916 leaders, fervently committed to the pure Fenian doctrine of achieving an Irish republic through force of arms. For him there could be no compromise on Irish independence, and all other goals were secondary. Modest and unassuming, he hated public speaking and had little personal ambition, but he was a relentless and ruthless conspirator who masterminded the Easter rising, and his thoroughness and tenacity were afterwards much admired by Michael Collins. His frail and inoffensive appearance concealed a fierce revolutionary spirit, and he was capable of great hatred, particularly for Irishmen he believed had betrayed their country, such as Hobson and MacNeill. During the rising those who observed Clarke commented on how happy he looked, the insurrection being for him the culmination of a decade's work and a life's ambition.

James Quinn

Sources

Thomas Clarke, *Glimpses of an Irish felon's prison life* (1922); Desmond Ryan, 'Stephens, Devoy, Tom Clarke', *University Review*, i, no. 12 (1937), 46–55; L. N. Le Roux, *Tom Clarke and the Irish freedom movement* (1939); William O'Brien and Desmond Ryan (ed.), *Devoy's post bag* (2 vols, 1948), ii, 330–31, 366, 395, 410–12; F. X. Martin, '1916—myth, fact and mystery', *Studia Hibernica*, vii (1967), 72–3; K. B. Nowlan, 'Tom Clarke, MacDermott and the IRB' in F. X. Martin (ed.), *Leaders and men of the Easter rising Dublin 1916* (1967); Piaras F. MacLochlainn, *Last words: letters and statements of the leaders executed after the rising at Easter 1916* (1971); León Ó Broin, *Revolutionary underground* (1976), 111, 133–4, 153–4, 165–6; Kathleen Clarke, *Revolutionary woman: Kathleen Clarke 1878–1972, an autobiography* (1991); Michael Foy and Brian Barton, *The Easter rising* (1999)

Con
Colbert

1888–1916

Cornelius ('Con') Colbert, republican revolutionary and soldier, was born 19 October 1888 in Moanlena, Castlemahon, Newcastlewest, Co. Limerick, son of Michael Colbert, small farmer, native of Athea, Co. Limerick, and Honora Colbert (née MacDermott), originally of Cooraclare, Co. Clare. His family on both sides had a tradition of Fenian and nationalist activity. When he was about three the family moved to Athea, where they resided in Galeview House, and his father farmed part of the old Colbert lands at Templeathea. He attended Athea national school, save for a brief period when, while living with relatives in Ballysteen, he attended Kilcolman national school. From childhood he had a lively interest in national affairs, local history, and the Irish language (still spoken at that time by many older people in west Limerick). Moving in early adolescence to live with a sister in Dublin, he continued his schooling under the Christian Brothers, completing primary education at St Mary's Place, and receiving secondary education at the O'Connell schools, North Richmond Street. (c.1905). Thereafter he obtained a clerkship in Kennedy's bakery, Parnell Street, remaining till his death.

Joining the Gaelic League, he became a fluent Irish-speaker, and an enthusiastic participant in the league's social, cultural and educational activities. He enrolled in Na Fianna Éireann, the national boy-scout organisation founded by Bulmer Hobson and Countess Markievicz, at the inaugural meeting (16 August 1909), and was soon appointed captain of a Dublin city branch. Highly proficient at military drill, having employed a British army instructor for private lessons, he conducted Fianna classes in drill, small arms, signalling, scouting, map reading, and first aid, frequently in the field outside Dublin. An active Fianna recruiting agent, he spent summer holidays on recruitment work cycling through the country, especially in the familiar landscape of his native Limerick. Appointed part-time drill instructor (1910–16) at St Enda's school by the headmaster, Patrick Pearse, who had experienced difficulty finding an instructor who could speak Irish, he indignantly refused Pearse's offer of a salary, expecting no remuneration for work undertaken in the national interest. Recruited into the Irish Republican Brotherhood, he became head of an IRB circle composed entirely of Fianna members, formed in 1912 by Hobson, the IRB Dublin centre. In July 1913 Colbert and others of the circle commenced secret drilling of IRB members at the National Foresters Hall, Parnell Square. A small man standing just over 5 ft (1.52 m) in height, with a quiet-spoken, earnest energy, Colbert pressed his charges hard; insistent on discipline and efficiency, he inspired respect and enthusiasm. He was among five Fianna and twelve IRB activists elected to the thirty-man provisional committee of the Irish Volunteers at the inaugural meeting in the Rotunda (25 November 1913). Appointed captain of F company, 4th battalion, Dublin Brigade, he was deeply involved in drill instruction, and selection and training of Volunteer officers. After the split in the Volunteer movement over the pledge by John Redmond to support the British effort in the first world war (September 1914), Colbert organised companies of the anti-war Irish Volunteers in Limerick and elsewhere. In the weeks immediately preceding the Easter rising he acted as bodyguard to Thomas Clarke.

On Easter Monday morning (24 April 1916), Colbert commanded a garrison of twenty men who established a 4th batallion outpost in Watkin's brewery, Ardee Street, but soon lost contact with the battalion's main position under Éamonn Ceannt in the South Dublin Union, where the first day's fighting was fierce. After a brief initial exchange with British troops advancing from Richmond Barracks towards the city centre, Colbert's garrison saw minimal action. Judging his position ineffective, early on Wednesday morning he moved his command to reinforce the larger garrison in Jameson's distillery, Marrowbone Lane, under Séamus Ó Murchu, closer to the Union complex. Whether he did so on his own initiative, or in consultation with the command of the Jacob's factory garrison, is not clear. Bypassed by the cordon of British troops encircling the city centre, repulsing the few small patrols that advanced near them, the Marrowbone Lane garrison—including seven Fianna scouts, and some two dozen women of Cumann na mBan, in an atmosphere of easy camaraderie and relative equality—were blissfully unaware of events elsewhere, and reputedly planned a victory ceilidh for the Sunday night. At the surrender Colbert assumed command of the combined garrison (Saturday 29 April). Court-martialled and sentenced to death (6 May), despite his minor role in the fighting Colbert was designated by intelligence agents for severe treatment owing to his pre-rising activities and connection with Pearse. He was shot by firing squad in Kilmainham jail (8 May), and buried in the common grave in Arbour Hill jail.

Aged twenty-seven, Colbert was one of the youngest of the insurgent leaders to be executed (and was described erroneously in contemporary accounts and some subsequent sources as being even younger). Owing to his youth and relatively junior rank, his execution was one of the most shocking to public opinion. Unmarried, he resided at 7 Clifton Terrace, Ranelagh. After the rising his sister Lila Colbert served on the committee of the Irish Volunteers Dependants' Fund. A parish hall and community centre dedicated to his memory was formally opened in Athea in 1974.

Lawrence William White

Sources

GRO (birth cert.); *Catholic Bulletin*, vi, no. 7 (July 1916), 402–3, 405 (photo); *Capuchin Annual 1942*, 362 (group photo), 452; Desmond Ryan, *The rising: the complete story of Easter week* (1949); F. X. Martin (ed.), *The Irish Volunteers 1913–1915: recollections and documents* (1963), 20–22, 30, 49, 96, 144, 155, 162; Max Caulfield, *The Easter rebellion* (1964); *Capuchin Annual 1966*, 212–13, 304; *Con Colbert memorial: Athea, County Limerick* (1966); J. M. McCarthy, *Limerick's fighting story* (c.1966), 223–6; Breandán MacGiolla Choille (ed.), *Intelligence notes 1913–16* (1966); NGI, *Cuimhneachán 1916: a commemorative exhibition of the Irish rebellion 1916* (1966); Martin Shannon, *Sixteen roads to Golgotha* (c.1966), 116–20; Margaret Ward, *Unmanageable revolutionaries: women and Irish nationalism* (1983); *1916 rebellion handbook* (1998 ed.) (photo); information from Kilmainham Jail Museum, and Allen Library

John Colthurst Bowen-Colthurst

1880–1965

John Colthurst Bowen-Colthurst, army officer and murderer, was born John Colthurst Bowen in Cork on 12 August 1880, eldest son of Robert Walter Travers Bowen JP (who changed the family name to Bowen-Colthurst in 1882 to meet the terms of a relative's will) and his wife, Georgina (née Greer). He was a cousin of the novelist Elizabeth Bowen and his mother approached Bowen's father for legal assistance when her son faced court martial in 1916. Bowen-Colthurst was educated in Germany, at Haileybury School in Hertford (1894–8), and at the Royal Military Academy, Sandhurst (1898–9), where he came second in his class. Bowen-Colthurst was commissioned a lieutenant in the 1st battalion Royal Irish Rifles and fought in the Boer war; he was taken prisoner at Reddersburg in April 1900 but was released after the fall of Pretoria. He received the Queen's Medal with four clasps for his service in South Africa. He served in India in 1901–8, taking part in 1904 in the British military incursion into Tibet led by Francis Younghusband. The mission turned into a full-scale occupation of Tibet, involving large casualties among the poorly armed Tibetan forces; Bowen-Colthurst received a medal and clasp for his service.

Bowen-Colthurst led a wild life as a young man but experienced a religious conversion in India and became an evangelical Christian; this led him to organise prayer meetings among the troops under his command and to develop a fanatical conviction that he was doing God's work in fighting for the crown. During the Curragh mutiny in summer 1914, while stationed with the 2nd battalion of the Royal Irish Rifles at Tidworth, near Salisbury, he quarrelled with his commanding officer, Lieutenant-Colonel W. D. Bird (an Englishman with whom he was on bad terms). Bowen-Colthurst informed Bird that 'he did not understand the Irish and never would' and that as 'an Irishman first and last and all the time' he refused to order his men to fire on the peaceful citizens of Belfast—their own kindred (the regiment's recruiting centre was in Belfast)—to please a lot of politicians (Taylor, 19–20). This considerably embittered relations between Bird and Bowen-Colthurst in the opening stages of the first world war: at one point during the retreat from Mons, Bowen-Colthurst (who may have been suffering from shellshock) was temporarily relieved of his command after he started to march his company back towards the Germans, declaring that retreat was bad for morale and it was better to fight to the death.

On 15 September 1914, while the battalion held defensive positions at the Aisne during the Allied counter-offensive after the battle of the Marne, Bowen-Colthurst led a force in a frontal attack on a German trench; he seems either to have misunderstood an order to reconnoitre or simply to have attacked on his own initiative. He achieved a short-lived success but was soon driven back, his men suffering heavy casualties; Bowen-Colthurst himself was wounded in the chest and right arm. He appears to have been in a frenzied state—he attempted to refuse medical treatment until he had used his knowledge of German to interrogate prisoners. Despite a critical report from Bird, Bowen-Colthurst escaped punishment as he claimed that his immediate superior (subsequently a casualty) had acquiesced in his interpretation of his orders by committing more men to support the attack. This incident foreshadows Bowen-Colthurst's later actions in Dublin during the Easter rising, and demonstrates his ability to rationalise and bend facts to justify himself retrospectively.

After hospital leave he was found to be suffering from nervous exhaustion and to have limited mobility in his right arm. His only brother, an officer in the Leinster Regiment, was killed in action in March 1915. From April to July that year Bowen-Colthurst undertook home service with the 11th Rifle Brigade; he was then posted to Portobello barracks, Dublin, where he performed recruiting duties. In this context he may have encountered the women's rights activist and pacifist Francis Sheehy-Skeffington, who was engaged in an anti-recruiting campaign in Dublin.

The outbreak of the Easter rising on Monday 24 April 1916 drove Bowen-Colthurst into a frenzy of activity; he later claimed that he feared a general rising and wholesale massacre and lived in imminent expectation of an attack on the barracks (which was subject to intermittent sniping). He led troops from the barracks on several patrols during which he fired randomly at figures in lighted windows (in the belief that they might be snipers) and threw bombs into buildings. On 25 April Sheehy-Skeffington was brought into the barracks after being detained crossing Portobello bridge. At around 11.00 p.m. that day Bowen-Colthurst led a raid on the tobacco shop belonging to the home rule councillor J. J. Kelly (whom he appears to have confused with the Sinn Féin councillors Tom Kelly and Seán T. O'Kelly), taking Sheehy-Skeffington with him as a hostage to be killed if the platoon was fired upon. As the troops made their way to Kelly's shop, Bowen-Colthurst arbitrarily shot dead a young man whom he stopped and questioned outside Rathmines church. The shop was bombed and two journalists found there, Thomas Dickson and Patrick McIntyre, were taken prisoner. Both men in fact held conservative views; Dickson was a unionist and McIntyre ran an anti-Larkin paper which had taken a pro-recruiting stand. (Bowen-Colthurst may have confused the *Searchlight*, a disreputable gossip sheet also published by McIntyre, with the separatist weekly the *Spark*.) The following morning Sheehy-Skeffington, Dickson, and McIntyre were taken into the barracks yard and shot without trial on the orders of Bowen-Colthurst, who later falsely claimed that they might have intended to escape; he further attempted to justify his actions by stating that he was as good an Irishman as they were

and had lost a brother in the war. Later on 26 April, when out on patrol, Bowen-Colthurst interrogated the captured Labour councillor and Volunteer officer Richard O'Carroll before shooting him through the lungs and leaving him mortally wounded in the street.

Major Sir Francis Vane of the Munster Fusiliers, who was stationed at the barracks but had been absent on duty in Rathmines at the time of the shootings, protested to the barracks commander upon hearing of the killings in the barracks yard; he ordered Bowen-Colthurst removed from duty and confined to barracks. Bowen-Colthurst protested that Vane was a rebel and a pro-Boer—he was a supporter of home rule, who had publicly denounced British reprisals against civilians during the Boer war— and that he ought to be shot. Vane found that the higher military authorities took little interest in the case: General Maxwell regarded Bowen-Colthurst as 'a hot-headed Irishman' (Townshend, 290); Major Price (director of intelligence) told Vane that those killed probably deserved it. On Friday of Easter week Vane was relieved of his duties and ordered to hand over the barracks defences to Bowen-Colthurst, who promptly threatened to arrest Hanna Sheehy-Skeffington when she came to enquire about her husband. That evening Bowen-Colthurst raided the Sheehy-Skeffington house and took away large amounts of manuscript material (most of which was never returned), which was sifted for any evidence of treasonable activities (even a child's drawing of a Zeppelin attacking a ship was regarded as evidence). Bowen-Colthurst was later placed in charge of a detachment of soldiers going to Newry. Vane, however, made his way to London and reported directly to Lord Kitchener, who immediately ordered Bowen-Colthurst's arrest. Although this was not the only case of military personnel running amok during the Easter rising and committing murder, Bowen-Colthurst's case involved five murders over several days and implicated several other soldiers and junior officers, who had carried out, or made no attempt to question, his orders. The case was raised in parliament by John Dillon and became a *cause célèbre*.

Bowen-Colthurst was court-martialled at Richmond barracks on 6 and 7 June 1916, found guilty but insane, and committed to Broadmoor Asylum for the Criminally Insane. He did not give evidence in his own defence but numerous character witnesses were called, and T. M. Healy, representing Hanna Sheehy-Skeffington, engaged in incisive and highly publicised cross-examination of other officers present in Portobello barracks about their acquiescence in Bowen-Colthurst's actions. This failed to satisfy Vane and Hanna Sheehy-Skeffington (who complained that Bowen-Colthurst had been under no restraint during his court martial and was allowed to live at a hotel with his family); as a result of their campaign a commission of enquiry headed by Sir John Simon met in August 1916. Its report (submitted in September and published in November 1916) established a greater degree of *ex post facto* knowledge by the military authorities than had previously been believed. Vane (who was discharged from his recruiting duties and refused permission to fight on the western front) and Hanna Sheehy-Skeffington (who refused offers of compensation for her husband's murder) regarded the verdict of insanity as part of a cover-up, doubted whether Bowen-Colthurst was in fact insane, and believed that his activities had been tacitly approved by senior pro-unionist military figures who wished to exacerbate the rising in the hope of killing off home rule. Vane compared official silence on the murders with the condemnation of the court martial and execution by the Germans of the nurse Edith Cavell for espionage. Vane did not believe that the cabinet had been complicit in the cover-up; Hanna Sheehy-Skeffington did, and regularly contrasted the punishments inflicted on her for her subsequent political activities with the leniency shown to Bowen-Colthurst.

While there was certainly an attempt at concealment, it is more likely to have proceeded from military and official self-protection than from a political conspiracy. Monk Gibbon, who had been present at Portobello barracks, pointed out that while Bowen-Colthurst certainly suffered from mental abnormality, his subsequent attempts to falsify evidence and hide his actions suggest that he may not have been legally insane, since the McNaghten Rules, which then governed the matter, required that the defendant should be either ignorant of the nature of his actions or unaware that they were wrong. The Bowen-Colthurst case was sometimes referred to by advocates of a pardon for British soldiers executed during the first world war as an example of shellshock being accepted as a legal defence for crimes by an officer, while it was not regarded as excusing soldiers charged with desertion.

Bowen-Colthurst was released from Broadmoor to a private asylum in January 1919; he was subsequently released as sane and emigrated to British Columbia. His family home at Oakgrove House, Dripsey, Co. Cork, was destroyed by the IRA in April 1920; according to local tradition this was done specifically to preclude the possibility he might return and settle there. His principal income derived from investments; he owned a fruit farm but this was more a hobby than a source of income. On 2 April 1910 Bowen-Colthurst married Rosalinda Laetitia Butler; they had three sons and one daughter. After Laetitia's death on 1 August 1940 he married Priscilla Mary Bekman; they had a son and a daughter. Bowen-Colthurst died of a coronary thrombosis at Penticton, British Columbia, on 11 December 1965. In 1981 Monk Gibbon recalled him as 'a sadistic maniac, a political bigot mixed up with religion' (Levenson, 231); his military career (as well as its final acts) can be seen as a reminder of the dark and brutal side of the Irish involvement in empire.

Patrick Maume

Sources

Sinn Fein rebellion handbook, Easter 1916: a complete narrative of the rising (1916), 84–90; Elizabeth Bowen, *Bowen's Court* (1942); Max Caulfield, *The Easter rebellion* (1964); Monk Gibbon, *Inglorious soldier* (1968); Leah Levenson, *With wooden sword: a portrait of Francis Sheehy-Skeffington* (1983); Tim Sheehan, *Lady hostage* (Dripsey, Co. Cork, 1990); Margaret Ward, *Hanna Sheehy-Skeffington: a life* (1997); Charles Townshend, *Easter 1916: the Irish rebellion* (2005); James W. Taylor, *The 2nd Royal Irish Rifles in the great war* (2005)

James Connolly

1868–1916

James Connolly, socialist and revolutionary leader, was born in Cowgate, Edinburgh, on 5 June 1868, the youngest in a family of three boys. His father, John Connolly, and his mother, Mary McGinn, were both born in Ireland in 1833, possibly in Co. Monaghan, and emigrated to Scotland. From their marriage in St Patrick's parish, Cowgate, in 1856, they lived among the Irish immigrant community in that slum quarter of Edinburgh where John worked as a manure carter for the city council. Mary was a domestic servant who died at the age of fifty-eight in 1891; her husband survived her by nine years before he died of a cerebral haemorrhage in 1900.

EARLY LIFE AND SOCIALIST BEGINNINGS

Of the three Connolly children, the eldest, John, born in 1862, worked as a labourer until he joined the army in 1877, and served in India before returning to work in Edinburgh as a temporary carter in the late 1880s. He became active in the growing labour and socialist movements in the city until his political activity caused his council employers to dismiss him. Of the second son, Thomas, born in 1866, almost nothing is known apart from his having worked as a compositor's hand before emigrating, after which no trace of him remains. An early beneficiary of the introduction of universal primary education, James attended St Patrick's Catholic primary school in Cowgate until 1878. Thereafter he went to work successively as a printer's devil, a bakery hand, and a factory labourer in a mosaic works. Although his formal education was brief and minimal, he became and remained an avid and reflective reader. In 1882 he followed in his brother John's footsteps by enlisting in the first battalion the King's Liverpool Regiment, and though almost nothing is known of his seven years or so in the army, he may have served in India and almost certainly served in Ireland, probably at Cork, Castlebar, the Curragh, and Dublin. It was in Dublin that he met Lillie Reynolds, a domestic servant from a Wicklow Protestant family. They married in Perth, Scotland, in April 1890.

Very soon after his marriage he found work in Dundee, but later in 1890 they settled in Edinburgh, where Connolly worked, like his father, as a manure carter. Connolly was still a practising Catholic and the couple undertook to rear the children of the marriage as Catholics, which they duly did—all six daughters and one son receiving a Catholic education. While he abandoned religious practice and religious belief in the early 1890s, Connolly returned to the Catholic fold in the last days before his execution.

The time of his marriage and return to Edinburgh coincided with the upsurge of the 'new unionism' in Britain and Ireland—that is, the development, for the first time in the history of urban labour, of militant, mass-membership trade unions of general workers. It also coincided with a significant growth of socialism, both Marxist and Christian, and in industrial Scotland these developments were especially marked. James followed his brother John in active involvement in both developments, joining the Socialist League in Dundee in 1889 and helping to organise trade unionism among the carters of Edinburgh in 1890. It is evident that his love of reading took him deeply into the socialist literature of the time, and he began associating with leading figures of the Scottish labour movement. One of the most important of these, who became his mentor and lifelong friend, was John Leslie, who, like the Connollys, came from the working-class Irish immigrant community of Edinburgh. A founder of the Scottish Socialist Federation in 1889, Leslie wrote a brilliant pamphlet, *The present position of the Irish question* (1894), which was undoubtedly the most decisive influence on the young Connolly apart from Marx and Engels.

It was Leslie who brought Connolly actively into the socialist movement, to which he remained passionately committed for the rest of his life. Another influence was James Keir Hardie, the Ayrshire miners' leader, the first independent, working-class socialist to be elected to the house of commons, and the founder in 1893 of the political mass movement the Independent Labour Party (ILP). James succeeded his brother John as secretary of the Scottish Socialist Federation in 1892 and in the following year he joined Hardie's party. It was in this context that Connolly began to develop his direct, trenchant and critical writing style, contributing reports to the Marxist Social Democratic Federation's journal, *Justice*, and articles to local Scottish papers and labour journals.

THE MOVE TO DUBLIN

In these years, between 1890 and 1896, his and Lillie's first three children, Mona, Nora, and Aideen, were born; having lost his job as a carter in 1894 and failed as a cobbler, Connolly became dependent on his developing abilities and energies as propagandist for socialism and the labour movement precariously to support his growing family. His desperate straits led him to consider emigration to Chile, but in 1896 an appeal by John Leslie in the pages of *Justice* led to the offer of employment in Dublin as organiser for the Dublin Socialist Club, at £1 per week. However small the socialist movement may have been in Britain in the nineteenth century, in Ireland it barely existed. Robert Owen in the 1820s, the chartists in the 1840s, the First International in the 1860s and 1870s, and William Morris's Socialist League and Henry Hyndman's Social Democratic Federation in the 1880s had all failed to make an imprint on Irish soil. In the 1890s there were very small groups of Fabian socialists and branches of the ILP in Belfast and Dublin, the latter forming the Dublin Socialist Club, which included the brothers Thomas, Daniel, and William O'Brien, the last of whom was destined to be one of Connolly's closest associates in Dublin and who came to dominate the Irish labour movement for four decades after Connolly's death.

Given the minuscule membership of the socialist organisations and the hostile climate for socialism and socialists in Ireland, Connolly's livelihood as a professional propagandist continued to be precarious and had to be supplemented by various labouring jobs. Still he brought to his new role in Dublin all the passion and commitment to the cause of working people and socialism that he had developed in Scotland. His arrival in Dublin in May 1896 constituted a decisive break in his career, entailing as it did for any socialist the need to confront the challenge of nationalism. His earliest Scottish years as an activist showed no especial concern for, or interest in, Ireland or in the politics of Irish identity, though the very Irish names he gave his children clearly testify to a strong ethnic consciousness, and the interest that his mentor Leslie took in the Irish question should be taken into account. However, from the moment of his arrival in Ireland Connolly had no choice but to take a position on the ideology that dominated Irish political life.

He rapidly arrived at a view that the future for socialism and the working class in Ireland lay in an independent republic rather than in continued union with Britain or in a federal arrangement involving home rule. This was quickly reflected in his and his colleagues' decision to disband the Dublin Socialist Club and to establish in its place the Irish Socialist Republican Party (ISRP). His manifesto for the new party was radical indeed, calling for free education and child health care, nationalisation of transport and banking, and a commitment to the further extension of public ownership. He expounded his developing views on the interrelationship of Irish socialism and republicanism in articles he sent to Keir Hardie's newspaper, *Labour Leader*, and to the Belfast nationalist journal, the *Shan Van Vocht*. In 1897 these were brought together and published by the ISRP as the booklet *Erin's hope*. Here, as in his propaganda in public meetings at Dublin's Custom House and Phoenix Park, he drew on the ideas of the Irish nationalist revolutionary of 1848, James Fintan Lalor, whose writings called for the creation of an agrarian cooperative republic. While his fellow British socialists were sympathetic to Irish nationalist aims, they stopped at the point where home rule might begin and were not prepared to envisage a separate republic across the Irish Sea.

Connolly persisted and developed his views on socialism, nationalism and the workers' cause extensively in the pages of his own weekly journal, the *Workers' Republic*, which he began in 1898 with the aid of a £50 loan from Keir Hardie. It brought him to prominence in Dublin radical circles as he joined with Irish advanced nationalists in verbal attacks on the monarchy, the empire and British rule in Ireland. Indeed, his agitation on the occasion of Queen Victoria's visit to Dublin in 1898 led to a police raid on the ISRP's premises and the temporary destruction of his printing press. The paper folded after twelve issues but he managed to relaunch it briefly in 1899.

THE DEVELOPMENT OF CONNOLLY'S SOCIALISM

Connolly's growing reputation in Dublin was due in equal measure to his work for trade-union organisation in the capital and his journalism. His was a strong voice for the new trade unionism of general labour as distinct from the traditional and conservative craft unions. In 1901 he was elected a delegate to the Dublin trades council where he represented the United Labourers' Union. From the outset of his public career Connolly combined his commitment to trade unionism and socialism in a way that made his version of Marxism distinctive. His approach differed from the state socialist Marxism of the Second International, the Leninist orthodoxies of the Third International, and the Marxism of the Social Democratic Federation. He developed a Marxist syndicalist position, distinguished by his own perspective, understanding and strategy, which was to make a major contribution to that tradition in international socialism in his later years, and especially from 1910 to 1913. Yet his syndicalism also differed profoundly from its continental European counterpart in that the latter had an aversion to politics and relied exclusively on the revolutionary potential of the general strike.

These matters were to become evident in later years, but from the turn of the century Connolly engaged in electoral politics as much as in trade-union organisation and socialist evangelism. He sought election to Dublin city council in the municipal elections of 1902 and 1903 with a marked lack of success, but made sufficient impact to be attacked in press and pulpit as an atheist, which he certainly was not: he was to develop a distinctive position also on the relationship of socialism and religion.

In the meantime his circumstances went from bad to worse. His propaganda appeared to be making few converts and his ISRP colleagues did

little to inspire or support him: his wages were often unpaid even as his family expanded with the birth of a fourth child, Ina, in November 1896, a fifth child, Maire, and then a sixth, a son, Roddy, in 1901. Money he managed to raise for the *Workers' Republic* was diverted by his colleagues into subsidising a drinking club for ISRP members—the last straw for Connolly, who was a strict teetotaller. He managed to supplement his uncertain income by speaking tours in England and Scotland, and in 1902 secured an invitation from Daniel DeLeon's Socialist Labor Party of America to undertake a lecture tour in the United States from September 1902 to January 1903. On his return, a row over the use and abuse of ISRP funds, which he had raised, led to bitter recriminations, his resignation, and the collapse of the party. The success of his American tour, however, made it possible for him to return to the USA in September 1903, where he would work as socialist agitator and union organiser for the next seven years. It was the hope of the Marxist revolutionary Socialist Labor Party (SLP) that Connolly would win many Irish-American workers to their cause.

THE AMERICAN YEARS, 1903–10

Connolly's seven years in America saw him working initially as an insurance salesman and collector in Troy, New York, which enabled him to bring his family to join him in the autumn of 1904; tragically, his eldest daughter, Mona, died in an accident on the very eve of their departure. Having lost his insurance employment, he worked for the Singer Sewing Machine Company in Newark for a year. During this time he was active in the SLP and was later elected to its national executive, despite a bruising doctrinal quarrel with its leader, DeLeon. This dispute centred on three items in the credo of the SLP, namely, the 'iron law of wages', the question of marriage, and the position of socialism in regard to religion. Connolly's debate with DeLeon on these matters was presented initially in his article, 'Wages, marriage and the church', published in the SLP's *Weekly People*, in April 1904. Connolly dissented from the official party line concerning the 'iron law of wages', originally laid down by the German socialist Ferdinand Lassalle, which stated that every nominal wage increase gained by workers would be quickly and exactly offset by a corresponding increase in prices. Connolly argued that Marx himself had rejected this proposition. Although a technical point, it had implications for Connolly as a syndicalist, who saw in mass trade unionism an instrument for effecting economic and social change.

Of greater significance was their disagreement over the issue of conventional morality respecting monogamous marriage and the relationship of socialism to religion and morality. Against the prevailing Marxist orthodoxy on historical materialism and atheism, Connolly tried to argue that socialism was concerned exclusively with economics and politics, and that the holding of certain religious beliefs was entirely consistent with being a socialist; furthermore, to the extent that a given set of religious beliefs might involve an egalitarian and humanitarian commitment, they could assist the cause of socialism. In addition, at a practical or strategic level, it made no sense to antagonise potential socialist support by irrelevant attacks on religious beliefs or those who held them. Connolly had abandoned the practice of his Catholicism from around 1893, but he never launched attacks on it in America, Britain, or Ireland. Further disputes with DeLeon arose in 1907, leading DeLeon to denounce Connolly and Connolly to sever his links with the sectarian SLP and join the much larger reformist Socialist Party of America, led by Eugene Debs. Having lost his job with Singer, Connolly was eventually able to secure a regular, if modest, income as speaker and organiser for Debs's party in 1909.

By that time Connolly was already involved in a major new development, launched in 1905 when Big Bill Haywood established the Industrial Workers of the World (IWW), or 'Wobblies' as they came to be known. A militant new labour organisation, the IWW promoted the ideology of revolutionary syndicalism or industrial unionism, recruiting among the huge mass of unskilled and general labour in the USA. The IWW aimed to pursue social and economic revolution through the agency of 'one big union', using mass action and sympathetic strikes. Joining it soon after its launch, Connolly became one of its most active and prominent propagandists, gaining widespread recognition in the movement for his tract *Socialism made easy*, published in Chicago in 1909. In industrial unionism he saw the potential for a socialist movement that, while remaining democratic, would be capable of developing the structures for a socialist republic. He himself successfully recruited Irish and Italian workers in New York for the IWW.

RETURN TO IRELAND

His commitment to promoting socialism among the Irish was evident in his foundation of the Irish Socialist Federation in 1907, and it was through its agency that he began to re-establish links with socialists in Ireland, notably with his former ISRP colleague, William O'Brien. By 1908 both he and O'Brien's Dublin socialists were considering the possibility of his coming back to be organiser for the newly emerging Socialist Party of Ireland (SPI). In January 1908 he established a radical journal, *The Harp*, as the organ of the Irish Socialist Federation and in 1909 he transferred its production to Dublin. In the next year he accepted an offer of speaking engagements in Ireland, Scotland, and England, and arrived back in Ireland on 26 July 1910. The Dublin to which he now temporarily returned was much changed in its radical politics, with the arrival on the scene three years before of the syndicalist agitator and union organiser Jim Larkin. His establishment of the Irish Transport Union as 'one big union' in 1909 was to transform labour relations in Ireland and the politics of the labour movement. It was mainly Larkin who persuaded the SPI to try to raise the finances that would enable Connolly as its national organiser to resettle permanently in Ireland. At the end of 1910 Connolly brought his family back to Dublin.

The period after his return saw much of the most significant theoretical and practical work of his life. In 1910 he published the important tract *Labour, nationality and religion*, written to rebut the attacks of the Jesuit Father Kane on socialism and to contest the contemporary orthodoxy that Catholicism and socialism were irreconcilable. In the same year he also brought to publication his most famous work, *Labour in Irish history*. This was the first substantial exposition of a Marxist interpretation of Irish history. Highly original in some if its findings, it argued for the continuity of a radical tradition in Ireland, and sought to debunk nationalist myths about Ireland's past and to expose the inadequacies of middle-class Irish nationalism in providing a solution for Ireland's ills.

From being national organiser for the SPI in 1910 he went on in 1911 to become Ulster organiser for the Irish Transport and General Workers' Union (ITGWU). In Belfast he encountered the stranglehold of sectarianism and although he managed a limited success in recruiting Catholic workers into the union he never really came to terms with the nature and strength of working-class political unionism. In May 1911 he issued 'A plea for socialist unity in Ireland' in the pages of the Scottish labour journal *Forward*, attacking the Belfast Independent Labour Party for its opposition to home rule. He thereby precipitated a famous controversy with the Belfast socialist William Walker, who argued that the future of socialism depended on the continuing union with Britain. For Connolly, Walker's position was one of false internationalism, and the only true socialist internationalism lay in a free federation of free peoples.

While he continued his promotion of industrial unionism he also continued to promote the political dimension of the labour movement in Ireland. With Larkin, O'Brien, and other radical elements in the Dublin trades council he managed to get the Irish Trade Union Congress at its meeting at Clonmel in 1912 to commit to the formation of the Irish Labour Party. That special combination of syndicalism and politics was reflected nominally in the new title, the Irish Trade Union Congress and Labour Party. In the midst of his hectic political and union organising activities Connolly continued to write, notably on the theme of socialism and nationalism at a time (1911–14) when the constitutional future of Ireland went into political crisis. Much of his writing at this time appeared in book form in 1915 as *The reconquest of Ireland*, where he argued that Irish freedom meant securing the common ownership of all Ireland by the Irish. Yet his experience in Belfast made it clear that a significant proportion of its working class had no time for Irish freedom, and that some of the north's socialist leaders sought the triumph of socialism within the continued political union of Britain and Ireland.

Whatever Connolly hoped to achieve in Belfast in terms of union growth and socialist progress was quickly overtaken by the events of the lockout and general strike in Dublin from August 1913. He was summoned to Dublin to assist Larkin in the leadership of this conflict, and, when the struggle was lost and Larkin left for America in 1914, Connolly took over as acting general secretary of the defeated Transport Union. At the same time he took over the editorship of Larkin's *Irish Worker* paper, as well as being commander of the Irish Citizen Army, which had been set up in November 1913 as a workers' defence force.

REVOLUTIONARY ACTIVITIES AND THE EASTER RISING

To the disastrous defeat of the locked-out and striking workers was now added the calamitous outbreak of world war. This drove him into an advanced nationalist position and, though he never abandoned his socialist commitment, the social revolution took a back seat. The growing militancy of Ulster unionist opposition to home rule, the British government's postponement of plans for home rule in the face of unionist opposition, the growing prospect of the partition of Ireland, the outbreak of world war, and the consequent collapse of international socialism all contributed to his adopting an extreme nationalist stance. As he wrote in *Forward* in March 1914: 'the proposal of the Government to consent to the partition of Ireland...should be resisted with armed force if necessary'. Added to this, the 'carnival of slaughter' that was the world war drove him to incite 'war against war', and to make tentative overtures to the revolutionary IRB. By late 1915 his increasing militancy at a time when the IRB had decided on insurrection caused them in turn to approach him; by late January they and he had agreed on a joint uprising. The Transport Union headquarters at Liberty Hall became the headquarters of the Citizen Army as he prepared it for revolt. It was ironic that Connolly, who had in the distant past denounced 'Blanquism' or 'insurrectionism' and who had ever argued that political freedom without socialism was useless, now joined forces with militant nationalists in an insurrection that had nothing to do directly with socialism. It appears that he had become convinced that national freedom for Ireland in the prevailing circumstances was a necessity before socialism could advance.

In the event, he led his small band of about two hundred ICA comrades into the Easter rising of 1916. His Citizen Army joined forces with the Volunteers, as the only army he acknowledged in 1916 was that of 'the Irish Republic'. As commandant general of the Republic's forces in Dublin he fought side by side with Patrick Pearse in the General Post Office, until surrendering on 29 April. Badly injured in the foot, he was court-martialled along with 170 others, was one of ninety to be sentenced to death, and was the last one of the fifteen to be executed by firing squad. He was shot dead, seated on a wooden box, in Kilmainham jail on 12 May 1916. He was buried in the cemetery within Arbour Hill military barracks. His wife and six of his children survived him.

REPUTATION AND LEGACY

Along with his executed comrades, Connolly entered the pantheon of Irish national heroes. However, for one whose public life until almost its end had been committed to the working classes of Britain, America, and Ireland, and to the cause of international socialism, the impact of this commitment is problematic. It can be argued that the great achievement of his final years, as a revolutionary socialist, was to bring the most militant elements of the Irish labour movement to the forefront of the anti-imperial fight against the British empire, giving Irish labour a central place in the national struggle. Thereby he gave national and international significance to a body of labour militants far in excess of what was warranted by their numbers. He was, however, to prove irreplaceable, and those who followed him in the leadership of socialism and the labour movement in Ireland, whatever their strengths and abilities, lacked that unique combination of personal passion, vision, insight, experience, and charisma, and the movement under his successors failed to capitalise on the position he had secured for it. The syndicalist ideal of 'one big union' as the vehicle for the realisation of the workers' republic, though it looked promising with the revival of ITGWU fortunes from 1917, failed to materialise, and in the end fell victim to the disruptive power of Jim Larkin's mercurial personality and to the entrenchment of a socially conservative ruling class.

Recognition of the significance of his social and economic writings came quickly, if critically, from unlikely quarters—notably in 1920, when another Jesuit, Fr Lambert McKenna, published *The social teachings of James Connolly*. However, despite biographical studies by Desmond Ryan, Nora Connolly-O'Brien, R. M. Fox and others, the writings themselves remained unpublished until the 1960s. From late in that decade a new generation began to revisit his life and make his work available in the context of a new phase of political and social conflict in Ireland. There is no James Connolly archive as such. There is a valuable discussion of his letters and writings in Donal Nevin's *James Connolly: 'a full life'* (2005). Manuscript sources relating to his career and its aftermath are in the NLI (William O'Brien papers, Thomas Johnson papers, Cathal O'Shannon papers, Dublin trades council minutes, Adolphus Shiels papers) and UCD Archives (Thomas McPartlin papers, Desmond Ryan papers). An extensive bibliography is to be found in W. K. Anderson, *James Connolly and the Irish left* (1994), and T. Horikoshi (ed.), *The political writings of James Connolly* (1980) has a comprehensive list of his journalistic work.

Connolly's memory is preserved in many different forms in Ireland and elsewhere. One of Dublin's three main railway stations, that in Amiens Street, was named Connolly Station in his memory in 1966. On the eightieth anniversary of his execution (12 May 1996) a memorial by Eamonn O'Doherty, located near the Custom House in Dublin and facing Liberty Hall, was unveiled by the Irish president Mary Robinson. His name is borne by several trade union and Labour party halls and buildings, including those of SIPTU (Services, Industrial, Professional and Technical Union) in Cork, Shannon, Thurles, Tipperary, Tralee, and Waterford, and by streets in places including Ballina, Clonakilty, Midleton, and Sligo. There are well-known drawings and portraits of him by Seán O'Sullivan and Robert Ballagh (first exhibited in 1971; latterly in the NGI). A famous set of labour murals in what was originally the headquarters of the Dublin bakers' trade union, Four Provinces House, Harcourt Street, was destroyed when the building was demolished for development. A photographic record (in private hands) was made of the murals, which included a fine representation of Connolly speaking at Belfast's docks. His Belfast

years are also marked by a plaque on the Falls Road, where he and his family lived during 1911–13. A plaque in his honour was erected in June 1968 on George IV Bridge, near his birthplace in Cowgate, Edinburgh, through the efforts of the Edinburgh and District Trades Council. There is a fine bust of Connolly with a commemorative plaque in Troy, New York, where he spent the years 1903–05.

Fergus A. D'Arcy

Sources

L. McKenna, *The social teachings of James Connolly* (1920); D. Ryan, *James Connolly: his life, work and writings* (1924); H. W. Lee and E. Archbold, *Social democracy in Britain* (1935); N. C. O'Brien, *James Connolly: portrait of a rebel father* (1935); R. M. Fox, *James Connolly: the forerunner* (1946); C. D. Greaves, *The life and times of James Connolly* (1961); O. D. Edwards and B. Ransom (ed.), *James Connolly: selected political writings* (1968); O. D. Edwards, *The mind of an activist: James Connolly* (1971); *James Connolly: selected writings*, ed. P. Berresford Ellis (1973); S. Levenson, *James Connolly: socialist, patriot and martyr* (1973); C. Reeve and A. B. Reeve, *James Connolly and the United States: the road to the 1916 rebellion* (1978); *The political writings of James Connolly*, ed. T. Horikoshi (1980) (incl. list of journalistic writings); H. Patterson, *Class conflict and sectarianism: the Protestant working class and the Belfast labour movement, 1868–1920* (1980); B. Ransom, *Connolly's Marxism* (1980); R. D. Edwards, *James Connolly* (1981); James Connolly, *Collected works* (2 vols, 1987–8); A. Morgan, *James Connolly: a political biography* (1988); E. O'Connor, *Syndicalism in Ireland* (1988); K. Allen, *The politics of James Connolly* (1990); W. K. Anderson, *James Connolly and the Irish left* (1994) (incl. bibliography); J. L. Hyland, *James Connolly* (1997); Donal Nevin, *James Connolly: 'a full life'* (2005)

Sean Connolly

1882–1916

Sean Connolly, actor, trade unionist, and republican, was born 12 April 1882 at 10 Seafort Avenue, Sandymount, Dublin, third child and eldest son among eight daughters and eight sons of Michael Connolly, seaman, and Mary Connolly (née Ellis). When his father ceased seafaring to work on the Dublin docks, the family moved to the northside city centre, firstly to Bella Street, where his mother practiced midwifery and ran a ground-floor shop in their home, secondly to Gloucester Street (latterly Sean MacDermott Street). Educated at North William Street national school and St Joseph's CBS, Fairview, he entered Eason's stationers as a despatch clerk (1897).

At an early age he joined the Gaelic League. In *Pictures in the hallway* (1942), Sean O'Casey describes conversing in Irish with Connolly on their first meeting in Eason's warehouse about this time and paints a vivid portrait of his fellow employee:

> young and handsome; young and firm; young and kindly…
> gentle but strongly built…a musical voice, a dark tenor,…
> calling the papers to be placed together to form a parcel for
> some country newsagent (O'Casey, 340–42).

Trained in the Inghinidhe na hÉireann acting class, he appeared in the first production of 'An scrabhadóir' by Tomás Ó hAodha (1866–1935) at the 1909 Oireachtas. Acting in various productions in Irish and English, he drew acclaim for his facility in both dramatic and comic roles and his fine singing voice. He joined the Abbey Theatre (January 1913), his regular appearances including the first European production of Rabindranath Tagore's 'The post office' (May 1913).

Active in the ITGWU during the 1913–14 lockout, he joined the Irish Citizen Army (ICA). In *Drums under the window* (1945), O'Casey recounts participating with Connolly in the Howth gun-running (26 July 1914). Alongside his sister (Mrs Katherine Barrett) and Helena Molony, he was prominent in the ICA's Liberty Players, popular for their Sunday night revues, in which Connolly revelled in satires and patriotic dramas by James Connolly and Arthur Griffith. When the ICA marched through Dublin against a Mansion House recruitment meeting (September 1914) addressed by John Redmond, John Dillon, and British prime minister H. H. Asquith, the cortège halted outside the old parliament building (Bank of Ireland), College Green, where Sean Connolly led a mass rendition of 'A nation once again'. By then employed as clerk in the motor tax office, City Hall, Connolly was usually the best-dressed man at ICA mobilisations.

Appointed captain on the eve of the Easter rising, he commanded the ICA contingent that operated in the Dublin Castle area on Monday 24 April, under orders to seize key positions, including the castle entrance, and thereby seal off the castle approaches. (Why Connolly's contingent did not attempt to seize the lightly guarded castle itself has been a matter of speculative historiographical debate regarding the planning and execution of the rising.) When the duty constable, James O'Brien, slammed shut the castle gates against them, Connolly fired what was probably the first shot of the rising when he shot O'Brien dead. While six of his troops secured the castle guardroom, Connolly occupied the nearby City Hall with his main body of nineteen men and women, establishing therein his primary base of operation. Within an hour, while occupying a position on the building's roof, he was killed by a sniper's bullet from the castle tower. The widely reported tradition that he was shot while running up the tricolour is not verified by Molony's eyewitness account (Caulfield,

125). The garrison, under heavy attack, surrendered that night. Connolly's sister, Kathleen Barrett, and three brothers—Eddie, George, and Matt—were also in the ICA's castle area contingent, while a fourth brother, Joseph, served in the General Post Office and St Stephen's Green.

With his handsome looks, singing and acting talents, modest demeanour, and noble idealism touched with the fanatic ('maybe dangerous, for, like Robespierre, he believes what he says' (O'Casey, 342)), Connolly made a lasting impression on many. Lady Gregory composed a verse elegy; it has been suggested that O'Casey partly based the character of Jack Clitheroe in *The plough and the stars* (1926) on him, and that W. B. Yeats had him in mind when he wrote of his drama *Cathleen ni Houlihan* (in which Connolly once played) having 'sen[t] out certain men the English shot'.

Connolly married (1910) Christine Swanzey (*c.*1888–*c.*1978) of Dublin; they had two sons and one daughter. His widow married secondly Joseph McCarthy, garda sergeant.

Lawrence William White

Sources

An Claidheamh Soluis, 3 Meitheamh 1916 (obit.); *Catholic Bulletin*, vi, no. 7 (July 1916), 404–5, 407 (portrait photo.); Dorothy Macardle, *The Irish Republic* (1937), 177; R. M. Fox, *History of the Irish Citizen Army* (1943), 80–83, 107, 116, 113–17, 134, 136, 139, 141, 147–50, 227, 230; Desmond Ryan, *The rising: the complete story of Easter week* (1949), 117–19; Lennox Robinson, *Ireland's Abbey Theatre: a history 1899–1951* (1951), 106–13 (cast lists); *Fifty years of Liberty Hall: the golden jubilee of the Irish Transport and General Workers' Union 1909–1959* (1959), 68, 69 (portrait between 40–41); Max Caulfield, *The Easter rebellion* (1964) (indexed as 'Connolly, John'); Frank Robbins, *Under the starry plough: recollections of the Irish Citizen Army* (1977), 47, 84, 98–9, 131 (portrait); Hugh Hunt, *The Abbey: Ireland's national theatre 1904–1978* (1979), 195; Uinseann MacEoin (ed.), *Survivors* (1980), 201–2, 214n; David Krause (ed.), *The letters of Sean O'Casey*, ii: *1942–54* (1980), 46–7; Margaret Ward, *Unmanageable revolutionaries: women and Irish nationalism* (1983); Diarmuid Breathnach agus Máire Ní Mhurchú, *Beathaisnéis*, iii 1992), 84–6 (under Ó Conghaile, Caoimhín (1912–79)); Sean O'Casey, *Autobiographies*, i (1992 ed.), 340–42, 642, 655; Padraic O'Farrell, *Who's who in the Irish war of independence and civil war 1916–1923* (1997), 20; *1916 rebellion handbook* (1998), 4, 11–12, 272; information from Mary Travers (niece)

Edward Daly

1891–1916

Edward Daly, republican, was born 28 February 1891 at 26 Frederick Street, Limerick city, the only son and youngest among ten children of Edward Daly (1848–90), Fenian and wood-measurer, and Catherine Daly (née O'Mara), dressmaker. An uncle, John Daly, had acted as national organiser for the IRB until imprisoned in 1884. Edward's sister Kathleen married the IRB leader Tom Clarke. The family endured some financial insecurity in his infancy until provided for by another uncle, James Daly, an emigrant returned from Australia in great prosperity. His upbringing was profoundly coloured by the Fenian nationalism of mother, aunt, and sisters, praying daily for the release and well-being of his uncle, and for Irish independence. Schooled first by Presentation nuns at Sexton Street, then by the Christian Brothers at Roxboro Road, he completed his academic education at Leamy's commercial college (1906). Initially groomed to inherit John Daly's bakery, he was sent to take up an apprenticeship in a Glasgow bakery (1907), but finding the airless heat of ovens damaging to a somewhat frail constitution, he came back to Limerick to work as a rather shy, though cheerful, clerk in Spaight's timber yard, his father's old employer.

In 1912 he moved to a clerkship in a builders' providers in Dublin, and then to a post in May Roberts and Co., wholesale chemists, and took a room with Kathleen and Tom Clarke on Richmond Road, Fairview. Thrilled by the inaugural meeting of the Irish Volunteers at the Rotunda (25 November 1913), he was among the first to enlist, as a private in B company, 1st battalion, telling his sister later that it was what he had always hoped for. By early 1914 he was appointed captain of B company, drawn from a poor inner-city parish. He pored over books on military tactics and history, and concentrated on the principles of drill and dress. On 26 July 1914 he impressed his superiors with his clever self-possession while in command of B Coy marching to and from Howth as arms were landed and cached; he was made commandant of 1st battalion by Patrick Pearse on 10 March 1915. It seems that plans in embryo for the Easter rising were confided to him and his vice-commandant, Piaras Beaslaí; there are clear indications that he had been a junior member of the IRB for some years. At the funeral of O'Donovan Rossa on 1 August 1915 he assumed charge of the four Dublin Volunteer battalions. Days before the rising he was required to detain Bulmer Hobson to prevent leakage of information.

He mobilised 1st battalion before noon on Easter Monday, 24 April; at first, to his disappointment, only about 150 of 400 men showed up. The plan to hold streets and buildings from Broadstone railway station to Cabra and to Parnell Street could not be realised. The Four Courts and buildings along Church Street to North King Street were occupied, to the consternation of many local inhabitants, and barricades were bundled together at strategic intersections. For several days shops remained open, and civilians were escorted through the district, some to a working bakery. Fierce resistance by Seán Heuston in the Mendicity Institution delayed open British attack on Daly's positions until 26 April, after Volunteers captured the Bridewell police station and the Linenhall barracks. By 27 April battalions of the South Staffordshires and Sherwood Foresters encircled the district. Despite relentless assaults down Church Street, supported by an armoured car, British forces were unable to penetrate more than 150 yards between the morning of 28 April and 2.00 p.m. on 29 April, when Daly received the order from Pearse to surrender. His command was disciplined and concerned for civilian welfare, and neatly anticipated British offensive tactics, and his manner was sober and contained. After

standing as a prisoner in teeming rain in front of the Rotunda on Saturday night, he was identified on Sunday morning and sentenced the following night to be executed. After a visit by three of his sisters he was shot by firing squad at 4.00 a.m. on Thursday 4 May, and buried in a mass grave at Arbour Hill. He never married.

Desmond McCabe

Sources

Louis N. Le Roux, *Tom Clarke and the Irish freedom movement* (1936); Max Caulfield, *The Easter rebellion* (1964); Paddy Holohan, 'The Four Courts area', *Capuchin Annual 1942*, 231–7; Anon., 'The story of Limerick and Kerry in 1916', *Capuchin Annual 1966*, 338, 359–60 (portrait); Martin Shannon, *Sixteen roads to Golgotha* (1966), 148–55; J. M. McCarthy (ed.), *Limerick's fighting story* (1966), 137–50; Desmond Ryan, *The rising: the complete story of Easter week* (1969 ed.); G. A. Hayes-McCoy, 'A military history of the 1916 rising' in Kevin B. Nowlan (ed.), *The making of 1916: studies in the history of the rising* (1969), 258–9, 268, 279, 281–3, 292; Helen Litton (ed.), *Revolutionary woman: Kathleen Clarke, 1878–1972, an autobiography* (1991) (portrait), 11–23, 38, 44–9, 63, 72–3, 118–23; Daly archives, University of Limerick

Helen Gifford
Donnelly

1880–1971

Helen Ruth ('Nellie') Gifford Donnelly, republican activist, was born 9 November 1880 at 26 Cabra Parade, Phibsborough, Dublin, fifth child and second eldest daughter among six daughters and six sons of Frederick Gifford (1835/6–1917), a well-to-do solicitor, and Isabella Julia Gifford (née Burton; 1847/8–1932). Her father, a Catholic, reared by maternal aunts in Nenagh, Co. Tipperary, after his mother died at his birth, was probably the illegitimate son of a father who left anonymous instructions regarding his education for the law, which was financed by the solicitors' benevolent fund. Commencing practice c.1877, he had offices at 5 Bachelor's Walk, Dublin, until 1900, and thereafter at addresses on Dawson Street. Her mother, reared in a family of twenty-three children (of whom eighteen survived) in Co. Clare, was rigorously Protestant in religion, and a domineering personality; she was a niece of the painter Frederick Burton. All twelve children were reared in the Church of Ireland. The six sons all emigrated as young men, retained their parents' unionist politics, and pursued successful, but unremarkable, careers. The six daughters all were active for varying lengths of time in nationalist politics. The most prominent careers were pursued by the two youngest, the artist Grace Gifford (1888–1955), and the journalist and broadcaster Sydney Czira ('John Brennan') (1889–1974).

Reared from the late 1880s in the family home at 8 Temple Villas, Palmerston Road, Rathmines, Nellie Gifford, characterised as 'nonintellectual' by the school authorities during her years at Alexandra College, trained as a domestic economy instructor, and worked some seven years at a series of six-month postings in country areas of Co. Meath. City-born and -bred, amid the sparsely populated, flat, and featureless grazing lands she felt herself 'out on the prairies of America' (Czira, 44). Frequently lodging in labourers' cottages, she observed conditions among the landless rural poor, and became an enthusiastic supporter of the cattle-driving campaign of the radical land agitator and nationalist MP Laurence Ginnell. Educating her sisters on the land issue, she in turn was influenced by their emerging nationalism and feminism. On returning home to Dublin, she was involved with them in the Irish Women's Franchise League, and became part of the circle of Countess Constance Markievicz. She acted in several stage plays, including the successful comedy 'Eleanor's enterprise' by George Birmingham (James Owen Hannay), produced in the Gaiety theatre (11 December 1911) by the Independent Dramatic Company of the countess's husband, Count Casimir Markievicz.

A strong supporter of the labour movement, during the 1913 lockout she accompanied James Larkin when, disguised as an elderly and infirm clergyman, he checked into the Imperial hotel and briefly addressed a Sackville Street crowd from a balcony, thereby precipitating the 'bloody Sunday' police baton charge (31 August); posing as the 'elderly gentleman's' niece, Nellie did all the talking to hotel staff lest the ruse be revealed by Larkin's pronounced Liverpudlian accent. A founding member of the Irish Citizen Army (ICA), she gave lessons on camp cookery in Liberty Hall. She was one of several middle-class women prominent in the body, attracted by its ethos of sexual equality beyond that within nationalist organisations, owing largely to the feminist convictions of James Connolly. Establishing an employment bureau in Irish Volunteers headquarters on Dawson Street, she found jobs with sympathetic employers for recruits to the movement arriving from abroad; she thus assisted Michael Collins on his arrival from London, and introduced him to her future brother-in-law Joseph Plunkett, whom Collins served as ADC during the 1916 Easter rising.

Though two of her sisters, Grace and Muriel, were married to signatories of the proclamation of the Republic, Nellie was the only one of the

Gifford sisters actively to participate in the rising. Serving with the ICA's St Stephen's Green contingent, she supervised the garrison's commissariat in the College of Surgeons building. Contending with a serious shortage of food stores throughout the week, she organised procurement of foodstuffs by commandeering from shops and bread vans, and by courier from other garrisons, and oversaw the cooking and delivery of rations to troops in the college and outlying posts. Arrested at the surrender, she was a prisoner in Kilmainham jail when, unknown to her, her sister Grace married Joseph Plunkett in the prison chapel hours before his execution. One of twelve women to be detained after the release of most women prisoners on 8 May, she was transferred to Mountjoy jail prior to her release on 4 June. Making her way first to England and then to the USA (late 1916 or early 1917), she joined several other women veterans of Easter week in lecturing on the rising throughout America. While in America she married (1918) Joseph Donnelly, of Omagh, Co. Tyrone. Separating from her husband, she returned to Ireland with their year-old daughter Maeve in 1921.

Despite receiving an £800 inheritance on her father's death in September 1917 (her four surviving sisters each received £500), she frequently experienced straitened financial circumstances. She broadcast children's stories on Radio 2RN (later Radio Éireann) (1920s–30s), and wrote occasional journalism for the *Irish Press* and other newspapers. Unlike the four of her sisters who converted to Roman Catholicism, she remained a staunch Protestant, deeply sceptical toward the Catholic faith. Though modifying her republican convictions, she remained devoted to preserving the historical record of the independence movement. Impressed by the influx of visitors to the 1932 Eucharistic Congress, but reportedly infuriated by a concurrent display of Catholic religious artifacts in the National Museum of Ireland, she organised a small exhibition there of 1916 memorabilia, and campaigned tirelessly for a permanent exhibition treating recent Irish nationalist history. As secretary of the 1916 research committee, she personally contacted and negotiated with prospective donors, thereby amassing a substantial body of material pertinent to nationalist organisations, the Easter rising, and the war of independence, which formed the basis of the present NMI collection. She was a sometime secretary of the Old IRA Association, an early member of the Old Dublin Society (mid 1930s), and a founding member of the Kilmainham Gaol Restoration

Society (*c.*1960). A lifelong animal lover, she cared for countless stray and neglected dogs and cats, a predilection passed on to her daughter. She died on 23 June 1971 at the Gascoigne nursing home, Dublin.

The eldest of the Gifford sisters, Katherine Anna ('Katie') Gifford Wilson (1875–1957), was living with her husband in his native Wales in 1916. After his death in the 1918 influenza epidemic, she returned to Ireland, became active in Sinn Féin and Cumann na mBan, and was registrar of the first Dáil Éireann loan. She was imprisoned during the civil war, because, according to family tradition, she was mistaken for her better-known and more politically active sister Grace, though she continued to be detained after Grace's arrest. University educated, she worked for a brief while in Radio 2RN, and for some years as a teacher of French.

The third sister, Ada Gertrude Gifford (1882–*c.*1953), and the sixth and youngest, Sydney Madge Gifford Czira, were both living in America at the time of the rising, where they were active in supporting the Irish nationalist interest. The fourth sister, Muriel Enid Gifford (1884–1917) was married to the 1916 leader Thomas MacDonagh.

Lawrence William White and Patrick Long

Sources

GRO (birth certs.); NAI: Census of Ireland 1901, www.census.nationalarchives.ie; *Thom*; R. M. Fox, *History of the Irish Citizen Army* (1943), 161–2, 230; Desmond Ryan, *The rising: the complete story of Easter week* (1949); *Irish Times*, 21 September 1957 (d. notice); Max Caulfield, *The Easter rebellion* (1964); Maurice Gorham, *Forty years of Irish broadcasting* (1967); Jacqueline Van Voris, *Constance de Markievicz: in the cause of Ireland* (1967); Edd Winfield Parks and Aileen Wells Parks, *Thomas MacDonagh: the man, the patriot, the writer* (1967); *Irish Times*, 24 June 1971 (obit., d. notice); Sydney Czira, *The years flew by* (1974); Frank Robbins, *Under the starry plough: recollections of the Irish Citizen Army* (1977); Johann A. Norstedt, *Thomas MacDonagh: a critical biography* (1980); Margaret Ward, *Unmanageable revolutionaries: women and Irish nationalism* (1983); Diana Norman, *Terrible beauty: a life of Countess Markievicz* (1987); Margaret Ward, *Maud Gonne: Ireland's Joan of Arc* (1990); Ruth Taillon, *The women of 1916: when history was made* (1996); Sinéad McCoole, *Guns and chiffon: women revolutionaries and Kilmainham gaol: 1916–1923* (1997), 24, 31, 46, 48; Alan Hayes (ed.), introduction to *The years flew by: the recollections of Madame Sidney Gifford Czira* (2000 ed.), pp ix–xx; Marie O'Neill, *Grace Gifford Plunkett and Irish freedom: tragic bride of 1916* (2000); Pádraig Yeates, *Lockout: Dublin 1913* (2000); Joanne Mooney Eichacker, *Irish republican women in America: lecture tours 1916–1925* (2003); Sinéad McCoole, *No ordinary women: Irish female activists in the revolutionary years, 1900–1923* (2003); information from Patrick F. Wallace and Michael Kenny (National Museum of Ireland); NUI archive; Anne Clare; and Dara Redmond

Ivor
Guest

1873–1939

Sir Ivor Churchill Guest, 3rd baronet and 1st Viscount Wimborne, lord lieutenant of Ireland (1915–18), was born 16 January 1873 in London, eldest of five sons of Sir Ivor Bertie Guest (1835–1914), 1st Baron Wimborne, and his wife, Cornelia Henrietta Maria, eldest daughter of John Winston Spencer Churchill, 7th duke of Marlborough. He was educated at Eton and Trinity College, Cambridge, but did not graduate. As captain and honorary major in the Dorset Imperial Yeomanry, he saw service in the Boer war. After unsuccessfully contesting Plymouth as a Conservative in 1898, he was returned unopposed for that constituency in a by-election (1900–06). Joseph Chamberlain's tariff reform proposals persuaded Guest to cross the floor of the house with his cousin, Winston Churchill, and at the general election of 1906 he was returned as Liberal MP for Cardiff (1906–10). Chairman of the royal commission on coast erosion and afforestation (1909–10), he became a member of the privy council in 1910 and at this time accepted a peerage (as Viscount Wimborne) to strengthen the government's representation in the house of lords. Until his father's death (1914), he sat as Baron Ashby St Ledgers. He was paymaster-general (1910–12) and lord-in-waiting to George V (1913–15).

After the outbreak of war in 1914, Wimborne was appointed to the staff of Lt-Gen. Sir Bryan Mahon, then commanding a division at the Curragh. Shortly afterwards, on 16 February 1915 he was appointed lord lieutenant of Ireland, which post he held from 1915 to 1918, except for three months (May–August 1916). Wimborne had a proven interest in Irish affairs, having spoken frequently in the lords in support of the home rule bill; however, his appointment was greeted warily by the chief secretary, Augustine Birrell, who thought him naïve and the type who 'if not backed up in one direction, will go a-whoring in the other' (Ó Broin, *The chief secretary*, 135). However, Birrell was a willing guest at the convivial social events organised in the viceregal lodge by the hospitable Wimborne and his wife (m. 10 February 1902), the former Alice Katherine Grosvenor, daughter of the 2nd Baron Ebury. Lady Cynthia Asquith, on a visit to Dublin, noted in her diary that the lord lieutenant was 'a fairly frank bounder…[with] a terrible way of flapping his furry eyelids at one', and an inveterate womaniser who 'really ought to restrain himself with the natives' (Asquith, 127–8).

Wimborne threw himself enthusiastically into his new position. On the suggestion of John Redmond he became director of recruiting and travelled to different parts of the country, where he reported that he was agreeably surprised by his reception. Determined to be well informed, he demanded that the under-secretary, Sir Matthew Nathan, brief him fully. Nathan, who considered himself answerable only to Birrell, did so reluctantly and incompletely. From the beginning of 1916 Wimbourne began agitating for measures to be taken against the Irish Volunteers, but was constantly dissuaded by Birrell and Nathan. However, his early recommendations for action stood Wimborne in good stead with Asquith's government after the 1916 rising. On being told that the cabinet demanded his resignation, he reluctantly tendered it but was able to point to his explicit instructions to Nathan on Easter Sunday to arrest the rebel leaders immediately; he held himself blameless that these instructions were deferred while Nathan consulted Birrell, absent as usual in London. The Hardinge commission, appointed in May 1916, found Birrell primarily responsible for the rising and entirely exonerated Wimborne, who was allowed to return to Dublin in August and continue as lord lieutenant. His evidence had been corroborated by his influential aide, Sir Basil Blackwood. The latter, however, privately criticised Wimborne's role during the rising:

His Ex simply *swilled* brandy the whole time...he was superlatively theatrical and insisted on his poor secretaries using the most melodramatically grandiloquent language down the telephone...He was delighted to think he was at last really in the limelight (Ó Broin, 182–3).

Dismayed at news of General Maxwell coming to assume command, Wimborne had wanted to negotiate with the rebels before the general arrived and declared that he would hang Eoin MacNeill but let the others off.

Wimborne could do little to prevent the Irish political situation unravelling over the next two years; however, he found his personal position improved, since the new chief secretary, H. E. Duke, consulted him and gave him a greater say in affairs. In 1918 the question of introducing conscription for Ireland resurfaced as a matter of urgency. Wimborne was pessimistic about the measure—he favoured introducing conscription and home rule simultaneously and interdependently, though he expected widespread opposition. However, Bonar Law was unwilling to risk antagonising the Ulster unionists. Wimborne was replaced in May as lord lieutenant by Lord French, who as a military man was judged better able to enforce conscription.

Returning to England, Wimborne devoted himself to sport and to adding to his art collection, and ceased to take an active part in politics, though he spoke in the lords in favour of the establishment of the Irish Free State. His sympathy with the Labour party allowed him at the time of the general strike in 1926 to get the trade union leaders in touch with the government, and so helped accelerate a settlement. In the 1931 crisis he supported the all-party government and was elected first president of the National Liberal party. He died at home in Wimborne House, Arlington Street, London, on 14 June 1939 and was survived by two daughters and a son, Ivor Grosvenor Guest (1903–67), who succeeded him as 2nd viscount.

Bridget Hourican

Sources

Dictionary of national biography (London); Max Caulfield, *The Easter rising* (1963); León Ó Broin, *Dublin Castle and the 1916 rising* (1966); Lady Cynthia Asquith, *Diaries, 1915–18* (1968); León Ó Broin, *The chief secretary* (1969); Thomas Jones, *Whitehall diary*, iii (1970); Burke, *Peerage* (2000)

Seán
Heuston

1891–1916

Seán (John J.) Heuston, revolutionary, was born 21 February 1891 in
Dublin, the son of John Heuston, clerk, and Maria Heuston (née
McDonald) of 24 Lower Gloucester Street. Educated locally by the
Christian Brothers, he did well in the intermediate examination and in
1908 began working for the Great Southern and Western Railway
Company (GSWR) as a clerk and was posted to Limerick. In 1910 he
joined Na Fianna Éireann, the republican boy scout movement, and
helped build up a Fianna troop in Limerick of over 250 boys. Transferring
to Dublin in 1913 with the GSWR, he continued to work with the Fianna,
becoming vice-commandant of its Dublin brigade and director of training
on its headquarters staff. In November 1913 he was a founding member
of the Irish Volunteers. A close associate of Con Colbert, he instructed
Fianna members in drill and musketry at Patrick Pearse's school at St
Enda's. In July 1914 he led the Fianna contingent at Howth that unloaded
hundreds of Mauser rifles from the *Asgard*.

By 1916 he was captain of D company, 1st battalion, of the Irish
Volunteers' Dublin Brigade. At the outbreak of the Easter rising, he
mobilised his men at Mountjoy Square on Monday 24 April, and, after

a circuitous march to the quays, seized the Mendicity Institute (a decaying eighteenth-century building on Usher's Island used as a poorhouse). With about fourteen men, Heuston ordered out its occupants and began to fortify the building. In taking this action he appears to have been acting on the direct orders of James Connolly, commandant-general of the Dublin forces who was based in the GPO, rather than his battalion commandant Edward Daly, whose headquarters was just across the Liffey at the Four Courts. Soon after seizing the building, his men opened fire on a British unit marching down the north quays, killing an officer and wounding nine men. The Mendicity Institute was a key position in preventing troops who had arrived at Kingsbridge station from linking up with other units in the city centre. Heuston's men defended the building tenaciously and were reinforced by a dozen men sent from the GPO. Over the next two days they came under heavy fire and were surrounded by hundreds of troops. By Wednesday 26 April the besiegers were close enough to throw grenades into the building, wounding several Volunteers. Heavily outnumbered, his men hungry, exhausted, and short on ammunition, Heuston expected to be overrun at any moment. At about midday on Wednesday he decided to surrender (despite the protests of some of his men) and his unit was taken to Arbour Hill detention barracks.

On 4 May he was tried by court martial at Richmond barracks. During his trial he strongly challenged the validity of the documentary evidence produced by the prosecution, but was found guilty and sentenced to death. Although a relatively junior officer, Heuston probably received a death sentence because he had held an independent command and inflicted significant casualties on British forces. Lodged in Kilmainham jail, on the eve of his execution, Sunday 7 May, he was visited by his mother, his sister Theresa, his brother, Fr Michael Heuston, OP, and Fr (later Cardinal) Michael Browne, who later remarked that Heuston seemed 'quite serene' (MacLochlainn, 113). He wrote a last letter to his sister Mary, a Dominican nun, stating that he had no regrets about his actions and that the independence of Ireland was there for the taking if the Irish people wanted it badly enough. Attended by the capuchin priest Fr Albert, he was shot by firing squad at Kilmainham jail on 8 May 1916 and buried at Arbour Hill.

Small collections of papers relating to Heuston are held in the NLI and Kilmainham jail. A statue (1943) by Laurence Campbell stands in the People's Gardens in the Phoenix Park. In 1966 Kingsbridge Station was renamed Heuston Station and the King's Bridge over the Liffey renamed Heuston Bridge.

David Murphy

Sources

Fr Albert, OFM, 'How Seán Heuston died', *Capuchin Annual* (1942), 343–4; Desmond Ryan, *The rising* (1949); Martin Shannon, *Sixteen roads to Golgotha* (1966), 107–14; Piaras F. MacLochlainn (ed.), *Last words: letters and statements of the leaders executed after the rising at Easter 1916* (1971), 107–17; D. J. Hickey and J. E. Doherty, *A dictionary of Irish history since 1800* (1980); Patrick O'Farrell, *Whos who in the Irish war of independence* (1997); Michael Foy and Brian Barton, *The Easter rising* (1999); Charles Townshend, *Easter 1916* (2005)

Bulmer Hobson

1883–1969

(John) Bulmer Hobson, nationalist, was born 14 January 1883 at 5 Magdala Street, Belfast, the son of Benjamin Hobson, a grocer who was from a Quaker family established in Ireland since the time of Oliver Cromwell, and his wife, Mary Ann Bulmer, a Yorkshire radical.

FAMILY INFLUENCES AND EARLY LIFE

Hobson's father was a Gladstonean home ruler. His mother was active in the Belfast Naturalists' Field Club (lecturing on archaeology) and the suffragette movement. Her friends included Ada MacNeill, a member of the Gaelic League, who maintained a lifelong connection with Hobson. (He later mistakenly claimed that MacNeill was the fiancée of Roger Casement.) Mary Ann Hobson belonged to the Irishwomen's Association organised by Alice Milligan and 'Ethna Carbery' (Anna Johnston); Milligan acquainted Bulmer with the works of Standish James O'Grady, which 'opened up…new ranges of hitherto unimagined beauty'. The ancient heroes 'became my constant companions… far more real than the crude town in which I lived' (Hobson, 1). Hobson subscribed to Milligan's and Carbery's separatist monthly, *Shan Van Vocht* (1895–8). The 1898 centenary of the rebellion of the United Irishmen added them to his pantheon, and he became a republican. He soon also joined the artistic and antiquarian circle around F. J. Bigger.

Hobson was educated at the Friends' school, Lisburn. After leaving school at the age of sixteen, Hobson supported himself through haphazard clerical jobs. In 1900 he founded the Ulster Debating Club for boys. In 1901–2 he was secretary of the Belfast Tír na nÓg branch of the Gaelic League. As secretary of the first Antrim county board of the GAA, he successfully resisted proposals that policemen should be permitted to join, though he resigned over the GAA's reluctance to encourage youth clubs. In 1902 he founded a boys' group, Fianna Éireann, which was soon crippled by financial problems and Hobson's other commitments. At the first Glens of Antrim feis in 1904 Hobson befriended Casement and they corresponded regularly. Casement saw Hobson as a substitute son; Hobson admired Casement's idealism, anger at injustice, and financial sacrifices for cultural and political nationalism. They shared a love for the Glens of Antrim, where they often hiked and camped; in later life Hobson recalled these excursions as proof of Casement's heterosexuality, on the grounds that Casement had never taken advantage of this close proximity to make advances to him.

In 1901–3 he trained as a printer, and he retained a lifelong interest in publishing and fine printing. In 1902 he and David Parkhill decided: 'Damn Yeats, we'll write our own plays!' (Hanna Bell, 1), and in 1904 they co-founded the 'Ulster branch of the Irish Literary Theatre'; it had to be renamed the Ulster Literary Theatre, after the Abbey Theatre in Dublin (which had developed out of the Irish Literary Theatre, founded by W. B. Yeats and his associates) refused responsibility for it. Its first production was Hobson's historical drama 'Brian of Banba', inspired by a poem by Milligan offering the apparently hopeless struggle of the young Brian Bórama (Boru) as a model for modern separatists. The theatre was associated with a literary magazine, *Uladh* (1904–5), the contributors to which included Joseph Campbell. Because of his political commitments Hobson drifted away from the group, which survived into the 1930s, its programme dominated by kitchen comedies.

Membership of the IRB

From 1901 Hobson belonged to Cumann na nGaedheal, a front organisation for the Irish Republican Brotherhood, and in 1904 was sworn into the IRB by Denis McCullough; they joined other young men (including Seán MacDermott and Patrick McCartan) in displacing the older Belfast leadership of the brotherhood. In 1906 they founded the Dungannon Clubs, another front organisation for the IRB, which maintained republican separatism against the dual-monarchist 'Hungarian policy' of Arthur Griffith. The clubs' mouthpiece was the *Republic*, a Belfast weekly established by Hobson in December 1906, which published several writers associated with Bigger and the Ulster theatre. Hobson also debated with home rulers at public meetings in Ulster and Scotland. His working life was precarious: he lost one job because of his membership of the Gaelic League and another through his anti-recruiting activities. He visited America early in 1907, where he met IRB veterans and established contact with John Devoy, becoming Irish correspondent for Devoy's *Gaelic American*.

In May 1907, the *Republic* merged with the Dublin journal the *Peasant*, edited by W. P. Ryan with Hobson as deputy editor. When the Dungannon Clubs merged with Griffith's Sinn Féin shortly afterwards, Hobson became vice-president of the merged organisation. From 1907 younger IRB men associated with the Belfast group (including Hobson), and the veteran former prisoners Tom Clarke and John Daly challenged the IRB leadership in Dublin, which was finally deposed in 1911. Hobson moved to the capital in 1908, and became 'centre' of the Teeling circle of the IRB; in 1911 he was elected chairman of the Dublin centre's board and the Leinster board, and a member of the IRB supreme council. He was a particular friend of Clarke, who idealised him as a new John Mitchel and hoped that he could one day win over Ulster Protestants to separatism. In 1909 the *Peasant* became the *Irish Nation and the Peasant*, remaining under Ryan's editorship with major contributions by Hobson.

In August 1909 Hobson and Constance Markievicz co-founded a republican boy scout movement, Na Fianna Éireann, which borrowed its name and some characteristics from Hobson's Belfast youth club but was more explicitly military in its orientation. Hobson was its first president, though Markeivicz later replaced him. Hobson and Markievicz briefly shared a large house in Co. Dublin, combining Fianna duties with an unsuccessful horticultural enterprise, which gave rise to some tension with Markievicz's husband. (Hobson's son later interpreted some of his father's descriptions of eccentric behaviour by the countess as indicating sexual advances that Hobson was too idealistic and sexually naïve to recognise or reciprocate; Hobson himself did not regard them in this light.) In 1912 Hobson founded an IRB circle for Fianna members.

After reading the writings on popular resistance by James Fintan Lalor in 1901, Hobson had begun to advocate this form of action; in 1909 his handbook, *Defensive warfare*, was published by the west Belfast branch of Sinn Féin. But the following year Hobson and his allies resigned from Sinn Féin over policy differences with Griffith, and founded a monthly journal of their own, *Irish Freedom* (edited by Hobson), and several Freedom clubs.

In July 1913 Hobson organised drilling for members of the IRB in Dublin in preparation for the founding of a volunteer force, and he was one of the IRB group that persuaded Eoin MacNeill to found the Irish Volunteers, against the advice of MacNeill's old friend and Gaelic League associate P. H. Pearse, who warned him against such extremists as Hobson. Hobson became secretary of the Volunteer executive in December 1913, to the disquiet of the Clarke–MacDermott group within the IRB, who were alarmed at Hobson's assumption of such a prominent position. Hobson believed that once the Volunteers had been founded, IRB members should regard non-IRB Volunteers as colleagues and work with them on equal terms within a broad group encompassing nationalists of different opinions. By contrast, Clarke and MacDermott and their associates believed that the IRB should be controlled by a tight-knit internal caucus, which could manipulate the Volunteers as a whole and use non-IRB members of the leadership for its own ends while keeping them ignorant of its true strategy.

These tensions were compounded by Hobson's arrogant air: he was acutely conscious that he had already been a separatist when MacDermott was a member of the Ancient Order of Hibernians, and he later claimed that MacDermott had never quite shaken off the Hibernians' fondness for wire-pulling and intrigue. Hobson was also compromised by his friendship with Casement, whose eccentricities and government service aroused suspicions that he was a government spy. Hobson used *Irish Freedom* to promote Casement's view that Ireland's best interests lay in forming an alliance with Germany against Britain; during an American speaking tour in March 1914 Hobson passed a message to this effect from Casement to Devoy for transmission to the German ambassador.

In the first half of 1914 Hobson drew closer to MacNeill, becoming his principal adviser. In June, when John Redmond threatened to set up

his own volunteer organisation if he was not allowed to nominate half of the Volunteers' executive committee, most of the IRB element in the Volunteer leadership favoured refusal. Hobson, however, persuaded MacNeill and the executive majority to accept Redmond's nominees, thereby avoiding a crippling split. Clarke, suffering from the after-effects of long imprisonment and the tensions of his political activity, interpreted Hobson's actions as treason: he accused Hobson of selling himself to Dublin Castle and they never spoke to each other again. Pearse, whom Hobson had sworn into the IRB, was now allied with the intransigents, but he accepted Hobson's good faith and interceded when Devoy sacked Hobson from the *Gaelic American*. Rather than split the IRB, Hobson left the supreme council and the editorship of *Irish Freedom*, but he retained his other IRB positions and remained active in the brotherhood, helping to organise the Howth and Kilcoole gun-runnings in July 1914. At this time he also resigned from the Society of Friends, having long abandoned Quaker pacifism; he remained a non-denominational Protestant, and later had difficulty obtaining a dispensation to marry a Catholic.

THE EASTER RISING AND ITS AFTERMATH

After the outbreak of the first world war and the split between Redmondite and MacNeillite Volunteers, Hobson became the driving force of the MacNeill group, which favoured a defensive strategy and guerrilla warfare. When he discovered that the Pearse group was actively preparing a pre-emptive rising, in March 1916 Hobson urged MacNeill to confront them, but MacNeill refused to press the issue after receiving assurances from Pearse. On the Thursday of holy week 1916 Hobson learned of the impending insurrection and notified MacNeill; they confronted Pearse but MacNeill failed to act decisively against the plotters, and on the evening of Good Friday Hobson was lured to a meeting and detained until the outbreak of the rising.

Believing that the rebels had wrecked Ireland's hopes, Hobson took no part in the fighting; unlike MacNeill (who was more receptive to political symbolism and less unbending) he evaded arrest. Thereafter he was excluded from mainstream Irish nationalist politics: he was barred from the meeting at the Mansion House in 1917, when the second Sinn Féin party was founded, and ostracised by many former friends. He continued to believe in the efficacy of guerrilla warfare and held its effectiveness during the war of independence vindicated his original strategy. In 1918 he published the first volume of *A short history of the Irish Volunteers* (no more appeared) followed by an abridged edition of the life of Wolfe Tone, and in 1921 a selection of Tone's letters.

LATER CAREER

On 19 June 1916 Hobson married (Mary) Clare Gregan, formerly a secretary in the Irish Volunteer offices; they had a daughter and a son. On the foundation of the Irish Free State, Hobson became deputy director of the stamping department in the Office of the Revenue Commissioners; he held this position until his retirement in 1948. In 1929 he edited *A book of Dublin* for Dublin Corporation and in 1932 edited the *Saorstát Éireann official handbook*, a multi-author account of Irish life and culture commissioned by the government of W. T. Cosgrave. He took a strong interest in the Gate Theatre during its early period, helping to recruit support for it at the time of its foundation; he edited and published in 1934 the *Book of the Gate Theatre*. He also took an interest in Esperanto.

Hobson detested the cautious economic policies of post-independence Irish governments, describing them as 'economic unionists'. From 1923 he advocated reafforestation, believing that spin-off industries would end rural depopulation and stabilise the Gaeltacht. His position as a civil servant obliged him to publish much of his writing on such matters anonymously, as, for example, *The new querist* (1933), whose authorship Hobson acknowledged only when he reprinted it in his memoir of 1968. In 1935 he founded a monthly journal, *Prosperity* (which became *Social Justice* in 1936 and folded in 1937), advocating the proto-Keynesian social credit theories of Major C. H. Douglas; these argued that economic growth could be secured by printing extra money to finance public works while controlling the speculative activities of the banks. Hobson joined the Catholic social activists Father Edward Cahill SJ and Mrs Berthon Waters in the League Against Poverty. In 1936 they founded a monetary reform group, the League for Social Justice; they drafted the minority report of the banking commission (1938) equating monetary reform with the social doctrine of the papal encyclicals. Orthodox economists, including George O'Brien, were utterly dismissive of Hobson and his associates. Although monetary reform had cranky, far-right overtones, it was a serious, if underdeveloped, response to the deflation of the 1930s. Many poets and artists advocated social credit in the 1930s and several prominent British adherents of this policy were lapsed Quakers. Hobson's former Volunteer associate Eimar O'Duffy (whose satirical *King Goshawk* trilogy was published under Hobson's 'Martin Lester' imprint from the late 1920s), was also a monetary reformer. After his retirement Hobson informally advised Clann na Poblachta on such matters as reafforestation and breaking the link with sterling; his criticisms of the banks' dominance of the Irish economy were occasionally quoted by the Irish Green Party in the 1990s.

A major preoccupation of Hobson's later career was his support for Roger Casement and his denial of Casement's homosexuality. He denounced the accusation as despicable propaganda, a charge that was foreshadowed in 1908, when, in the *Gaelic American*, Hobson had publicised the Irish crown jewels scandal, with its homosexual overtones, as evidence of British degeneracy; he expanded on this in his 1968 memoir. Hobson and McCartan encouraged W. J. Maloney (who was based in America) to write *The forged Casement diaries* (1937), which advanced the now exploded theory that the diaries were Casement's transcription of material written by a Peruvian criminal. Hobson became Maloney's Dublin research assistant and oversaw the publication.

LAST YEARS AND ASSESSMENT

On his retirement from the staff of the Revenue Commissioners in 1948, Hobson moved from Dublin to Roundstone, Co. Galway. He was frequently consulted by scholars about the Volunteers and the events of 1916, and significantly influenced scholarly reassessments of the Easter rising. In retrospect Hobson criticised Pearse as a 'sentimental egotist' with a 'strain of abnormality', whose financial irresponsibility inflicted severe damage on vulnerable creditors (Edwards, 157, 337–8). Shortly before his death Hobson published a fragmentary memoir, *Ireland yesterday and tomorrow* (1968). Increasingly blind, he spent his last years with his daughter in Castleconnell, Co. Limerick, where he died on 8 August 1969.

Hobson's was a life of achievement, though the potential greatness once seen in him never came to fruition. His expectations were arrogantly high, his disappointment and frustration profound. 'The Phoenix of our youth has fluttered to earth such a miserable old hen', he lamented in 1953 (Dudgeon, 16). Many, like Sean O'Casey, thought Hobson vain and manipulative; others, like MacNeill, revered his quiet determination and selflessness. MacNeill's nephew, the novelist Brian Moore, who chose to have his ashes scattered at the Connemara graveyard where Hobson is buried, wrote: 'his body lay here in this small Connemara field, facing the ocean, under a simple marker was somehow emblematic of his life' (Patricia Craig, *Brian Moore* (2002)).

Hobson's papers are in the NLI, including his copy of the *Irish Freedom* anthology *The voice of freedom*, annotated with the authors of the anonymously published articles. The Maloney Papers in the New York Public Library have his extensive correspondence with Maloney in connection with *The forged Casement diaries*. UCD holds letters to Denis McCullough (McCullough papers, UCD Archives Department, P120) and Desmond Ryan (Ryan papers, UCD Archives Department, LA10). Police reports on Hobson's separatist activities are in the NAI. A few items of correspondence may be found in the *New Statesman* archive at the University of Sussex Library.

Patrick Maume

Sources

Belfast Telegraph, 29 March 1960; 25 July 1964; 9 August 1969 (interview with Hobson); *Irish Times*, 6 May 1961; F. X. Martin, *The Irish Volunteers, 1913–1915* (1963); F. X. Martin, *The Howth gunrunning* (1964); Bulmer Hobson, *Ireland yesterday and tomorrow* (1968); *Irish News*, 14 November 1968; 9 August 1969; *Irish Independent*, 9 August 1969; *Newsletter* (Belfast), 18 August 1969; Sam Hanna Bell, *The theatre in Ulster* (1972); F. X. Martin and F. J. Byrne (ed.), *The scholar revolutionary: Eoin MacNeill, 1867–1945, and the making of the new Ireland* (1973); León Ó Broin, *Revolutionary underground: the story of the Irish Republican Brotherhood, 1858–1924* (1976); Ruth Dudley Edwards, *Patrick Pearse: the triumph of failure* (1977); Michael Tierney, *Eoin MacNeill: scholar and man of action, 1867–1945*, ed. F. X. Martin (1980); Kathleen Clarke, *Revolutionary woman: Kathleen Clarke, 1878–1972*, ed. Helen Litton (1991); Thomas Hennessy, *Dividing Ireland: World War I and partition* (1998); Billy Mitchell, 'Hobson's choice', *Fourthwrite*, no. 2 (summer 2000); Jeffrey Dudgeon, *Roger Casement: the black diaries* (2002); Ben Levitas, *The theatre of nation: Irish drama and cultural nationalism, 1890–1916* (2002); W. J. McCormack, *Roger Casement in death; or, Haunting the Free State* (2002); Marnie Hay, 'Bulmer Hobson: the rise and fall of an Irish nationalist' (Ph.D. thesis, UCD, 2004); local history newscuttings, Belfast Central Library collection

Walter Edgeworth-Johnstone

1863–1937

Walter Edgeworth-Johnstone, soldier, DMP commissioner, and sportsman, was born at Kingstown, Co. Dublin, the eldest son of Robert Johnstone (1806–85), QC and county court judge, of Laputa, Co. Donegal, and his wife Doris (née Tivy). In 1838 a member of the Johnstone family had married into the Edgeworth family of Kilshrewley, Co. Longford (not the Edgeworths of Edgeworthstown), and subsequently some family members had taken the name Edgeworth-Johnstone. Educated at St Columba's College, Walter entered TCD in 1880, graduating BA in 1884. He played rugby and cricket for TCD, and played once for Ireland at rugby in 1884. After attending the Royal Military College at Sandhurst (1884–6), he was commissioned into the 1st West India Regiment in 1886. He served in the expedition against the Yonnie tribe in Nigeria, West Africa, in 1887 and was mentioned in dispatches. He also took part in the West African expeditions to the Tambaku country and Gambia, and was present at the captures of Tambi and Toniataba, again being mentioned in dispatches. In 1893 he was promoted to captain and transferred to the Royal Irish Regiment.

On his return to England his prowess as a sportsman secured him appointment as superintendent of gymnasia, southern district, in 1894; he later served as assistant-inspector of gymnasia (1895–8) and superintendent of gymnasia at the Curragh, Co. Kildare (1898–1902). He excelled at fencing and boxing as well as rugby and cricket and during his army career won numerous awards, including the army heavyweight boxing championship (1894), the amateur heavyweight championship of England (1895 and 1896), the Irish heavyweight championship (1895), the sabre challenge cup, royal military tournament (1896), and the amateur sabre championship (1898 and 1900). In 1888 he played for the Gentlemen of Ireland cricket team. He also published *Boxing: the modern system of glove-fighting* (1901). He belonged to several clubs, including the National Sporting, Kildare Street, Royal Irish Automobile, and the United Services clubs.

In January 1904 he was appointed RM for Dunfanaghy, Co. Donegal. Promoted lieutenant-colonel in 1906, he took command of the 4th (militia) battalion of the Royal Irish Regiment. Appointed chief commissioner of the Dublin Metropolitan Police (DMP) in January 1915, he was concerned by Dublin's traffic problems and initiated the stationing of constables on point duty at major intersections; he also introduced the wearing of white gloves by traffic policemen. More seriously, he looked upon the activities of the Irish Volunteers in the capital with great concern; on 7 April 1916 he reported to the under-secretary:

> The Sinn Fein party is gaining in numbers, in equipment, in discipline, and in confidence, and I think drastic action should be taken to limit their activities. The longer this is postponed the more difficult it will be to be carried out (Herlihy, 173).

At a meeting at the viceregal lodge on 23 April 1916 (the day before the outbreak of the Easter rising) he suggested that twenty to thirty Volunteer and Citizen Army leaders should be arrested simultaneously and interned in England, the rank and file disarmed, and all drilling and marching prohibited. During the rising he withdrew his men from the streets after three were shot dead. In May 1916 he gave evidence to the royal commission of inquiry into the causes of the rebellion. The commis-

sion praised the conduct of the unarmed DMP and noted that Edgeworth-Johnstone had given the government several warnings on which they could have acted before the rising.

Over the next few years Edgeworth-Johnstone faced the difficult task of commanding a civil police force in an increasingly militarised society. The DMP was armed briefly after 1916, but this decision was soon reversed despite protests from its members. During the war of independence (1919–21), shootings of uniformed DMP constables were few (although the detective 'G' division was specifically targeted by the IRA and suffered several fatalities) and the force had some success in maintaining public confidence in very difficult circumstances. One of the terms of the truce of July 1921 was that the DMP alone was to police Dublin. After the establishment of the Irish Free State the DMP was renamed Poilíní Átha Cliath and Edgeworth-Johnstone retired 30 April 1923. Most observers admitted that he had performed well in a difficult job: he was created CB (1918) and KBE (1924). He died 4 January 1936 at his London home, 1 Regent's Park Terrace, and was cremated at Golders Green cemetery.

In 1897 he married Helen Gunning Walker Walters; they had two sons and two daughters. His younger brother, Robert Johnstone (1872–1950), played rugby for Ireland (two caps in 1893) and in three test matches for Great Britain in their tour of South Africa in 1896. He joined the British army and was awarded the VC during the Boer war after he had suffered a serious wound and shown great courage at Elandslaagte on 21 October 1899. Another brother, Ralph Johnstone (d. 1915), was a medical inspector with the Local Government Board and played cricket and rugby (three caps in 1890) for Ireland.

David Murphy and James Quinn

Sources

Who's who (1936), 1,008; *Times*, 6 January 1936; *Who was who*, iii: *1929–1940*; F. X. Martin, '1916–Myth, fact and mystery', *Studia Hibernica*, vii (1967); Robert Edgeworth-Johnstone, *The Johnston(e)s of Magheramena and Laputa* (privately published, 1972); Louis McRedmond (ed.), *Modern Irish lives: dictionary of 20th-century Irish biography* (1996); Penny Bonsall, *The Irish RMs* (1997); *1916 rebellion handbook* (1998), 174–6, 273–4; Jim Herlihy, *The Dublin Metropolitan Police* (2001); information from Inspector John Duffy, Garda Síochána Museum, Dublin Castle

Thomas Kent

1865–1916

Thomas Kent (Ceannt), farmer, land agitator, and nationalist revolutionary, was born 29 August 1865 in Bawnard House, Castlelyons, near Fermoy, Co. Cork, fourth among seven sons and two daughters of David Kent, a substantial farmer (leasing 200 acres), and Mary Kent (née Rice). He received a national school education locally, and worked on his father's farm, until being sent at age nineteen to Boston to join two brothers who had emigrated previously. There he worked with a Catholic publishing and church furnishing firm, and participated in Irish cultural activities. Returning to Cork in 1889/90, he immediately became actively involved in the Plan of Campaign being organised by William O'Brien and the Land League. The Kent family had already come to wide attention during the agitation when the four brothers who had not emigrated to America (David, William, Edmund, and Richard) were all arrested under the 1887 Balfour coercion legislation and charged with conspiracy to evade payment of rents; three of the brothers had been convicted and served prison sentences. Soon after Thomas's arrival from America, he and William were arrested under the Balfour act and placed on summary trial on charges of conspiracy to encourage evasion of rent, resulting in terms of two months' imprisonment with hard labour in Cork jail for Thomas, and a longer sentence of six months with hard labour for

William, owing to his previous conviction. Huge crowds in Fermoy applauded the brothers on the occasions of their release. Of infirm health from this period, Thomas, along with his brothers, ceased to participate in nationalist politics after the split in the movement and the death of Charles Stewart Parnell in 1891. Until his late forties Thomas confined himself to the cultural nationalism of the Gaelic League, learning and promoting traditional Irish music and dancing, as a member of the Castlelyons branch. For a brief while he lived in South Africa, where his brother William had emigrated.

In January 1914 the Kent brothers were among the first recruits to the Cork Brigade of the Irish Volunteers. They helped organise the Castlelyons company (said to be the first teetotal Volunteer unit in Ireland), mustered equipment, and trained recruits in weaponry on the family farm. Working closely with Tomás MacCurtain and Terence MacSwiney, they were prominent in the recruitment of members and organisation of local companies throughout the county. Thomas was present at the historic graveside oration by Patrick Pearse at the funeral of the Fenian leader Jeremiah O'Donovan Rossa in Glasnevin cemetery, Dublin (1 August 1915), and he represented several Cork districts at the Irish Volunteers convention in the Abbey theatre, Dublin (October 1915). He and his brothers helped disrupt a British army recruitment rally in November 1915 at Dungourney, in east Co. Cork, by marching the local GAA club through the assembly with shouldered hurleys. Thomas was charged, alongside MacSwiney, with making seditious speeches at a Volunteer recruitment meeting at Ballynoe (2 January 1916), and was tried under the Defence of the Realm Act, but acquitted. Within weeks he was sentenced to two months' imprisonment for illegal possession of arms, arising from a police raid on Bawnard House on 13 January.

The youngest of the brothers, **Richard Kent** (1875–1916), was born 4 January 1875 at Bawnard House. Arrested and charged with conspiracy during the 1889 Plan of Campaign, he was acquitted owing to his youth. A fine athlete, well known in GAA circles, he worked for years on the family farm. He joined the Irish Volunteers in 1914, but seems not to have been as active as his older brothers.

At Easter 1916 four of the Kent brothers—Thomas, David (1867–1930), William (1873–1956), and Richard—were living at Bawnard with their octogenarian widowed mother. Throughout Easter week the brothers hid on neighbouring farms while awaiting mobilisation orders from Volunteer headquarters, then returned home on hearing of the surrender of the Dublin insurgents. On the early morning of 2 May, amid a roundup of Volunteer activists throughout the county, a party of constabulary approached Bawnard House to arrest one or more of the family. When the Kents refused them admission a gun battle ensued, during which RIC Head Constable William Rowe was killed and David Kent seriously wounded. The incident was the only armed clash in Co. Cork, and one of the few outside Dublin, associated with the Easter rising. Accounts of the incident by participating police and military vary substantially from those rendered in retrospective nationalist historiography. Apart from differences regarding the size of the police party and the firing of the first shot, nationalist chroniclers have asserted that the Kent family carried on a determined resistance for several hours (in which the aged matriarch assisted), refusing to surrender to the constabulary or military reinforcements, until they ran out of ammunition and gave up. Police reported that, after an hour's exchange of shots, gunplay had ceased after the wounding of David Kent, and a protracted siege transpired, until military arrived and the family surrendered; police also claimed that ammunition as well as rifles were found in the house after the affray.

As the family were surrendering, Richard Kent was shot and critically wounded while trying to burst through a hedge and escape arrest. He died the next day (according to the death certificate) in Fermoy military hospital (3 May 1916). He was unmarried. His remains were interred in the family vault at Castlelyons; a small crowd defied a military ban and attended the obsequies.

At Cork detention barracks on 4 May, Thomas and William Kent were tried under courts martial for the wilful murder of Head Constable Rowe. While William was acquitted, Thomas was found guilty and sentenced to death by firing squad. On 9 May he was executed, standing in an attitude of prayer, gripping a set of rosary beads. He too was unmarried.

David Kent was treated for his wounds for two weeks in Fermoy military hospital. Transferred from Co. Cork, where feelings were running high, he was tried by court martial at Richmond barracks, Dublin, for the wilful murder of Rowe, and aiding and abetting an armed rebellion (14–15 June). In a written statement read to the court he denied having had any part in the gun battle. William Kent testified that their deceased brother Richard—who he asserted had spent time in a 'lunatic asylum' owing to an 'accident'—seized a shotgun on seeing police outside the family home, and that any shooting coming from the house had been done solely by him. Prosecuting counsel observed that there had been four men in the house, and four guns, all of which had been fired. David Kent was found guilty on both counts and sentenced to death, with a strong recommendation to mercy on account of previous good character, as attested by an RIC district inspector. Amid the swing of public opinion pursuant to the fifteen executions of the previous month, the sentence was duly commuted to five years' penal servitude. After incarceration in several English prisons, he was released in the general amnesty of June 1917.

Popular esteem for the exploits of the Kent family was shown in January 1917 when an enormous cortège assembled at the funeral of the mother. David Kent served on the Sinn Féin national executive from October 1917 throughout the 1920s, and was elected for Cork constituencies to the first and second dáils. Taking the anti-treaty side in the civil war, he was re-elected as an abstentionist republican in the August 1923 and June 1927 elections, and continued to attend the legitimist republican second dáil. He died of influenza at Bawnard House on 16 November 1930.

William Kent was the first member of Sinn Féin to chair Cork County Council (1917), but by 1927 had left the party to join Fianna Fáil. Serving as TD for Cork East (1927–32, 1933–7), he broke with Fianna Fáil over the land annuities controversy and economic war, and contested the 1933 election for the Centre Party, which later that year merged with other parties to form Fine Gael. He left Fine Gael in 1934 after disagreeing vehemently with tactics of the Blueshirts, and completed his dáil tenure as an independent. He died at Bawnard House on 8 March 1956.

Desmond McCabe and Lawrence William White

Sources

GRO (birth, death certs.); *Catholic Bulletin*, vi, no. 8 (August 1916), 457–9; no. 9 (September 1916), 521 (portrait photographs in both nos.); William J. Flynn, *Oireachtas companion* (1928); *Cork Examiner*, 17, 20, 21 November 1930; 7–13 January 1933; 9, 10 March 1956; *Irish Press*, 10 October 1934; P. J. Power, 'The Kents and their fight for freedom', in *Rebel Cork's fighting story* (1947 ed.), 59–64; Desmond Ryan, *The rising: the complete story of Easter Week* (1949); Breandán MacGiolla Choille (ed.), *Intelligence notes 1913–16* (1966); National Gallery of Ireland, *Cuimhneachán 1916: a commemorative exhibition of the Irish rebellion 1916* (1966), 61–2, 71; Florence O'Donoghue, 'The Irish Volunteers in Cork, 1913–16', *Journal of the Cork Historical and Archaeological Society*, lxxi, nos. 213–14 (1966), 41–8; Patrick Power, 'The Kents of Bawnard, Castlelyons, and their fight for Irish freedom' in *Rebel Cork's fighting story: from 1916 to the truce with Britain* (1966 ed.), 33–8; Martin Shannon, *Sixteen roads to Golgotha* (*c.*1966), 162–7; Dorothy Macardle, *The Irish Republic* (1968 ed.); C. Desmond Greaves, *Liam Mellows and the Irish revolution* (1971); Piaras F. MacLochlainn, *Last words: letters and statements of the leaders executed after the rising at Easter 1916* (1971); Uinseann MacEoin (ed.), *Survivors* (1980); Michael Gallagher, *Political parties in the Republic of Ireland* (1985); National Graves Association, *The last post* (1985 ed.); Tomás O'Riordain, *Where martyred heroes rest: the story of the republican plot, Kilcrumper, Fermoy* (1987), 34–7; Brian M. Walker, *Parliamentary election results in Ireland 1918–92* (1992); Michael Gallagher (ed.), *Irish elections 1922–44: results and analysis* (1993), *passim*; Uinseann MacEoin, *The IRA in the twilight years, 1923–1948* (1997); Padraic O'Farrell, *Who's who in the Irish war of independence and civil war 1916–1923* (1997); *1916 rebellion handbook* (1998 ed.); Michael Laffan, *The resurrection of Ireland: the Sinn Féin party, 1916–1923* (1999); John M. Regan, *The Irish counter-revolution 1921–1936: treatyite politics and settlement in independent Ireland* (1999)

Kathleen Lynn

1874–1955

Kathleen Lynn, medical practitioner and political activist, was born 28 January 1874 in Mullafarry, near Cong, Co. Mayo, second oldest of three daughters and one son of Robert Lynn, Church of Ireland clergyman, and Catherine Lynn (née Wynne) of Drumcliffe, Co. Sligo. Despite aristocratic relations and a comfortable upbringing, her professional career was primarily concerned with the less well-off. Lynn's Mayo childhood, where poverty coincided with land agitation, may have motivated her to seek political and pragmatic solutions to socio-economic deprivation. After education in Manchester and Düsseldorf, she attended Alexandra College, Dublin. She graduated from Cecilia Street (the Catholic University medical school) in 1899, and, after postgraduate work in the United States, became a fellow of the Royal College of Surgeons in 1909. She was refused a position in the Adelaide Hospital because of her gender, and eventually joined the staff of Sir Patrick Dun's Hospital. Valuable experience was also gained at the Rotunda Lying-In Hospital. From 1910 to 1916 she was a clinical assistant in the Royal Victoria Eye and Ear Hospital, the first female resident doctor at the hospital, but was not allowed to return after the 1916 rising. Her private practice, at 9 Belgrave Road, Rathmines, was her home (1903–55).

An active suffragist and an enthusiastic nationalist, Lynn was greatly influenced by labour activists Helena Molony, Constance Markievicz, and

James Connolly. Her work in the soup kitchens brought her into close contact with impoverished families in Dublin during the 1913 lockout of workers. She joined the Irish Citizen Army (ICA) and taught first aid to Cumann na mBan. As chief medical officer of the ICA during the 1916 rising, she tended to the wounded from her post at City Hall, and her car was used for the transportation of arms and for Markievicz to sleep in. Imprisoned in Kilmainham, along with her close friends Helena Molony and Madeleine ffrench-Mullen, she complained bitterly about the cramped prison conditions.

A committed socialist, Lynn was an honorary vice-president of the Irish Women Workers' Union in 1917, and denounced the poor working conditions of many women workers. She was vice-president of the Sinn Féin executive in 1917, and her home was a meeting point for fellow Sinn Féin women, notably for meetings of Cumann na dTeachtaire (the league of women delegates). On the run from May to October 1918, she was sent to Arbour Hill detention barracks when arrested. The authorities agreed to release her, on the intervention of the lord mayor of Dublin, Laurence O'Neill, as her professional services were essential during the 1918–19 influenza epidemic. Despite her high political profile, Lynn is remembered, primarily, for her work in St Ultan's Hospital for Infants on Charlemont Street, which she established in 1919 with her confidante, Madeleine ffrench-Mullen. Its philosophy was to provide much-needed facilities, both medical and educational, for impoverished infants and their mothers.

Though she was active in south Tipperary during the war of independence, Lynn's national prominence faded after the heady 1913–23 period. In 1923 she was elected to Dáil Éireann as Sinn Féin candidate for Dublin County on the anti-treaty side, but did not take her seat. She failed to retain her seat in the June 1927 election, but was an active member of Rathmines Urban District Council from 1920 to 1930. She commented regularly on public-health matters such as housing and disease prevention. As council member of the Irish White Cross she endeavoured to help republicans and was very critical of the newly formed Irish Free State's attitude to anti-treatyites. At St Ultan's, Lynn fostered international research on tuberculosis eradication. In 1937, through the efforts of her colleague Dorothy Stopford-Price, the hospital introduced BCG (Bacillus Calmette-

Guerin) inoculation, which prevented TB. She also encouraged links with US and continental European medical practitioners. Ffrench-Mullen and Lynn visited the United States in 1925 to raise funds for St Ultan's and visit paediatric institutions. Lynn's interest in child-centred education was furthered in 1934 when Dr Maria Montessori visited St Ultan's.

Throughout her life Lynn preached the virtues of cleanliness and fresh air. She was involved with An Óige (the Irish youth hostel organisation) and gave them her cottage in Glenmalure, Co. Wicklow (which she had previously lent to Dorothy Macardle for the writing of *The Irish Republic*). Lynn's friend, the architect Michael Scott, designed a balcony outside her bedroom, where she slept for most of the year. A devout member of the Church of Ireland, she worshipped regularly at Holy Trinity church, Rathmines, but often criticised the Christian churches for losing sight of Christ's original teaching. After World War II, she was vice-chairman of the Save the German Children Society. She died on 14 September 1955 at St Mary's nursing home in Dublin and was given a full military funeral. Remembered primarily for her socio-political activism, she was part of a generation of women who were politicised in the 1910s and who devoted their later careers to maternal feminism. A portrait by Lily Williams is in the Royal College of Physicians of Ireland.

Margaret Ó hÓgartaigh

Sources

Kathleen Lynn diaries and St Ultan's papers, Royal College of Physicians of Ireland; Br Allen papers, Christian Brothers archive, Dublin; minute book of Cumann na dTeachtaire (NLI, Hanna Sheehy-Skeffington collection, MS 21,194 (47)); *Evening Mail*, 10 June 1916; 31 October 1918; Kathleen Murphy, obituary, *Journal of the Irish Medical Association*, xxxvii (1955), 321; Hazel Smyth, 'Kathleen Lynn MD, FRCSI (1874–1955)', *Dublin Historical Record*, xxx, no. 2 (March 1977), 51–7; J. B. Lyons, *Brief lives of Irish doctors* (1978), 159–60; Margaret Mac Curtain, 'Women, the vote and revolution' in Margaret Mac Curtain and Donncha Ó Corráin (ed.), *Women in Irish society: the historical dimension* (1978), 46–57; Pearl Dunlevy, 'Patriot doctor—Kathleen Lynn FRCSI', *Irish Medical Times*, 4 December 1981; Gearóid Crookes, *Dublin's Eye and Ear: the making of a monument* (1993); W. W. [Canon William Wynne], 'Kathleen Lynn', *Irish Times*, 9 April 1994; Margaret Ward, 'The League of Women Delegates and Sinn Féin 1917', *History Ireland*, iv, no. 3 (autumn 1996), 37–41; Margaret Ó hÓgartaigh, *Dr Kathleen Lynn and maternal medicine* (2000); Ó hÓgartaigh, 'St Ultan's, a women's hospital for infants', *History Ireland*, xiii, no. 4 (July/August 2005), 36–9; Ó hÓgartaigh, *Kathleen Lynn, Irishwoman, patriot, doctor* (2006)

John
MacBride

1865–1916

John MacBride, officer in the Boer army and republican, was born 7 May 1865 at Westport, Co. Mayo, the youngest of the five sons of Patrick MacBride and his wife, Honoria (née Gill), shopkeepers in the town. MacBride was educated at the Christian Brothers' school in Westport and at St Malachy's College, Belfast. A small, wiry, red-headed man, with grey eyes and a long nose, 'Foxy Jack' MacBride worked as a young man in a draper's shop in Castlerea, Co, Roscommon; he also involved himself in the GAA and the IRB in Mayo. When he moved to Dublin, to work in Moore's wholesale chemist business in Yarnhall Street, MacBride joined the advanced nationalist splinter group the Irish National Association, which he represented at an Irish republican convention in Chicago in 1895. The following year, possibly for health reasons, he emigrated to the Transvaal republic, where he worked on block B of the Langlaagte gold-mine outside Johannesburg. MacBride became leader of the pro-Kruger Irish uitlanders, which soon included Arthur Griffith, and which organised a '98 centenary commemoration in Johannesburg that rivalled that held in Dublin, and clearly demarcated the Irish as the 'odd man out' in uitlander society. Eighty years later, there were reports that at about this time MacBride and a woman of mixed race had a son together.

With the outbreak of the South African war in October 1899, MacBride organised an Irish commando, or Irish Transvaal brigade, of about 300 men to fight on the Boer side. Nominating as commander John Blake (1856–1907), an Irish-American and former US cavalry officer, MacBride accepted the role of second-in-command with the rank of major. He became a naturalised citizen of the republic and was made a justice of the peace. A good soldier and leader in the field, and fervently loyal to what in Ireland was called 'MacBride's brigade', MacBride, usually on his horse Fenian Boy, fought with his unit in Natal. For four months he guarded a 'long tom' Creusot siege gun on Pepworth Hill outside Ladysmith, and he fought in the battles of Talana Hill, Colenso and Tugela Heights. In his absence he was nominated to stand in February 1900 as an independent nationalist in the South Mayo by-election, following the resignation of Michael Davitt, but he lost to the Irish parliamentary party candidate by 427 votes to 2,401.

In May 1900 the Irish commando was in the van of the Boer retreat through the Orange Free State republic. MacBride's unit was one of the last of the republican forces to leave Johannesburg in front of the occupying British army. Deserted by Blake, MacBride commanded what was left of the unit from 7 June 1900, as it retreated across the eastern Transvaal, and he was still in command when the Irish commando disbanded and its surviving members crossed into Portuguese Mozambique at Komatipoort on 23 September 1900.

MacBride then travelled to Paris, and became involved with a small group of Irish nationalist expatriates dominated by Maud Gonne. At the suggestion of Arthur Griffith, at the end of 1900 MacBride went on an extended lecture tour of the United States; for part of this he was joined by Gonne. After returning to Paris, MacBride became a paid runner for the journalist Victor Collins. Despite advice from his friends, and probably dragooned into it by Maud Gonne herself, he married her on 21 February 1903 at the church of Saint-Honoré d'Eylau in Place Victor Hugo; she later said she thought she was marrying Ireland. The following year a son, Seán, was born. Beset by sharp differences in temperament and social status, the marriage was a failure and, amid bitter recriminations and accusations by Gonne of cruelty, infidelity and drunkenness, a separation was granted by a French court in 1906.

MacBride returned to Ireland, unmolested by the police. He was now a sad figure, respected for his war effort, but his reputation tarnished by

the break-up of his marriage. Treated with caution by advanced nationalists because of his heavy drinking, he was however a close friend of the republican Fred Allan (in whose house he lived for a while) and was elected to the supreme council of the IRB in 1911. He occasionally made speeches, and wrote a series of good articles on his wartime experiences for the *Freeman's Journal*. But the reality was that, even after he got a permanent job in 1910 as water bailiff in the port of Dublin, MacBride was regarded as unreliable and was politically marginalised by advanced nationalists; in the latter part of 1911 he was replaced on the IRB supreme council by Seán Mac Diarmada.

The 1916 rising in Dublin came as a surprise to MacBride. Stumbling on it by accident, he fell in with the 2nd battalion of Thomas MacDonagh, which occupied Jacob's factory. To MacDonagh's credit, he appointed MacBride his second-in-command. By all accounts MacBride (dressed in civilian clothes throughout) fought well and generally showed more initiative and decisiveness than his commanding officer. Before surrendering on 30 April he encouraged the men under his command to escape and take up the fight again at a later date, but never again to allow themselves to be cooped up in a building. He himself made no effort to escape or to disguise his identity. He was court-martialled on 4 May and condemned to death. General Blackader, who presided over the courts martial, described him as a 'brave man' and the 'most soldierly' of the defendants (Ó Broin, 26–7). MacBride was shot by firing squad in Kilmainham jail at 3.47 a.m. on 5 May 1916. Immortalised by his enemy W. B. Yeats as 'a drunken, vainglorious lout' ('Easter 1916'), nonetheless MacBride, conventional and limited though he may have been, was a dedicated soldier and nationalist who achieved martyrdom status in the pantheon of Irish republicanism.

Donal P. McCracken

Sources

NLI, Allan papers; O. J. O. Ferreira, 'MacBride, John', *Dictionary of South African biography*, iii (1977); León Ó Broin, *W. E. Wylie and the Irish revolution, 1916–21* (1989); Anthony J. Jordan, *Major John MacBride, 1865–1916* (1991); R. F. Foster, *W. B. Yeats: a life*, i: *The apprentice mage, 1865–1914* (1997); Donal P. McCracken, *MacBride's brigade: Irish commandos in the Anglo–Boer war* (1999); Michael Foy and Brian Barton, *The Easter rising* (1999); Anthony J. Jordan, *The Yeats–Gonne–MacBride triangle* (2000)

Seán Mac Diarmada

1883–1916

Seán Mac Diarmada (MacDermott), republican revolutionary, was born John Joseph McDermott in January 1883 (baptised 29 January) in Corranmore (Laghty Barr), Kiltyclogher, Co. Leitrim, eighth child and third son among five sons and five daughters of Donald McDermott (d. 1913), a small farmer and carpenter, and Mary McDermott (née McMorrow) (d. 1892), native of the nearby townland of Ardmoneen (Loughros Barr). Educated at Corracloona national school, he studied by correspondence course for a king's scholarship to train as a teacher, but twice failed the examination owing to deficiency at mathematics. After working briefly and unhappily as a gardener in Edinburgh (1904), he studied bookkeeping, shorthand and Irish at a night school near Dowra, Co. Cavan, and was deeply influenced by his teacher's nationalism (winter 1904–5). Moving to Belfast, he worked as a tramcar conductor (1905–6), until his dismissal for smoking on a tram platform.

THE RELENTLESS ORGANISER

Involved for a time in the Ancient Order of Hibernians (AOH), he soon converted to militant, physical-force republicanism. Joining a Dungannon club (1905), he met members of the secret Irish Republican Brotherhood (IRB), one of whom, victim of the purge of inactive members being conducted within the organisation's Belfast circle by Bulmer Hobson and Denis McCullough, recommended Mac Diarmada as his replacement.

Sworn into the IRB (1906), he joined eagerly in the reinvigoration of the body's Belfast organisation. Appointed full-time organiser, with a bicycle and small salary, of the Dungannon Clubs—the open organisation founded by Hobson and McCullough to promote republicanism in Ulster—he especially sought recruits from the AOH, exacerbating the considerable ill feeling between the rival bodies. When the Dungannon Clubs amalgamated with the Cumann na nGaedheal organisation of Arthur Griffith to form the Sinn Féin League (April 1907), Mac Diarmada became an organiser for the new body, founding local branches initially throughout Ulster and then nationally (1907–11). He canvassed extensively in the 1907–8 North Leitrim parliamentary by-election campaign waged for Sinn Féin by Charles Dolan.

At the instigation of McCullough, who was co-opted to the IRB supreme council in 1908, Mac Diarmada was appointed the brotherhood's national organiser (1908–16). He moved with Hobson to Dublin, where they allied with IRB veteran Thomas Clarke, recently returned from America, in urging a more active policy upon the semi-moribund organisation, and undermining the authority of the body's old-guard national leadership. Physically robust and gregarious, Mac Diarmada toured the country tirelessly by foot or bicycle or motorcar, engaged in the open activity of organising Sinn Féin clubs, and the clandestine activity of recruiting likely men into the IRB, thus weaving a vast web of personal contacts throughout Ireland. He was the chief operative implementing the IRB policy of infiltrating national cultural organisations, and placing IRB men in leadership positions within them. He himself was active in Dublin in the Gaelic League, the GAA (as a non-playing club member), a GAA pipe band, and the Celtic Literary Society. From 1908 he organised the annual Aonach na Nollag, a Christmas exhibition of Irish goods sponsored by Sinn Féin to promote development of native industries. He was manager of the monthly journal *Irish Freedom* (November 1910–December 1914), an initiative of McCullough and Clarke launched under the cover of the Dublin Wolfe Tone Clubs committee, and intended to express IRB opinion. Through 1910–12 the contest between IRB militants and moderates centred on first the launch, and then the control, of the newspaper, concluding in resignations of key old-guard leaders. During this time Mac Diarmada succeeded John MacBride as Connaught representative on the IRB supreme council (probably 1911).

In autumn 1911 Mac Diarmada was stricken with poliomyelitis; hospitalised for several months, and convalescing subsequently in the homes of friends, he was rendered partially disabled in the right leg (among other lasting chronic complications), and thereafter walked with a limp and the aid of a stick. He travelled to the USA as IRB delegate to the Clan na Gael convention in Atlantic City, New Jersey (October 1912), where he propounded the organisation's new activist philosophy and programme. From as early as 1911 he promoted the profile within republican circles of Patrick Pearse, recognising his potential value to the movement despite the initial guardedness of Clarke and others.

CONSPIRING FOR INSURRECTION

Elected secretary of the IRB supreme council (1913), Mac Diarmada constituted, with Clarke (treasurer) and James Deakin (president), the body's standing executive, empowered under the brotherhood's constitution to act for the supreme council between meetings. With Deakin distracted by business commitments, Clarke and Mac Diarmada exercised the powers of the executive to impose their policy upon the entire organisation, increasingly concentrating governance of the IRB into their hands alone. Among several top IRB activists involved in the launch of the Irish Volunteers, Mac Diarmada attended the initial organising meeting in Wynn's hotel (11 November 1913), and addressed one of the two overflow meetings at the paramilitary body's public launch in the Rotunda (25 November 1913), at which he was elected to the provisional committee. Perceiving with Clarke the Volunteers' potential as an IRB-controlled army capable of staging an armed rebellion, as a paid Volunteer organiser he established units countrywide while continuing his IRB recruitment, placing members of the secret organisation into key Volunteer commands. The controversy over co-option of nominees of John Redmond to the Volunteers' provisional committee (June 1914) caused Mac Diarmada's and Clarke's bitter and lasting estrangement with Hobson, who had agreed to Redmond's demand to avoid a split in the movement. During the Howth gun-running (26 July 1914) Mac Diarmada operated together with Clarke in a hired taxi as scouts for the Volunteer column returning with arms through Clontarf to Dublin, and conveyed several loads of rifles in the taxi to safe locations.

Instrumental in the decision of the IRB supreme council to stage an armed rising during the first world war, he joined Clarke in convening the secret meeting representing the spectrum of advanced nationalist leadership in the Gaelic League library, Parnell Square, that resolved to pursue that objective (9 September 1914). Over the ensuing winter the pair allowed the advisory military committee formed at the meeting to lapse, determining to confine planning for the rising within a much smaller, trusted, and more tightly controlled clique to obviate potential betrayal by informers and spies. Mac Diarmada was among the twenty members of the Volunteers' provisional committee who signed a statement (24 September 1914) repudiating Redmond's speech at Woodenbridge, Co. Wicklow, pledging support to Britain in the first world war. The ensuing Volunteers' split paradoxically enhanced his and Clarke's designs, by placing at their disposal a smaller, more militant, and more easily manipulated paramilitary organisation. Mac Diarmada was elected to the Irish Volunteers' general council at the body's first convention (October 1914), and to the central executive at the second convention (October 1915). After government suppression of *Irish Freedom* for its anti-war line (December 1914), Mac Diarmada was manager and registered owner of the new IRB organ, *Nationality* (1915–16). He was imprisoned for four months in Mountjoy jail (May–September 1915) after making a vigorous anti-recruiting speech to a Volunteer meeting at Tuam, Co. Galway.

On his release he and Clarke joined the secret military council—already consisting of Pearse, Joseph Plunkett, and Eamon Ceannt—assembled by Clarke during Mac Diarmada's imprisonment to devise the detailed plans for the rebellion. Amid a concurrent reorganisation of the IRB supreme council, Mac Diarmada engineered the election of the Belfast-based McCullough as president, thereby securing his and Clarke's unimpeded control of the executive. At its last meeting prior to Easter week (January 1916), the supreme council approved Mac Diarmada's motion for a rising at the earliest possible date, and sanctioned the existence of the military council. Mac Diarmada was prominent in initiating and conducting the discussions with James Connolly that resulted in the latter's approval of the plans for the rising and his co-option to the military council (January 1916), which subsequently co-opted Thomas MacDonagh as a seventh member.

Throughout the early months of 1916 Mac Diarmada was at the centre of the final logistical preparations for the rising. His role in the confused events immediately preceding the rising was critical. He and Plunkett most likely instigated circulation of the 'Castle document,' a purported leak suggesting an imminent government move to disarm the Volunteers, which conveniently supplied a plausible cover before the eyes of the Volunteers' moderate leadership for the final mobilisation activity. On Good Friday morning (20 April) Mac Diarmada persuaded Volunteer commander-in-chief Eoin MacNeill, who had learned the previous evening of the plan to rise on the Sunday, that the insurrection should proceed because the expected arrival of German arms made likely a government move to suppress the movement, but also increased the prospects for success. Mac Diarmada ordered the temporary detention of Hobson that evening, fearing his interference with the conspirators' intentions. When MacNeill learned on the Saturday of the loss of the arms ship and arrest of Roger Casement, and was made aware of the extensive subterfuges of Mac Diarmada and his fellow conspirators, he reversed his position and issued an order countermanding the Volunteers' scheduled Easter manoeuvres. Mac Diarmada secured the military council's decision on Sunday morning (23 April) (against Clarke's wish to proceed as planned) to delay the rising by one day, to allow time to rescind the countermand.

As a member of the provisional government into which the military council now transformed itself, Mac Diarmada signed the proclamation of the Republic. Throughout the rebellion he remained, in civilian clothes, with the headquarters garrison in the General Post Office, functioning as adjutant to Connolly (the commander-in-chief), and coordinating the operation of a field hospital in the building. From the Thursday evening, as Connolly weakened from wounds, Mac Diarmada and Clarke, though neither held officers' rank in the Volunteers, increasingly commanded the direction of the battle. Mac Diarmada ordered evacuation of the wounded to Jervis Street hospital on the Friday, and amid the confused evacuation of the burning GPO, rallied the troops to continue the manoeuvre in the face of withering hostile fire. With Pearse in military custody after agreeing to surrender on Saturday afternoon (29 April), Mac Diarmada read the surrender order to the garrison in the new headquarters in a Moore Street

shop, adding his own commendation of their gallantry. With calm logic, he quelled a section of the garrison who wished to fight on, stressing their duty to survive the rebellion, so as to some day 'finish the job'.

Among the party of prisoners held overnight outside the Rotunda hospital, and ridiculed for his physical disability by the officer-in-charge who confiscated his walking stick, the next day he was conducted to Richmond barracks under a slower escort separate from the main column of prisoners. After escaping identification by intelligence agents for some days, at his court martial (9 May) he conducted a spirited defence, challenging prosecution evidence, cross-examining witnesses, and demanding that all allegations against him be proved. Found guilty of participation in armed rebellion, he was acquitted on a lesser charge of causing disaffection among the populace. He and the severely wounded Connolly were the last two of the rebellion leaders to be executed by firing squad in the yard of Kilmainham jail (12 May), despite growing public disquiet, and protests by British and Irish politicians (both nationalist and unionist).

ASSESSMENT

Mac Diarmada's historical legacy is inseparable from that of Tom Clarke, his closest friend and political ally: as Clarke was the master mind behind the Easter rising, Mac Diarmada was the master machinist, the man who more than any other assembled and manipulated the various cogs of organisation. In the last critical months of planning and plotting, it was Mac Diarmada, with his genius for covert activity and intrigue, network of personal contacts, and comprehensive knowledge of the strength, calibre, and leadership of individual IRB and Volunteer units countrywide, who wielded the greater control over events, concealing certain of his machinations even from Clarke himself. His obsession with secrecy, perceived as essential to obviate informers, undermined the communications necessary to stage successful insurrection.

Ideologically a pure physical-force separatist, single-mindedly devoted to expelling British government from Ireland, he was hostile toward trade-unionism and socialist internationalism as impeding the development of native entrepreneurial industry and diluting national feeling. Dark-haired and handsome, he was an articulate and persuasive public speaker. His foremost asset as a revolutionary intriguer was said to be the simple and warm charm of his manner, which attracted and instilled confidence among a wide diversity of personalities. His example was cited by Michael Collins as the model for the latter's post-1916 reorganisation of the IRB, and strategic exploitation of the secret society as a personal power base in the conduct of armed insurrection.

Unmarried, from 1915 Mac Diarmada was romantically attached to Josephine Mary ('Min') Ryan, a Cumann na mBan activist and NUI graduate from a prosperous farming background in Tomcool, Co. Wexford, who later married Richard Mulcahy; Min and her sister were the last visitors prior to Mac Diarmada's execution. His brother Seamus MacDermott (1887–1962) emigrated to America (1914), was active there in Clan na Gael and the New York branch of the Irish Volunteers, and joined the staff of the *Gaelic American*, succeeding on the death of John Devoy as the paper's editor (1928–62). A statue of Mac Diarmada was unveiled in Kiltyclogher (1940). The family homestead and cottage in Corranmore, purchased by the state in 1964, is a national monument under the OPW. The railway station in Sligo town and a street in Dublin city centre bear Mac Diarmada's name.

Lawrence William White

Sources

Catholic Bulletin, vi, no. 7 (July 1916), 400–01, 403; *Capuchin Annual 1942*, 220–26, 306–7, 346, 365; Desmond Ryan, *The rising: the complete story of Easter week* (1949); Diarmuid Lynch, *The IRB and the 1916 insurrection* (1957); F. X. Martin (ed.), *The Irish Volunteers 1913–1915: recollections and documents* (1963), 25, 30, 49–50, 76, 79–80, 89, 95–6, 109, 144, 155, 162, 201–2; Max Caulfield, *The Easter rebellion* (1964); F. X. Martin (ed.), *The Howth gun-running* (1964); *Capuchin Annual 1966*, 156–7 (includes portrait drawing by Seán O'Sullivan), 170–78, 302–3; Breandán MacGiolla Choille (ed.), *Intelligence notes 1913–16* (1966); Martin Shannon, *Sixteen roads to Golgotha* (*c.*1966), 133–40; Charles J. Travers, 'Sean Mac Diarmada 1883–1916', *Breifne*, iii, no. 9 (1966), 1–46; F. X. Martin (ed.), *Leaders and men of the Easter rising: Dublin 1916* (1967); Kevin B. Nowlan (ed.), *The making of 1916: studies in the history of the rising* (1969), 164, 166, 169–73, 177–81, 186; León Ó Broin, *Revolutionary underground: the story of the Irish Republican Brotherhood 1858–1924* (1976); Ruth Dudley Edwards, *Patrick Pearse: the triumph of failure* (1977); Ciarán Ó Duibhir, *Sinn Féin: the first election 1908* (1993); *1916 rebellion handbook* (1998 ed.); Michael Foy and Brian Barton, *The Easter rising* (1999); Brian Barton, *From behind a closed door: secret court martial records of the 1916 Easter rising* (2002); Gerard MacAtasney, *Seán Mac Diarmada: the mind of the revolution* (2004); Charles Townshend, *Easter 1916: the Irish rebellion* (2005)

Thomas MacDonagh

1878–1916

Thomas MacDonagh, teacher, writer, and republican revolutionary, was born 1 February 1878 in Cloughjordan, Co. Tipperary, third child and eldest son among six surviving children (four sons and two daughters; three elder children had died in infancy) of Joseph MacDonagh (1834–94), native of Co. Roscommon, and Mary MacDonagh (née Parker), Dublin native of English parentage (her father had moved to Dublin to become compositor in Greek for Trinity College Press); both were national school teachers. His father (who claimed descent from the medieval Mac Donnchadha clan of Ballymote castle, Co. Sligo), the son of a small farmer, received through the efforts of his widowed mother and her brother, a parish priest, teacher training in Dublin. He met and married MacDonagh's mother while both were teaching in Cloghan, Co. Offaly; they were transferred to Cloughjordan the year before MacDonagh's birth. Both parents were averse to political partisanship ('great cry and little wool, like the goats of Connacht' in his father's estimate (Parks, 1)). While his father's was a jovial, kindly, indulgent personality, MacDonagh received from his mother (a convert before marriage from Unitarianism to Roman Catholicism) deep interests in music and literature, and a grave sense of high moral purpose.

After primary education under his father in Cloughjordan, MacDonagh studied under the Holy Ghost fathers at Rockwell College, Cashel, Co. Tipperary (1892–6), where in 1894 he entered the order's junior scholasticate to prepare for the Catholic priesthood. Joining the college faculty as teacher of English, French, and Latin literature (1896–1901), after experiencing a profound crisis of faith he abandoned his vocation for the priesthood for a career as teacher and writer. While senior master of English, French, and history at St Kieran's College, Kilkenny (1901–3), he attended a Gaelic League meeting for a lark, intending to scoff at the proceedings, but instead was moved to a conversion of Pauline peremptoriness, his self-described 'baptism in nationalism' (Norstedt, 26). Immersed in the league's social and cultural activities, elected to the Kilkenny branch executive committee, he attended summer language classes on Inishmaan, Co. Galway (1902), becoming in time a fluent Irish speaker and writer. Each of his first two volumes of poetry—*Through the ivory gate* (1902) and *April and May* (1903)—is redolent of the two successive obsessions of his early adulthood: the spiritual anguish suffered at Rockwell (charted from simple, naïve faith, through a brooding pessimism culminating in nightmarish despair, to restored emotional and spiritual balance in a devout but heterodox Catholic mysticism), and his conversion to Irish-Ireland nationalism.

Estranged from St Kieran's ethos by the latter enthusiasm, MacDonagh moved to a teaching post in the more religiously liberal and Gaelic setting of St Colman's College, Fermoy, Co. Cork (1903–8). After 1905 he drifted away from the language movement, disillusioned by the humourless and blinkered zealotry of the more ardent activists. Discovering a new obsession in concentrated pursuit of his career in literature, he wrote the lyric of a sacred cantata, 'The exodus' (1904), with music by Bendetto Palmieri, RIAM, performed at the RUI and awarded first prize at the 1904 feis ceoil. The exclamatory rhetoric and emotional excess of the piece—tolerable in the context of chorale composition—intruded upon the contemporaneous verse of 'The praises of beauty', published as the opening sequence of *The golden joy* (1906), a volume expressing MacDonagh's spiritual movement from Christian mysticism to neoplatonism in its assertion of devotion to ideal, spiritual beauty, not Christian faith, as the means to redemption, and its concept of the poet as divinely inspired mediator between the spiritual world and the physical. In subsequent years MacDonagh moved further toward a free-thinking, non-dogmatic spirituality.

Seeking wider intellectual contact and literary opportunities, MacDonagh moved to Dublin to become resident assistant headmaster and instructor of language and literature (1908–10) in St Enda's college, Cullenswood House, Ranelagh, the progressive, Irish-language school newly opened by Patrick Pearse, to whom he had become known through the Gaelic League. His first play, *When the dawn is come* (published concurrently with the Abbey Theatre production of November 1908), takes as protagonist an idealistic poet turned nationalist revolutionary in an Ireland fifty years in the future; flawed by windy dialogue and unresolved elements of plot, the play deals with the poet's internal conflicts, and his external differences with fundamentalist, fanatical comrades. Well known in Dublin literary and theatrical circles, MacDonagh formed a particularly close friendship with Joseph Mary Plunkett, whom he tutored in Irish and encouraged in poetical efforts, extending a determining hand toward production of the younger man's first book of verse, *The circle and the sword* (1911).

During his second year at St Enda's, MacDonagh read in English, French, and Irish at UCD, graduating BA (1910). Shaken by an unhappy love affair with writer and teacher Mary Maguire (Mary Colum), he resigned from St Enda's at the time of the school's move to Rathfarnham, Co. Dublin. After a restorative six weeks in Paris, he assumed a semi-reclusive residence in the lodge of Grange House, Rathfarnham (whose owner, Professor David Houston of the College of Science, became an intimate friend), engaged in writing, postgraduate research, and part-time teaching at St Enda's (1910–12). The poems of *Songs of myself* (1910), notwithstanding the transparent allusion of the title, largely retain the intensely subjective poetic voice characteristic of MacDonagh's oeuvre, in preference to a Whitmanesque identification of the self with the representative man. Awarded a first-class honours MA by UCD (October 1911)—his thesis on English Elizabethan prosody was published as *Thomas Campion and the art of English poetry* (1913)—he was appointed full-time assistant lecturer in English at the university (1911–16). As in his earlier posts, he was a lively and stimulating teacher, sincerely engaged with his students, albeit prone to discursiveness and abstraction; his lectures were remembered as 'never relevant and invariably interesting' (McCartney, 65).

With a coterie of close literary friends (Houston, Maguire, James Stephens, and Padraic Colum), MacDonagh was co-founder and associate editor of the *Irish Review* (March 1911–November 1914), a literary and topical monthly, initially without political affiliation, and attracting an impressive range of prominent contributors. The *Review* printed his second play, *Metempsychosis*, a satire of theosophy and related esoteric doctrines, with a wickedly accurate caricature of William Butler Yeats; the play was misinterpreted by contemporary audiences as serious comment when performed by the amateur Theatre of Ireland (1912). The volume *Lyrical poems* (1913) collected the works from MacDonagh's first three books that he wished preserved alongside new material, including mystical poems, nationalist ballads, and translations from the Irish, the latter comprising some of his sturdiest poetic achievement. From 1914 he managed the Irish Theatre in the Hardwicke Street Hall, Dublin, co-founded with Plunkett and Edward Martyn in reaction to the Abbey's prevailing diet of peasant comedy and Yeats's poetic drama, and producing original plays in Irish, in English by Irish authors, and translations into English from continental drama.

THE IRISH VOLUNTEERS

MacDonagh's third play, *Pagans* (produced by the Irish Theatre in April 1915, and published posthumously in 1920), holds interest for an autobiographical subtext: the central conflict between irresponsible bohemian individuality and socially respectable bourgeois domestic convention concludes with the protagonist declaring his newfound devotion to a reborn Irish nation, a resolution neither irresponsible nor conventional.

The theme reflects MacDonagh's own gradual progress from cultural nationalist to physical-force political separatist, initiated by his witnessing the police baton charge down Sackville Street on 'Bloody Sunday' during the 1913 Dublin lockout; thereafter he was active in the Dublin Industrial Peace Committee, whose efforts at independent mediation were frustrated by the employers' intransigence. Enrolling in the Irish Volunteers within a week of their formation (December 1913), and appointed to the armed body's governing provisional committee, he was elected a company captain (July 1914). Initially he regarded the body not as a vehicle for insurrection, but as an armed, militant pressure group, embracing the spectrum of nationalist opinion, in counter-balance to the Ulster Volunteers, to assure British implementation of home rule. His oratorical eloquence, punctuated by melodramatic posturing, contributed to his effectiveness in recruitment efforts countrywide. In association with Plunkett, who had purchased the *Irish Review* from Houston in June 1913, he turned the journal into a virtual mouthpiece for Volunteer policy until its demise in November 1914.

The outbreak of the first world war radicalised his outlook. He was among the twenty members of the provisional committee who repudiated the Woodenbridge declaration by parliamentary party leader John Redmond pledging Volunteer support for the British war effort. Although he attended the secret meeting of advanced nationalists (9 September 1914) that resolved to prepare for an armed insurrection during the course of the European war, and despite being sworn by March 1915 into the secret Irish Republican Brotherhood (IRB), he was not privy to the detailed planning for the rising until the last few weeks before Easter 1916. Serving on both the central executive and the general council after the Volunteers' first general convention (October 1914), he was appointed to the headquarters staff as director of training (December 1914). Appointed commandant of the 2nd battalion, Dublin Brigade (March 1915), he also became brigade commandant with authority over the four city and one county battalions. He assumed a major role in the organisation of the funeral of IRB veteran Jeremiah O'Donovan Rossa, and served as Volunteer acting commandant general for the funeral march (1 August 1915).

MacDonagh's vital importance as Dublin Brigade commandant was probably the reason for his co-option in early April 1916 to the IRB's secret military council, then finalising preparations for the rising; he was the last of the seven council members to be added. Another factor may have been his relationship with Volunteer Chief of Staff Eoin MacNeill, a UCD faculty colleague; in the final confused days before Easter Monday, MacDonagh was intermediary between the conspirators and MacNeill, when the latter became belatedly cognisant of the intended insurrection. Pursuant to the military council's decision on Easter Sunday morning to postpone the rising by one day to the Monday, MacDonagh in his capacity as brigade commandant signed an order confirming MacNeill's public announcement cancelling Easter Sunday manoeuvres, but ordering all volunteers to remain in Dublin pending further directives. At a subsequent final meeting with MacNeill he gave a feigned and trusted assurance that the insurrection had indeed been cancelled.

On Easter Monday morning (24 April), MacDonagh issued the order deploying the Dublin Brigade for muster, and as a member of the provisional government signed the proclamation of the Republic. His battalion divided between two mobilisation centres—a modification of plan to allow for the effects of MacNeill's countermand upon the number of available men—MacDonagh commanded a force of 150 volunteers that occupied Jacob's biscuit factory, Bishop Street, a strong position surrounded by a warren of narrow lanes. In the early afternoon an outpost of his command disregarded his orders by firing prematurely on an advance party of British troops advancing from Portobello barracks up Camden Street to relieve Dublin Castle, thereby forgoing the opportunity to enfilade the main party and inflict heavy casualties. Although snipers in the factory's immense towers harassed enemy patrols throughout the week, no further attempt was made to assault the garrison. MacDonagh's leadership through the week was erratic: hearty but indecisive, he tended inexplicably to amend or rescind orders.

On Sunday 30 April, MacDonagh, the senior Volunteer officer remaining in the field and occupying such an impregnable (if strategically ineffectual) position, initially declined to accept the surrender order issued the previous day, on the grounds that Patrick Pearse, being in enemy custody, had issued the directive under duress. After parleying with the British commander, General Lowe, he was conveyed by motorcar to the South Dublin Union. There, after conferring with 4th battalion commandant Éamonn Ceannt, he agreed to surrender. MacDonagh thereupon countersigned Pearse's order, which, dispatched to the other garrisons still in the field, effectively ended the rising. Convicted and sentenced to death, he was shot by firing squad in Kilmainham gaol on 3 May 1916, with Pearse and Thomas Clarke the first three of the insurrection leaders to face execution. The authenticity of a document widely circulated after the rising, purporting to be an ardent statement made by MacDonagh at his court martial, has been heatedly debated; transcripts of the proceedings made public in 1999 do not indicate that such a statement was made.

FAMILY

MacDonagh married (3 January 1912) Muriel Enid Gifford (1884–1917), sister of Grace Gifford, who married MacDonagh's intimate friend and revolutionary comrade Joseph Plunkett on the eve of his execution. They had been introduced in 1908, when Muriel was visiting St Enda's with her sisters Grace and Sydney, by the suffragist journalist Mrs N. F. Dryhurst, who coyly advised MacDonagh to 'fall in love with one of these girls and marry her', to which he laughingly replied: 'That would be easy; the only difficulty would be to decide which one' (Parks, 26). In the event, MacDonagh and the Gifford sisters were casual friends until autumn 1911, when he and Muriel had an intense and rapid courtship. They had one son, author and barrister Donagh MacDonagh, and one daughter, Barbara MacDonagh Redmond. Initially residing at 32 Baggot Street, at the time of the rising the family lived at 29 Oakley Road, Ranelagh.

Though active in both the Women's Franchise League and the nationalist organisation Inghinidhe na hÉireann, Muriel was the most domesticated and least ardently feminist of the Gifford sisters, highly attentive to her dress and grooming. Named by MacDonagh with David Houston as his joint literary executors, Muriel helped prepare for publication a compilation, *The poetical works of Thomas MacDonagh*

(October 1916), which included some previously unpublished material. Prone to physical illness and nervous disorder, she was emotionally devastated by her husband's death, and drowned while swimming in the sea off Skerries, Co. Dublin (9 July 1917). With public interest in the 1916 widows and their families already stimulated as a major focus of republican propaganda in the immediate aftermath of the rising, her funeral to Glasnevin cemetery was attended by an immense crowd of mourners.

Thomas MacDonagh's eldest sibling, Mary Josephine MacDonagh (1872–1954), entered the Sisters of Charity, teaching and ministering to the sick in the order's schools, hospitals and hospices in Dublin; her name in religion was Sister Mary Francesca. She was the only member of Thomas MacDonagh's family to visit him in Kilmainham jail on the eve of his execution.

Two of MacDonagh's brothers were politically active. The second eldest brother, John MacDonagh (1880–1961), fought in the Easter rising under Thomas's command in the Jacob's factory garrison, after which he was imprisoned in England. An actor and operatic tenor who had toured in Britain and America, from 1914 he was an actor-producer with the Irish Theatre, of which Thomas was co-founder, and revived the theatre in 1918 and for a few years in the early 1920s. He wrote plays (one of which, 'The Irish Jew', was performed on Broadway), and directed several motion pictures (including *Willie Reilly and his colleen bawn* (1920), filmed in the grounds of St Enda's). From 1926 he worked in the newly launched radio station 2RN (latterly Radio Éireann) as an actor and programme producer, and subsequently as a literary and drama critic.

The youngest MacDonagh brother, Joseph (1883–1922), took no part in the Easter rising, but was interned briefly thereafter owing entirely to his kinship with one of the insurgent leaders, and was compelled to retire from his civil-service position in Inland Revenue. After a time as headmaster of St Enda's (1916–17), he worked in income tax recovery and as partner in an insurance brokerage. Prominent in the post-rising reorganisation of Sinn Féin, he was imprisoned on several occasions in the 1917–21 period, and was continually on the run during the war of independence. Elected to the first and second dáils, he was director of the Belfast boycott, and deputised as minister for labour during the imprisonment of Countess Markievicz. Bitterly opposed to the Anglo–Irish treaty, he was imprisoned during the civil war. Falling seriously ill with acute appendicitis, he refused to sign the required form to secure release for medical treatment because doing so would implicitly recognise the legitimacy of the Free State government. Transferred at length to a private nursing home, he underwent an operation, but developed peritonitis, and died 25 December 1922.

ASSESSMENT

Yeats's assertion in 'Easter 1916' that Thomas MacDonagh at the time of his death 'was coming into his force' seems a considered assessment, both in terms of the man's poetry and his scholarship. MacDonagh's poetic reputation rests on a handful of late lyrics—some original ('The night hunt', 'The man upright'), some translations ('The yellow bittern')—in which for the first time he attained to a precision of imagery and a lucid colloquial diction that portended a breakthrough into a unique poetic voice. His foremost contribution to literature resides in his criticism. The posthumous publication *Literature in Ireland: studies Irish and Anglo-Irish* (1916), completed hastily amid the manifold preoccupations of his last year, while uneven and fragmentary in structure, contains a central core of coherent argument and demonstration. A scholarly synthesis of ideas current among the literary revivalists, the book is a pioneering definition of the distinctive character of Anglo-Irish literature and the influences that shaped it in directions different from the literature of England. Analysing the impact of Gaelic poetry and Hiberno-English speech on what he termed 'the Irish mode' in English-language poetry, MacDonagh's treatment of Irish and Anglo-Irish literature as occupying a shared cultural continuum adumbrated a critical approach not to be revived until the latter twentieth century.

Short in stature but of sturdy physique, with crispy brown hair and large grey eyes, MacDonagh had an open, verbose, ebullient persona ('a thousand opinions and the words to sustain them' (Shannon, 124)). His mischievous humour and infectious cheer masked profound inner turmoil and insecurity, the wracking doubt and despair exposed in his more personal poetry. A man of contrasting extremes, torn between contemplation and action, his life was a restless quest for meaning and fulfilment through some all-consuming commitment, a succession of withering disillusionments and fervent new beginnings. The Irish Volunteers were the last, and fatal, oscillation of the cycle.

Among several portraits, the most notable is the bronze head by Oisín Kelly in the common room of UCD, Belfield. The most moving elegy was composed in verse by Francis Ledwidge.

Lawrence William White

Sources

GRO (birth cert.); *Catholic Bulletin*, vi, no. 7 (July 1916), 395–7; Padraic Colum (ed.), introduction to *Poems of the Irish Revolutionary Brotherhood* (1916), ix–xxxvi: xxv–xxxi; *Capuchin Annual 1942*, 214–18, 368, 374–5; Donagh MacDonagh, 'Thomas MacDonagh,' *An Cosantóir*, v, no. 10 (October 1945), 525–34; Diarmuid Lynch, *The IRB and the 1916 insurrection* (1957); F. X. Martin (ed.), *The Irish Volunteers 1913–1915: recollections and documents* (1963), *passim*; Max Caulfield, *The Easter rebellion* (1964); *Capuchin Annual 1966*, 162–3, 214–18; Padraic Colum, 'Thomas MacDonagh and his poetry,' *Dublin Magazine*, v, no. 1 (spring 1966), 39–45; *Irish Times*, Easter rising supplement, 7 April 1966; Breandán MacGiolla Choille (ed.), *Intelligence notes 1913–16* (1966); F. X. Martin (ed.), *The Easter rising and University College Dublin* (1966); Martin Shannon, *Sixteen roads to Golgotha* (*c.*1966), 122–31; Marcus Bourke, 'Thomas MacDonagh's role in the plans for the 1916 rising', *Irish Sword*, viii (1967–8), 178–85; F. X. Martin (ed.), *Leaders and men of the Easter rising: Dublin 1916* (1967); Edd Winfield Parks and Aileen Wells Parks, *Thomas MacDonagh: the man, the patriot, the writer* (1967); Owen Dudley Edwards and Fergus Pyle (ed.), *1916: the Easter rising* (1968), 18–19, 149–52; *Memoirs of Desmond Fitzgerald: 1913–1916* (1968); Kevin B. Nowlan (ed.), *The making of 1916: studies in the history of the rising* (1969), 166, 172–3, 184–6, 219, 222, 226–32, 245–6, 257, 260–01, 271, 291, 298; Piaras F. Mac Lochlainn (ed.), *Last words: letters and statements of the leaders executed after the rising at Easter 1916* (1971); Sydney Czira, *The years flew by* (1974); León Ó Broin, *Revolutionary underground: the story of the Irish Republican Brotherhood 1858–1924* (1976); Ruth Dudley Edwards, *Patrick Pearse: the triumph of failure* (1977); Johann A. Norstedt, *Thomas MacDonagh: a critical biography* (1980); Roger McHugh and Maurice Harmon, *A short history of Anglo-Irish literature* (1982); Declan Kiberd, *Inventing Ireland* (1995); Kevin Rockett, *The Irish filmography* (1996); *1916 rebellion handbook* (1998 ed.); Michael Foy and Brian Barton, *The Easter rising* (1999); Patrick Maume, *The long gestation: Irish nationalist life 1891–1918* (1999); Donal McCartney, *UCD; a national idea: the history of University College, Dublin* (1999); Roche Williams, *In and out of school: in the home of the MacDonaghs* (1999); Declan Kiberd, *Irish classics* (2000); Pádraig Yeates, *Lockout: Dublin 1913* (2000); *Irish Times*, 5 May 2001; Brian Barton, *From behind a closed door: secret court martial records of the 1916 Easter rising* (2002); Charles Townshend, *Easter 1916: the Irish rebellion* (2005); Geraldine Plunkett Dillon, *All in the blood: a memoir* (2006); information from Dara Redmond

Eoin
MacNeill

1867–1945

Eoin (John) MacNeill, Gaelic scholar and nationalist politician, was born 15 May 1867 in Glenarm, Co. Antrim, sixth of eight children of Archibald MacNeill, baker, sailor and merchant, and his wife Rosetta (née Macauley).

Family background and education

MacNeill was profoundly influenced by his upbringing in the Glens of Antrim, a Catholic enclave which still retained some Irish-language traditions and was to become a major focus for Ulster-based Gaelic revivalists (especially in the period before the Great War). The fact that local Protestants shared with Catholics a veneration for St Patrick based on his association with Slemish, the existence of a few Irish-speaking Presbyterians in the Glens, and the strength of the Presbyterian liberal tenant-right tradition in Co. Antrim, led MacNeill to see Ulster unionism as a superficial product of elite manipulation; this perception might have seemed less convincing in the embattled borderlands of south Ulster. His father had been prosecuted in 1872 for participating in a demonstration against the first Orange march in the Glens by a lodge recruited among the Protestant lumpenproletariat by the local rector and land agent.

The MacNeill family attached considerable importance to education. All five sons had distinguished educational records, and the youngest daughter became a hospital matron and inspector of industrial schools.

(Her two elder sisters ran the family business.) MacNeill received his primary education in local schools, and his secondary education (1881–5) at St Malachy's College, Belfast, in whose collegiate division from 1885 he began his studies for the (examination-only) RUI after securing a modern languages scholarship. He secured a degree in constitutional history, jurisprudence and political economy in 1888 having attended law lectures at TCD and King's Inns.

In 1887 MacNeill obtained a junior clerkship in the accountant-general's office in Dublin law courts. He was the first clerk in the office to be appointed by competitive examination rather than patronage; he was also the first not to be a member of the Church of Ireland. (When he left in 1909, nine of the eleven clerks were Catholic; the others were Englishmen.) MacNeill's position as a civil servant attracted some criticism from separatist opponents within the Gaelic League. When MacNeill assisted in disrupting a meeting organised by William Martin Murphy to gather public support for a proposed Dublin international exhibition (denounced by Irish Irelanders as a denationalising project), the *Irish Independent* sneered at 'a civil servant masquerading as Robert Emmet' and MacNeill narrowly escaped dismissal.

MacNeill, the Irish language and the Gaelic League

From 1887 MacNeill took up the study of Irish. In 1890 he began to study Old and Middle Irish in his spare time under the Jesuit scholar Edmund Hogan; this led him to study Irish history and to learn spoken Irish through annual visits to the Aran islands (1891–1908). These studies, and the bitter political factionalism of the Parnell split (in which MacNeill was strongly anti-Parnellite), led MacNeill to develop a theory of Irish identity which stressed cultural factors (especially the language) over state power; in later life he accused those historians (generally imperialist) who equated the progress of civilisation with the growth of state power of 'worshipping the Beast and his image'. This distrust of state absolutism echoed his strongly held Catholicism, though he was not necessarily clericalist.

He contributed articles on the Irish language to the *Irish Ecclesiastical Record* and the *Gaelic Journal*, and in 1893 took a leading role in the group of clerks who founded the Gaelic League under the inspiration of

Douglas Hyde's *The necessity of de-anglicising Ireland*. From 1893 to 1897 MacNeill acted as unofficial (and unpaid) secretary to the Gaelic League. The burden of work this entailed brought on a nervous breakdown which left him with an abiding lassitude and a distaste for correspondence. (He developed a tendency to write letters forcefully setting out his position, but not posting them.) MacNeill edited the *Gaelic Journal* (1894–7), co-edited *Fáinne an Lae* (1898–9), and became the first editor of *An Claidheamh Soluis* (1899–1901), without pay. In 1898 he nominated Patrick Pearse as a member of the Gaelic League executive, and they worked together on the publications committee. The fact that Pearse and MacNeill are generally thought of in connection with their roles in the Irish Volunteers tends to obscure the length of their personal friendship and professional association in the Gaelic League; this underlay MacNeill's willingness to accept Pearse's assurances in 1914–16, and his lasting indignation at the revelation that his friend had systematically misled him.

In 1902 MacNeill took a leading role in establishing an Irish-language printing business, which eventually involved him in heavy losses. In 1903 he became vice-president of the Gaelic League in succession to Fr Michael O'Hickey. In 1909 he was appointed to the chair of early (including medieval) Irish history at UCD (incidentally forfeiting his civil-service pension rights); he took a leading role in the campaign to make Irish compulsory for matriculation in the new university, publishing *Irish in the National University: a plea for Irish education* (1909).

THE IRISH VOLUNTEERS

On 1 November 1913 MacNeill published an article, 'The North began' in *An Claideamh Soluis*. He claimed that the creation of the Ulster Volunteers marked the inception of a popular movement which would end by overthrowing the decayed feudal leadership of unionism, suggested that Edward Carson was a crypto-nationalist, and called for the formation of Irish Volunteers on the Ulster model. (MacNeill's view of Carson as crypto-nationalist, which he only abandoned after the outbreak of the Great War, reflected the unionist leader's participation in a protest campaign against Irish over-taxation in the late 1890s; MacNeill attached great importance to the taxation issue as a means of converting Ulster

unionists. His practice of advocating cheers for Carson at early Irish Volunteer meetings caused some difficulties.) As a result of his article, MacNeill was approached by a group of separatists associated with the Irish Republican Brotherhood, who asked him to take the lead in organising the Irish Volunteers (launched 11 November 1913).

MacNeill is often seen as a straightforward Redmondite loyalist manipulated by the IRB. In fact, it is clear that he had his own agenda; he hoped that John Redmond could use the Volunteers' existence to demand an end to compromise and pressurise the Liberals into granting home rule. (MacNeill believed H. H. Asquith never intended to grant home rule and was secretly encouraging Ulster resistance to provide a pretext for abandoning the bill; this belief derived from memories of Asquith's earlier association with the Liberal imperialist faction who had regarded home rule as a political liability after the retirement of Gladstone.) When Redmond, having initially opposed the Volunteers, demanded that as civil leader of the Irish nation he should control this military force, MacNeill replied that a nation's military forces should not be controlled by the leader of a single party and suggested that by joining the Volunteers the Irish people had given MacNeill a mandate independent of Redmond. When Redmond threatened to establish his own rival organisation, MacNeill was persuaded by Bulmer Hobson to give in to avoid nationwide disruption; this set the pattern for the organisation's subsequent history in which a faction led by MacNeill with Hobson as his chief counsellor was intrigued against by IRB militarists centred on Tom Clarke and allied to Pearse.

MacNeill and 1916

On the outbreak of war in August 1914, MacNeill initially hoped that Redmond's suggestion in parliament that the Volunteer forces should take over the defence of Ireland represented an attempt at non-involvement, but Redmond's Woodenbridge speech (20 September) advocating recruitment for overseas service precipitated the final split. As editor of the weekly *Irish Volunteer* newspaper, MacNeill accused Redmond and his followers of mental and moral corruption, while proclaiming that both British parties were joined in a conspiratorial 'continuity coalition' to defeat home rule, and only the existence of the Volunteers could prevent this. This view of the government as determinedly and systematically hostile underlies both the MacNeill group's resistance to the IRB project of a pre-emptive rising (they believed it would inevitably be suppressed by the government, which would take the opportunity to abandon home rule) and MacNeill's reluctance to split the Volunteers by confronting the conspirators. (A memorandum which MacNeill prepared for presentation to the Volunteer executive but never produced for discussion advocates the defensive strategy on both practical and moral terms; the contrast between the sensibilities of MacNeill and Pearse is indicated by the difference between MacNeill's invocation of Catholic casuistry on the conditions for a just war and Pearse's deployment of apocalyptic and devotional rhetoric to present the rising as a supreme act of sacrificial faith.) MacNeill's associates appear to have had a better grasp of the prospects for guerrilla warfare than their opponents, though the latter could see the defensive strategy as leaving the initiative with the government.

Early in April 1916 the IRB group convinced MacNeill that a crackdown was imminent by producing a forged 'Castle document' (possibly based on genuine contingency plans). Only on Maundy Thursday (20 April) did he discover that the IRB group was using preparations for a general mobilisation on Easter weekend to bring about a rising on Easter Sunday. MacNeill initially acquiesced, but after discovering that an arms ship sent from Germany had been sunk and that the Castle document had been forged, he sent out messengers around the country ordering a general demobilisation, following this up with an advertisement in the *Sunday Independent*. This decision delayed the rising for a day and largely frustrated it outside Dublin. MacNeill was arrested after the suppression of the rising, court-martialled, sentenced to life imprisonment, and deprived of his UCD chair (he was reinstated after his release in June 1917).

POLITICAL CAREER 1918–27

Despite recriminations he took an active role in the reconstituted Sinn Féin party. In 1918 he was elected to the first Dáil Éireann for Sinn Féin as agreed nationalist candidate for Derry City and as representative of the NUI. In May 1921 he was re-elected for both constituencies in the elections for the northern parliament and southern parliament (second dáil) respectively.

In January 1919 MacNeill was appointed minister for finance in the first dáil government; he was relegated to minister for industries when Michael

Collins was appointed to the finance portfolio in April 1919. MacNeill's three eldest sons were active in the IRA. In mid 1920 he witnessed large-scale sectarian violence in Derry city. He was arrested in November 1920 and remained in jail until released on 30 June 1921. In August 1921 he was elected speaker of the second dáil. In this capacity he presided over the Anglo–Irish treaty debates, attempting unsuccessfully to get both sides to agree to ratify the treaty with an explanatory declaration on disputed points. He spoke in favour of the treaty, but as speaker did not vote.

In 1922 MacNeill was elected as a pro-treaty TD for Clare; he was re-elected in 1923. During the civil war he was a strong supporter of the government's reprisal policy. He is alleged to have been one of the two strongest advocates (with Ernest Blythe) of the summary execution of four imprisoned republicans in retaliation for the assassination of Seán Hales; when Thomas Johnson, the Labour leader, protested in the subsequent dáil debate that such measures were rendering the government morally indistinguishable from the previous British administration, MacNeill retorted that the old regime had used force to suppress the will of the people, whereas the current government was stern in order to uphold the people's will. MacNeill experienced personal tragedies. His sister Anne McGavock, already suffering terminal illness, came south from Glenarm to plead unsuccessfully for the life of Erskine Childers; the siblings quarrelled and were not reconciled. His second son, Brian, joined the anti-treaty forces and was killed during fighting in Sligo; MacNeill convinced himself that (authentic) reports that his son and those with him had been killed after surrendering were republican propaganda devised to torment him.

As minister for education (1922–5), MacNeill was largely inactive, because he saw the primary responsibility for education as lying with the churches rather than the state; his principal legacy was the stringent implementation of compulsory Irish. In these respects he set a pattern for state education policy which lasted until the 1960s. His ministerial role was further diminished in 1924, when he became the Irish representative on the Boundary Commission. There is some evidence that he expected the failure of the commission and accepted the position in the knowledge that he would serve as a scapegoat, but his maladroit behaviour made his position worse. Seeing the commission as a quasi-judicial body, he made no attempt to inform his cabinet colleagues of developments (he was not imitated in this by the Northern Ireland representative) and by acquiescing when he was outvoted on the points at issue he strengthened the legal position of the other commissioners. In November 1925, when a leak revealed that the border would be virtually unchanged, he resigned as commissioner and as minister. In the June 1927 general election he stood as a Cumann na nGaedheal candidate for the NUI, but received little support from his party.

ACADEMIC CAREER 1927–45

His narrow defeat ended his political career and he returned to academic life. He chaired the Irish Manuscripts Commission from its foundation in 1928; he was president of the newly founded Irish Historical Society (1936–45), the RSAI (1937–40) and the RIA (1940–43).

On 19 April 1898 MacNeill had married Agnes Moore; they had four sons and four daughters. He retired from his professorship in 1941 and died of abdominal cancer on 15 October 1945 at his residence, 63 Upper Leeson Street, Dublin.

INTELLECTUAL ACHIEVEMENT

MacNeill's interest in early Irish history grew out of his interest in the Irish language. According to himself, it was a chance remark of his father's that awakened his interest in the language, but it was also the circumstances of time and place. The Glens of Antrim were one of those districts in which, in the second half of the nineteenth century, the language was just slipping beyond the horizon. A sense of the loss of a language and of the culture embodied in the language, and a consequent impoverishment of national distinctiveness, a sense of a break with a shared tradition that had lasted since the dawn of Irish history—all this was enough to make him desire to recover what had been lost. This desire would, in him, work towards making him an historian, especially of that first period of Irish history, just as it led him to learn the language and to promote it in the Gaelic League. His first ambition was to learn the Irish of the Glens, about which he would later write, but a meeting in 1890 with Eugene O'Growney, professor of Irish at Maynooth, and a subsequent decision to become a pupil of Edmund Hogan (1917), widened his ambitions. In 1891, on O'Growney's advice, he visited Inishmaan in the Aran islands, the principal resort at that time for scholars wishing to learn to speak Irish. He returned annually until 1908. At the same time he soon became not so much Hogan's pupil as, in MacNeill's own words, 'my professor's apprentice'. Hogan, as Todd professor in the RIA, was working on an edition of the Middle Irish text 'Cath Ruis na Ríg'. MacNeill became his assistant, subsequently writing that 'he made me do all the spade-work', a contribution handsomely acknowledged by Hogan. This was hugely advantageous, since MacNeill was thereby introduced, under supervision, to skills he would later need: reading and comparing manuscripts, establishing a text, translation, textual commentary, and compiling a vocabulary. When he himself, with Hogan's encouragement, went on to edit texts on his own, he chose three Middle Irish poems about the legendary Battle of Mucrama; here he was dealing with one of the principal Irish 'origin legends', stories that purported to recount the beginnings of the early Irish political order. One of his major contributions was his discussion of 'the Irish synthetic historians' and their construction, partly out of such origin legends, of a pre-Patrician history for Ireland.

MacNeill's contributions to early Irish scholarship may be placed under three headings: first, 'Where does Irish history begin?', the title of one of his lectures; second, the history and hagiography of St Patrick; and third, early Irish law. The first was his main preoccupation up to the Great War, the second a comparatively brief phase arising out of his imprisonment in Mountjoy, while the third occupied him especially from 1923 to 1934. The synthetic historians had been successful in creating a history that established a line of narrative from the book of Genesis to early Christian Ireland. This history was later given memorable expression in Geoffrey Keating's *Foras Feasa ar Érinn*; and, down the centuries, what began as a learned construction became the standard view of the Irish past. A scholarly Irish history could not exist until the Milesian legend embodied in *Lebor Gabála Érenn*, 'The book of the settlement of Ireland', had been analysed and mere fiction separated from what might be history and from what was history. For MacNeill, establishing a scholarly history did not entail throwing away all early Irish narrative about the centuries before St Patrick: the strategy was to isolate those stories and aspects of stories that were inconsistent with the Milesian legend. The most important of these was the Ulster cycle, which cast doubt on the antiquity of an all-Ireland kingship of Tara.

Another prerequisite was a critical analysis of the medieval collections of genealogies, which in their overall structure presupposed the Milesian legend and yet contained a mass of essential material about early Irish royal dynasties: MacNeill's 'Notes on the Laud genealogies', published in 1911, supplied a model study of how to work on these extraordinarily voluminous sources. A further approach to the half-known period between the fall of the Western Roman Empire and the seventh century was epigraphy, a subject mainly cultivated by MacNeill's colleague, R. A. S. Macalister. MacNeill wrote two papers for the RIA that occupy a central position in his most fertile period as an historian, 1900–14. One was principally linguistic, 'Notes on the distribution, history, grammar, and import of the Irish ogham inscriptions', in one section of which he proposed a rule (subsequently known as 'MacNeill's law') governing an early Irish sound-change. The other, 'Early Irish population-groups: their nomenclature, classification, and chronology', used evidence from the ogham inscriptions, in conjunction with annals, genealogies, and hagiography, to establish changes in the way collective groups were described from the time of Ptolemy's Geography up to the Viking period. In these two papers, MacNeill's conjunction of linguistic and historical skills can be seen to their best effect. In his more general books, *Phases of Irish history* (1919) and *Celtic Ireland* (1921), his preoccupation with the beginnings of Irish history are just as apparent as in his more specialised work.

At the same time, MacNeill was also giving major assistance to Hogan's last and greatest work, *Onomasticon Goedelicum*, taking over a position that had been occupied by his elder brother, Charles (1862–1958). The *Onomasticon* has ever since been an indispensable tool for early Irish historians and editors of texts: not only did it collect together a vast mass of references to places, peoples and dynasties from medieval Irish texts, only some of them in print, but it also drew on the pioneering work of John O'Donovan and William Reeves. MacNeill was always concerned with the where as well as the when of Irish history: perhaps the most valuable strand in his work on St Patrick from 1923 to 1934 was his analysis of the topography of the Tripartite Life of St Patrick. This source offers the first comprehensive single view of the geography of power in Ireland and the related geography of churches; and MacNeill's account corrected several misconceptions, and has ever since been a *vade mecum* for early Irish historians.

Two elements in MacNeill's account of the Patrician material have not endured so well. The first is his over-valuation of the evidence linking St Patrick with Ulster. MacNeill is seen at his best and at his worst close to home—at his best in his correction of earlier views on the boundary between Dál Riata and Latharna (the church of Glore and, therefore, his birth place, Glenarm, belonged to the latter); and at his worst in his attempt to show that the *Silva Focluti*, 'the Wood of Fochloth', mentioned in Patrick's *Confessio*, was to be located in Ulster, and, therefore, that the story of Patrick in slavery on Slemish propounded by the seventh-century hagiographers, Tírechán and Muirchú, was historical. The other contention that soon came under damaging fire was his claim that the Tripartite Life embodied Tírechán's own revision of his earlier *Collectanea*.

MacNeill was capable of misjudging texts and issues, as in his dating 'The Book of Rights', *Lebor na Cert*, to the reign of Brian Bórama. Yet even his mistakes were often fruitful for the discipline, since they usually contained some element of truth and they elicited further research. Sometimes his views now look closer to the truth than they did to his immediate successors, as with the kingship of Tara. Sometimes, too, the occasional rash speculation has been exaggerated: he did not think that the Book of Rights as we have it went back to the time of Benignus, disciple of St Patrick, merely that Benignus could have been responsible for an earlier text on the same topic, a text written in Latin. Moreover, his mistakes pale into insignificance beside what the leading Irish medieval historian of the next generation, D. A. Binchy, called 'his uncanny sense of communion with a long-dead past'. The truth is that he had read widely and sympathetically in the primary sources, and he had a sense of how all the elements of society fitted together into a functioning whole. He was the first historian of early medieval Ireland of whom this can be said, and his work thus marks the start of a new era in the subject he made his own.

POLITICAL REPUTATION

MacNeill's reputation has been dominated by his role in relation to the 1916 rising. Early accounts written by admirers of Pearse generally presented MacNeill as comically ineffective or even treacherous, and displayed little concern for accurately recounting his actions or for understanding his motives. MacNeill's later years were distressed by this; he frequently explained himself to friends, and composed fragmentary memoirs. His version of events, however, attracted little attention until 1961 when F. X. Martin edited for publication in *Irish Historical Studies* two self-justificatory memoranda prepared by MacNeill in 1915 and 1917. MacNeill's historical reputation was further rehabilitated through the efforts of his son-in-law Michael Tierney, who arranged the publication of the essay collection *The scholar revolutionary* (edited by F. J. Byrne and F. X. Martin), and who himself undertook an official biography of MacNeill (edited for publication by F. X. Martin after Tierney's death). The Northern Ireland crisis after 1969 and the reassessment of Pearse's messianic nationalism in an Ireland increasingly less receptive to Catholic valorisations of sacrifice contributed to the re-evaluation of MacNeill; it is arguable that this exaltation of MacNeill as 'man of peace' underestimates the extent to which he and Pearse shared terms of reference, while differing on strategy. Even MacNeill's sceptical and iconoclastic nephew Brian Moore revered his integrity, and saw him as embodying the idealism of the Revival generation (as well as some of its limitations). In the long run, MacNeill's reputation is more likely to rest on his epochal contributions to language revival than on his ambivalent and chequered political career, which combined selfless dedication with weak execution and considerable capacity for self-deception.

Patrick Maume and Thomas Charles-Edwards

Sources

MacNeill papers in UCD Archives and NLI; Eoin MacNeill, *Shall Ireland be divided?* (1915); *Dictionary of national biography 1941–1950* (London) (entry by D. A. Binchy); F. X. Martin and F. J. Byrne (ed.), *The scholar revolutionary: Eoin MacNeill, 1867–1945, and the making of the new Ireland* (1973); Michael Tierney, *Eoin MacNeill: scholar and man of action 1867–1945*, ed. F. X. Martin (1980); Charles Townshend, *Political violence in Ireland* (1983); Pádraig Ó Snodaigh, *Two godfathers of revisionism: 1916 in the revisionist canon* (1991); J. A. Gaughan (ed.), *The memoirs of Senator Joseph Connolly: a maker of modern Ireland* (1996); Patrick Maume, *The long gestation: Irish nationalist life 1891–1918* (1999); Patrick Maume, 'Anti-Machiavel; three Ulster nationalists', *Irish Political Studies* (1999); *Oxford dictionary of national biography* (2004)

Peadar Macken

1878–1916

Peter Paul ('Peadar') Macken, trade unionist and revolutionary, was born 29 June 1878 at 13 Nassau Place (now part of the Setanta building, Nassau Street), Dublin, youngest of three children of George Macken, house painter, and Anne Macken (née Shanahan) (d. 1901), both of whom were originally from Portarlington, Queen's Co. (Laois). He had two older sisters. His father was a strong nationalist and treasurer of the Regular Operative House Painters' Trade Union, and president of its successor, the Dublin Metropolitan House Painters' Trade Union (DMHPTU). Educated at CBS, Westland Row, where he was a contemporary of Patrick Pearse, Peter became an apprentice house painter and took evening classes at the Metropolitan School of Art. Like his father, he held strong nationalist views and became president of the Oliver Bond Society, set up to commemorate the centenary of the 1798 rising; he had earlier joined the William Orr Society in February 1897 but was unhappy at its domination by members of the Irish parliamentary party. In 1899 he took the oath of the IRB.

A strong Irish Irelander, he joined the Celtic Literary Society and acquired a good knowledge of the Irish language, teaching Irish classes at the '98 Oliver Bond club in Parnell Square and sometimes using the Irish

form of his name, Peadar Ó Maicín. In 1901 he founded the St Patrick's branch of the Gaelic League in Dublin and with Sinéad Ní Fhlannagáin (later Sinéad de Valera) founded another branch of the league in Balbriggan. At the 1903 Gaelic League oireachtas he received teaching certificates, and won a gold medal in examinations for the Fleming Companionship. In 1904 he was awarded a scholarship by the Keating branch of the Gaelic League to attend courses in the Munster College, Ballingeary, Co. Cork. To improve his proficiency in Irish he often undertook painting jobs in Gaeltacht areas, working for the Congested Districts Board and the Commissioners of Irish Lights, and on his travels wrote regular articles for *An Claidheamh Soluis*. In 1912 he contributed articles on the Irish language to Pearse's journal *An Barr Buadh*. He made a point of writing in roman type and advocated its use to simplify the learning of Irish. He also wrote articles in Irish and English for Arthur Griffith's papers *United Irishman* and *Sinn Féin*. One of Macken's great interests was the variant of Hiberno-English spoken in Dublin, which he believed was strongly influenced by the Irish language.

Active in socialist politics, he was a member of a unity committee formed to bring together opposing elements of the Irish socialist movement which led to the founding of the Socialist Party of Ireland in August 1909; he later delivered lectures on socialism and Irish nationalism to the party. Like his father, he was active in the affairs of the DMHPTU, and in 1911 was instrumental in restoring its fortunes after two senior officials absconded with the union's funds and records. At a by-election in June 1912 he was elected for the Dublin Labour party as alderman for the North Dock ward on Dublin Corporation. He remained a member of the corporation until January 1914, serving on the improvements committee, but his attendance at meetings was sporadic.

In 1912 he became a member of the resident committee of Sinn Féin, and was nominated as its representative on the provisional committee of the Irish Volunteers in 1913, remaining in the MacNeillite Irish Volunteers after the split in 1914. He was also on the Volunteers' county sub-committee and the committee that organised the funeral of Jeremiah O'Donovan Rossa in 1915, and was a member of the IRB. During the

Easter rising he took part in the fighting at Boland's Mills, where he was shot dead 27 April 1916, by one of his own men who had run amok, and who was in turn shot dead. Macken was buried in St Brigid's plot in Glasnevin cemetery. A branch of the Gaelic League was named after him in 1917 and the street where he died is now named Macken Street. He never married and lived all his life at 13 Nassau Place.

Marie Coleman

Sources

NAI: Census of Ireland 1901, www.census.nationalarchives.ie (accessed March 2013); Dublin City Archives: *Dublin Corporation diary* (1913), *Reports and printed documents of the corporation of Dublin* (1913, 1914), *Minutes of the municipal council of the city of Dublin* (1912, 1913); Martin Daly [Stephen McKenna], *Memories of the dead* (1916); Charles Callan, 'A philosopher with a slow smile: Peadar Macken, 1878–1916', *Labour History News*, v (autumn 1989), 5–9 (photo); *Beathaisnéis*, iii; Declan Kiberd (ed.), *Sinn Féin rebellion handbook, 1916* (1998 ed.)

Michael
Mallin

1874–1916

Michael Thomas Mallin, trade unionist and revolutionary, was born 1 December 1874 at Ward's Hill in the Liberties in Dublin, the eldest of six surviving children (four boys and two girls) of John Mallin, a boatwright and carpenter, and his wife Sarah (née Dowling), a silk winder. He was educated at Denmark Street national school, Dublin, and on 21 October 1889 joined the Royal Scots Fusiliers (in which his uncle James Dowling was a pay sergeant) as a drummer boy, enlisting for twelve years, and was stationed at the Curragh. On 1 June 1891 he was promoted to drummer (the rank he held throughout his service); as part of his training he learned the flute and violin and studied music theory. He also became a useful lightweight boxer and the best shot in his company. In 1896 his battalion went to India, where he served for six years. He took part in the Tirah campaign (1897–8) against insurgent tribes on the north-west frontier and contracted malaria, from which he suffered sporadically for the rest of his life. While serving in India, Mallin became disillusioned with military life and sympathetic to the Indian struggle for independence. In a letter home he recorded his wish that 'it was for Erin that I was fighting and not against these poor people' (Hughes, 36). He longed for his discharge from the army, which finally came on 18 December 1902. On 26 April 1903 he married Agnes Hickey of Chapelizod, Co. Dublin.

They had met in Dublin nine years earlier and corresponded throughout his service overseas.

Mallin was apprenticed as a silk weaver at Atkinson's poplin factory in Dublin and by 1908 had become a qualified weaver and secretary of the Silk Weavers' Union. Active in socialist politics, he was a member of a unity committee formed to bring together opposing elements of the Irish socialist movement, which led to the founding of the Socialist Party of Ireland in August 1909. Mallin was secretary of the Silk Weavers' Union during a bitter four-month strike (March to June 1913) and wrote accounts of the dispute for the *Irish Worker*. After the strike he was forced out of Atkinson's and tried various ways to earn a living: opening a newsagent's shop, starting a chicken farm and running a cinema, all of which proved unsuccessful. He supplemented his income by teaching music to local children and won several medals for conducting bands such as the Dublin Fife and Drum Band (1913–14). In May 1914 he took over the ITGWU's Emmet Fife and Drum Band and became a member of the union, moving his family to Emmet Hall, headquarters of the union's Inchicore branch. When James Connolly took command of the Irish Citizen Army in October 1914 he appointed Mallin his chief of staff. Mallin, a devout Catholic and temperance advocate with a passion for music and books (especially ancient history and the novels of Joseph Conrad), was a popular and respected figure among his comrades. Although gentle and soft-spoken, he had a firm side to his character and insisted on strict discipline. Connolly had a high opinion of his abilities and left the business of organising and training the force largely to him. Mallin put his military experience to good use in welding the Citizen Army into a disciplined and well-drilled unit, leading it on outdoor manoeuvres including mock attacks on public buildings, and performing well in drill contests against the Irish Volunteers. As an ex-soldier, he was adept in obtaining arms and ammunition from serving soldiers to equip the Citizen Army. He also wrote articles on guerrilla warfare derived from his experience in India which were published in the *Workers' Republic* from August 1915.

In April 1916, on the Saturday prior to the Easter rising, Mallin was given the Irish Volunteer rank of commandant, and appears to have

known of the plan weeks in advance. On Easter Sunday evening his instrumental quartet, known as the 'Workers' Orchestra', in which he played the flute, held an improvised concert for Citizen Army members in Liberty Hall. He led the Citizen Army force that occupied St Stephen's Green on Monday 24 April, digging trenches in the park and erecting barricades on the surrounding roads; he appointed Constance Markievicz as his second-in-command. As dawn broke on Tuesday they came under fire from a machine gun on the roof of the Shelbourne hotel, suffering several casualties. Mallin himself had to drag a wounded man to safety and had a close shave when a bullet went through the brim of his hat. He was forced to withdraw to the College of Surgeons on the west side of the Green, a safer position but one of little strategic value. The decision to occupy a park overlooked on all sides by high buildings was a serious mistake, as was the failure to seize the Shelbourne, which dominated the area. Over the next few days Mallin ordered sporadic attacks on nearby British army positions, but his force was out-manned and out-gunned and their isolated forays had little effect. Having received Connolly's confirmation of the order to lay down arms, Mallin surrendered along with his garrison of 109 men and 10 women on 30 April. Tried by court martial in Richmond barracks on 5 May, he denied holding a commission in the Citizen Army and claimed to be an ordinary soldier who had taken command of the St Stephen's Green garrison on Markievicz's orders. Mallin was especially anxious to avoid execution for the sake of his family but, as a senior figure in the Citizen Army and head of an independent command that had inflicted a number of casualties on crown forces, he was regarded as a ringleader and sentenced to death. His anguish at leaving his pregnant wife and four young children was clearly evident in a letter written to Agnes on the eve of his execution. He was shot by firing squad in Kilmainham jail on 8 May 1916 and buried at Arbour Hill.

His fifth child, Mary Constance (1916–2005), was born four months after his death. His wife struggled to raise the young family and died of tuberculosis in 1932. In his last letter to his wife Mallin had expressed the wish that his two youngest children should enter religious life: his son Joe (b. 1914) became a Jesuit priest and his daughter Una (b. 1908) a Loreto sister; another son, Seán (1906–77), also became a Jesuit. His eldest son, Séamus (1904–82), served with the anti-treaty IRA in 1922 and was imprisoned for two years by the Free State government for possession of a rifle. He graduated as an engineer from UCD in 1926 and became head engineer of the fisheries division of the Department of Agriculture and the first chairman of Bord Iascaigh Mhara (1952–62).

Marie Coleman and James Quinn

Sources

Bureau of Military History: 'Statement of Thomas Mallin', WS 382; 'Statement of James O'Shea', WS 733; *Catholic Bulletin* (July 1916), 399–400; R. M. Fox, *The history of the Irish Citizen Army* (1943), 5–7, 90–92, 96–8, 105–7, 156–67; Liam Ó Briain, 'St Stephen's Green area', *Capuchin Annual 1966*, 219–36; Frank Robbins, *Under the starry plough: recollections of the Irish Citizen Army* (1977); *Irish Times*, 2 July 1982; 23 April 2005; Piaras F. MacLochlainn (ed.), *Last words: letters and statements of the leaders executed after the rising at Easter 1916* (1990); Michael Foy and Brian Barton, *The Easter rising* (1999); Donal Nevin, *James Connolly: 'a full life'* (2005); Charles Townshend, *Easter 1916* (2005); Brian Hughes, *16 lives: Michael Mallin* (2012)

Constance
Markievicz

1868–1927

Constance Georgine Markievicz, Countess Markievicz, republican and labour activist, was born 4 February 1868 at Buckingham Gate, London, eldest of the three daughters and two sons of Sir Henry Gore-Booth of Lissadell, Co. Sligo, philanthropist and explorer, and Georgina Mary Gore-Booth (née Hill) of Tickhill Castle, Yorkshire. She was taken to the family house at Lisadell as an infant, and retained a strong attachment to the west of Ireland despite her frequent sojourns in Dublin and abroad.

She was born into a life of privilege. Descended from seventeenth-century planters, the Gore-Booths were leading landowners who entertained lavishly at Lissadell, and enjoyed country pursuits including riding, hunting and driving. An active and demonstrative child, she was known for her skill in the saddle and for her friendly relations with the family's tenants. She and her favourite sister, Eva, were brought up in a manner that reflected their class and social standing. They are recalled as 'two girls in silk kimonos' in the poem 'In memory of Eva Gore-Booth and Con Markiewicz' (October 1927) by W. B. Yeats. Educated at home, they were taught to appreciate music, poetry and art, and in 1886 they were taken by their governess on a grand tour of the Continent. Constance made her formal debut into society in 1887 when she was presented to Queen Victoria at Buckingham Palace.

She hoped to study art, but faced opposition from her parents who disapproved of her ambition and refused to fund her studies. They finally relented in 1893, and she went to the Slade School of Art in London. On her return to Lissadell, she took up the cause of women's suffrage, presiding over a meeting of the Sligo Women's Suffrage Society in 1896. But she remained interested in art, and in 1898 her parents were persuaded to allow her to go to Paris to further her studies. While in Paris she met fellow art student Count Casimir Dunin-Markievicz, a Pole whose family held land in the Ukraine. They were married in London in 1900 and a daughter, Maeve, was born the following year. The couple returned to Paris in 1902, leaving their daughter in the care of Lady Gore-Booth. The family was reunited in Dublin in the following year, but from about 1908 Maeve lived almost exclusively with her grandparents at Lissadell.

Markievicz and her husband became involved in Dublin's liveliest cultural and social circles, exhibiting their paintings, producing and acting in plays at the Abbey theatre, and helping to establish the United Arts Club. She and her husband separated amicably about 1909. Her conversion to Irish republicanism dates from about 1908 when she joined Sinn Féin and Inghinidhe na hÉireann (Daughters of Ireland). She also helped to found and became a regular contributor to *Bean na hÉireann* (Woman of Ireland), the first women's nationalist journal in Ireland. She continued to advocate women's suffrage, but devoted most of her time to overtly nationalist causes such as the establishment in 1909 of Na Fianna Éireann, a republican youth movement. By 1911 she had become an executive member of Sinn Féin and Inghinidhe na hÉireann, and was arrested that year while protesting against the visit to Dublin of George V.

Markievicz became increasingly interested in socialism and trade unionism. She spoke in 1911 at a meeting of the newly established Irish Women Workers' Union and remained a strong supporter. An advocate of striking workers during the lockout of 1913, she organised soup kitchens in the Dublin slums and at Liberty Hall. Markievicz became an honorary treasurer of the Irish Citizen Army, and was instrumental in merging Inghinidhe na hÉireann with Cumann na mBan, a militant women's republican organisation which was established to support the

Irish Volunteers. Fiercely opposed to Irish involvement in the British war effort, she co-founded the Irish Neutrality League in 1914, and supported the small minority who split from the larger Volunteer organisation over the issue of Irish participation in the war. She remained active in labour circles, co-founding in 1915 the Irish Workers' Co-operative Society, while also participating in the military training and mobilisation of the Citizen Army and the Fianna.

An aggressive and flamboyant speaker who enjoyed wearing military uniforms and carrying weapons, Markievicz was known for her advocacy of armed rebellion against British authority. She welcomed the Easter rising, acting as second-in-command of a troop of Citizen Army combatants at St Stephen's Green. As British troops occupied buildings surrounding the park, it became a death trap for the Citizen Army who were forced to seek refuge in the College of Surgeons. After a week of heavy fire, Markievicz and her fellow rebels surrendered. She was originally sentenced to death for her part in the rebellion, but this was commuted on account of her sex; she was transferred to Aylesbury prison and was released under a general amnesty in June 1917, having served fourteen months. While being held at Mountjoy prison just after her surrender, she had begun to take instruction from a Roman Catholic priest, and shortly after returning to Ireland she was formally received into the church. Notoriously ignorant of the finer points of Catholic theology, she none the less embraced her new faith wholeheartedly, claiming to have experienced an epiphany while holed up in the College of Surgeons.

Markievicz threw herself behind Sinn Féin: she was elected to its executive board and was one of the many advanced nationalists arrested in 1918 on account of their alleged involvement in a treasonous 'German plot'. During her incarceration, she was invited to stand as a Sinn Féin candidate for Dublin's St Patrick's division at the forthcoming general election. She was the first woman to be elected to the British parliament, but like all Sinn Féin MPs she refused to take her seat at Westminster. On her release and return to Ireland in March 1919, she was named minister for labour in the first Dáil Éireann, a position that bridged her commitment to labour and to the fledgling republic. Arrested again in

June for making a seditious speech, she was sentenced to four months' hard labour in Cork, the third time she had been incarcerated in four years. After her release Markievicz continued to defy British authorities by maintaining her work for Sinn Féin and the dáil. Such political activity became more dangerous and difficult after the outbreak of the Anglo–Irish war in early 1919 and Markievicz spent much of this time on the run and in constant danger of arrest. She was arrested again in September 1920 and sentenced to two years' hard labour after a long period on remand. Released in July 1921 in the wake of a truce agreed between the British government and Irish republicans, she returned to her ministry, but any hope of political stability was dashed by the split in republican ranks over the Anglo–Irish treaty of December 1921. Dressed in her Cumann na mBan uniform, Markievicz addressed the dáil in a characteristically theatrical fashion, condemning the treaty and reiterating her advocacy of an Irish workers' republic. Re-elected president of Cumann na mBan and chief of the Fianna in 1922, she reaffirmed her opposition to the treaty through those organisations.

As an active opponent of the treaty, Markievicz refused to take her seat in the dáil and was once again forced to go into hiding while former comrades became embroiled in a civil war. She composed anti-treaty articles and continued to engage in speaking tours to publicise the republican cause. Elected to the dáil for Dublin South in August 1923, she refused to take the oath of allegiance to the king and, like other elected republicans, she thus disqualified herself from sitting. She was arrested for the last time in November 1923 while attempting to collect signatures for a petition for the release of republican prisoners, and went on hunger strike until she and her fellow prisoners were released just before Christmas. Removed from parliamentary politics and increasingly detached from her former republican colleagues—some of whom remained suspicious of female politicians and of Markievicz in particular—she remained committed to the republican ideal, producing numerous publications which focused more on former glories than on disappointing contemporary realities. She joined Fianna Fáil when it was established in 1926, finally breaking her ties with Cumann na mBan, which opposed the new political party. She stood successfully as a Fianna Fáil candidate for

Dublin South at the June 1927 general election, but hard work and often rough conditions had taken their toll, and her health began to fail. She was admitted to Sir Patrick Dun's Hospital and, declaring that she was a pauper, was placed in a public ward, where she died on 15 July 1927; she was buried in Glasnevin cemetery.

Senia Paseta

Sources

Eva Gore-Booth and Esther Roper, *Prison letters of Countess Markievicz* (1934); Brian Farrell, 'Markievicz and the women of the revolution', in F. X. Martin, *Leaders and men of the Easter rising: Dublin 1916* (1967), 227–303; Anne Marreco, *Rebel countess: the life and times of Countess Markievicz* (1967); Jacqueline Van Voris, *Constance Markievicz: in the cause of Ireland* (1967); Sean O'Faolain, *Constance Markievicz* (1968); Elizabeth Coxhead, *Daughters of Erin: five women of the Irish renaissance* (1969); Eibhlin Ní Éireamhoin, *Two great Irish women: Maud Gonne MacBride and Countess Markievicz* (1971); Margaret Ward, *Unmanageable revolutionaries: women and Irish nationalism* (1983); Anne Haverty, *Constance Markievicz: an independent life* (1988); Diana Norman, *Terrible beauty: a life of Constance Markievicz* (1988)

John
Maxwell

1859–1929

Sir John Grenfell Maxwell, soldier, was born 12 July 1859 at Aigburth, Liverpool, second son of Robert Maxwell, merchant, and his wife, Maria Emma Maxwell, daughter of Vice-Admiral John Pascoe Grenfell. He was educated at Cheltenham College and the Royal Military College, Sandhurst (1878–9), and commissioned into the 42nd foot (the Black Watch) in 1879. Nicknamed 'Conky' because of his large nose, Maxwell spent most of his military career in Egypt. He served during the 1882 Egyptian war, and in the Gordon relief expedition of 1884–5. He was on the staff of his cousin General Sir Francis Grenfell and of Grenfell's successor as sirdar (commander) of the Egyptian army, Sir Herbert (later Earl) Kitchener. In the late 1890s he commanded troops during the reconquest of the Sudan. In February 1900 he was appointed to command a brigade during the Boer war (1899–1902), with which he took part in the capture of Pretoria; he was subsequently military governor of Pretoria and in charge of the notorious camps, set up by Lord Kitchener (C-in-C, South Africa), where Afrikaner civilians were concentrated. He was knighted in 1900. In 1902 he became chief staff officer to the duke of Connaught and served him while he was successively C-in-C in Ireland (1902–4), inspector-general of the forces (1904–7), and C-in-C in Malta (1907–8). Maxwell was promoted major-general in 1906, and from 1908 to 1912 commanded the

British troops in Egypt, after which, having no military appointment, he went on half-pay. In 1892 he married Louise Semina, daughter of Charles William Bonynge, a wealthy Irish-American. They had one daughter.

At the start of the first world war Maxwell briefly headed the British military mission at the French headquarters, but in September 1914 he resumed command of the troops in Egypt, where he successfully organised defences against a Turkish attack in February 1915 and presided over the huge expansion of his command as Egypt became a major British imperial military base, both for the ill-fated Gallipoli campaign (1915–16) and for operations in Palestine. In March 1916, having been superseded as general officer commanding in Egypt by Sir Archibald Murray, he was recalled home and was seeking further employment when the Easter rising broke out the following month. On Easter Thursday, 27 April, he was appointed C-in-C in Ireland. He was not the first choice of Lord Kitchener (now secretary for war), who favoured Sir Ian Hamilton, also available following the evacuation of Gallipoli, where he had been in command. But the prime minister, Asquith, anxious not to offend Irish sensibilities, objected: Hamilton had come under Irish nationalist criticism for the bungled landings at Suvla Bay on Gallipoli in August 1915, during which the 10th (Irish) division had suffered heavy casualties.

Equipped with sweeping martial law powers, Maxwell's task was to crush the rebellion and restore order. Taking into account the scale of the rising, its wartime context, and the widely held assumption that it had been fomented by the Germans, Maxwell's initially stringent security policy is scarcely surprising. He had little to do with the actual ending of the fighting, as the defeat of the rebels was inevitable by the time he arrived to take command in Dublin. But he was primarily responsible for government policy in the immediate aftermath of the rising. In a series of courts martial, 171 prisoners were tried and 90 death sentences were imposed, of which Maxwell confirmed fifteen, which were carried out over a ten-day period. More than 300 other Volunteers, detained at the end of the hostilities, were immediately transported to camps in Britain. They were joined shortly afterwards by 1,800 men from among some 3,500 men and women (most of whom had taken no active part) arrested immediately after the rising, a procedure which clearly radicalised many of those involved. By imposing these draconian measures, Maxwell has been credited with powerfully accelerating the shift in Irish nationalist feeling away from Redmondite constitutionalism towards the militant separatism of Sinn Féin.

It is difficult to see what else Maxwell (or any other military governor of Ireland at the time) could have done. Although, seen with hindsight, his actions undoubtedly exacerbated the political situation in Ireland, his limited conception of how law and order had to be restored reflected both the inchoate nature of British policy-making generally towards Ireland, and the overriding imperative of maintaining domestic order while the United Kingdom was engaged in the titanic struggle of the first world war. That Maxwell, a middle-ranking general of no great reputation, was selected to go to Dublin reflects, moreover, how comparatively low down Ireland was in the scale of British political priorities in 1916. Maxwell himself was not unaware of the political consequences of wartime decision-making and, for example, opposed the introduction of conscription in Ireland, but he took much of the blame for the changing Irish political landscape and was effectively dismissed in November 1916. He was posted to the comparative backwater of the British domestic northern command, where he remained until the end of the war. After serving on Lord Milner's mission to inquire into the future government of Egypt (1919–20), he was not re-employed in the army and retired in 1922. Plagued by ill health in his later years, on his doctors' advice Maxwell went to South Africa, where he died (at Newlands, Cape Province) on 21 February 1929. There is a collection of Maxwell papers preserved at Princeton University Library.

Keith Jeffery

Sources

George Arthur, *General Sir John Maxwell* (1932); Thomas Pakenham, *The Boer war* (1979); Eunan O'Halpin, *The decline of the union: British government in Ireland, 1892–1920* (1987); Michael Foy and Brian Barton, *The Easter rising* (1999); *Oxford dictionary of national biography* (2004)

Helena Molony

1883–1967

Helena Molony, actress, republican, trade unionist, and feminist, was born 15 January 1883 at 8 Coles Lane, off Henry Street, Dublin, the younger of one daughter and one son of Michael Moloney, grocer, of that address, and Catherine Moloney (née McGrath). Orphaned at an early age, she had an unhappy relationship with her stepmother, whom her father had married shortly before his death. Helena probably received a Catholic secondary-school education. Throughout adult life she styled her surname 'Molony', though some sources erroneously employ the spelling 'Moloney'. Self-described in reminiscence as 'a young girl dreaming about Ireland' (Fox (1935), 120), she was deeply moved on hearing (August 1903) a speech by Maud Gonne and soon joined Gonne's women's organisation Inghinidhe na hÉireann. Adopting the pseudonym 'Emer' for Inghinidhe work (by which name she was called within Gonne's circle of republican women the rest of her life), in 1907 she became the organisation's secretary. Opposed to the socially conservative and dual-monarchist policies advocated by Sinn Féin's Arthur Griffith in the *United Irishman*, she assisted Gonne in launching Ireland's first women's periodical, the monthly *Bean na hÉireann*, to advocate 'militancy, separatism and feminism' (Fox (1935), 121). Molony edited the journal (1908–11), and wrote its 'Labour notes' (from 1910), thus initiating her involvement with the trade union movement. She was introduced (1908) by Bulmer Hobson to

Constance Markievicz, whom she brought into the nationalist and feminist movements, and whom she assisted in the founding (1909) and early operation of the republican scouts' organisation, Na Fianna Éireann. During Dublin protests against the impending visit of King George V (July 1911), she was arrested for throwing a stone at portraits of the monarch and his consort outside a Grafton Street shop. Jailed after refusing to pay the fine, she was the first Irishwoman of her generation imprisoned for a political offence, but served only several days of a one-month sentence before the fine was paid for her by Anna Parnell.

Trained in the Inghinidhe acting class by Dudley Digges, she began acting professionally in 1911. Acclaimed for her performance in 'Eleanor's enterprise' by George Birmingham—produced by the Independent Dramatic Company run by Count and Countess Markievicz (December 1911)—she was invited to join the Abbey Theatre, where, amid interruptions occasioned by political activity and time abroad, she appeared regularly until the 1916 rising, and intermittently for several years thereafter, playing in first productions by Lady Gregory, Lennox Robinson, Brinsley McNamara, and others. During the 1913 Dublin lockout, Molony employed her theatrical experience to make up the disguise of James Larkin as an aged clergyman, in which guise he entered the Imperial hotel and from a balcony briefly addressed a crowd in Sackville Street, resulting in the 'bloody Sunday' police baton charge (31 August). Over ensuing months Molony played in 'The mineral workers' at the Abbey, and between her scenes addressed strike meetings at Liberty Hall.

When the Irish Women Workers' Union (IWWU) was reorganised as an affiliated branch of the Irish Transport and General Workers' Union (August 1915), Molony, on the recommendation of James Connolly, was elected general secretary. Manager of the Liberty Hall workers' clothing co-operative (which manufactured cartridge belts prior to the Easter rising), she was secretary of the Irish Citizen Army (ICA) women's group, and performed in the ICA acting troupe. On Easter Monday 1916 she was attached to the ICA contingent, commanded by fellow Abbey actor Sean Connolly, that operated in the Dublin Castle area. She supervised the nine women of the City Hall garrison in establishing a first-aid station and commissariat, and witnessed Connolly being shot dead by a sniper. Arrested on the garrison's surrender that night, Molony was one of five women interned in England until her release from Aylesbury jail (December 1916). Returning forthwith both to politics and the Abbey stage, she appeared in the first Irish production of Chekhov's 'Uncle Vanya' (February 1917); serving briefly on the Sinn Féin executive, she attended the October 1917 ard fheis that reconstituted the organisation as a republican party.

Although resuming her post as IWWU general secretary in 1917, she was replaced in a 1918 reorganisation by Louie Bennett, under whom she served for a time as deputy. She remained an IWWU official for over twenty years, her republicanism and social radicalism often in conflict with the union's moderates, led by Bennett and Helen Chenevix. Active in the ICA until 1923, during both the war of independence and civil war (in which she was anti-treaty) she served in various capacities, including training, propaganda, and courier of arms and messages. She strenuously supported the contemporary workers' soviets and factory seizures. Pressured by Bennett to concentrate on trade-union duties, she abandoned the stage in a last, memorable performance in Lennox Robinson's 'Crabbed youth and old age' (November 1922). At intervals in the 1920s and 1930s she urged reorganisation of the trade unions along industrial lines, partly to resolve rancorous jurisdictional disputes between Irish-based and cross-channel unions, partly out of abiding syndicalist conviction. When the Irish Labour Party and Irish Trade Union Congress (ITUC) split into separate organisations (1930), she led a losing fight to keep both bodies committed to the socialist objective of workers' control of industry. Her abiding concern was the organisation of domestic workers, for which she led periodic, albeit largely fruitless campaigns. Her 1930 visit to the USSR accentuated ideological tensions within the IWWU. She was active, often alongside Maud Gonne, in the Women's Prisoners' Defence League, the People's Rights Association, and the Anti-Partition League. On the founding executive of Saor Éire (September 1931), under pressure from Bennett she resigned within one month. As IWWU organising secretary (1929–41), she was prominent in effecting the union's growth to over 5,000 members, representing one-quarter of the country's women trade unionists. Serving several one-year terms on the ITUC executive (1921–2, 1933–8), as congress vice-president (1935–6) she unsuccessfully opposed those provisions of the conditions of employment act that allowed the displacement of women workers by men. Vice-chair of the 1936 trade union commission of inquiry, she defended the IWWU's status as an all-female body on the grounds that women constituted a separate economic class. She was the second woman (after Bennett) to be elected ITUC president (1937–8), but ill health prevented her delivering the annual presidential address. Under pressure over alleged wartime IRA associations, she retired on health grounds in October 1941.

A fervent speaker and 'doughty fighter for the working class' (Jones, 165), Molony retained a passionate commitment to her early revolutionary ideals into a time when both the nationalist and trade union movements eased into moderation and institutionalised respectability. After living through her twenties on a small family bequest, for many years she led a precarious and unsettled existence, often reliant on friends for accommodation. Bouts of depression, heavy drinking, and physical illness often occasioned absence from work, and contributed to her induced retirement. She never married. From the 1930s she had a close relationship with psychiatric doctor Evelyn O'Brien, with whom she lived on the North Circular Road and, from 1966, on Strand Road, Sutton. She died in their Sutton home on 28 January 1967, and was buried in the republican plot, Glasnevin cemetery.

Frances Clarke and Lawrence William White

Sources

GRO; R. M. Fox, *Rebel Irishwomen* (1935), 119–32 (interview); R. M. Fox, *History of the Irish Citizen Army* (1943), 108, 136, 150, 154, 185, 231; Lennox Robinson, *Ireland's Abbey theatre: a history 1899–1951* (1951), 106–13, 128, 132–4 (cast lists); Maire Nic Shiubhlaigh, *The splendid years: recollections* (1955), 142–3; *Fifty years of Liberty Hall* (1959) (portrait between 40–41); *Irish Press*, 30 January 1967 (obit.); *Irish Times*, 30 January (obit.), 1 February 1967; Hugh Hunt, *The Abbey: Ireland's national theatre 1904–1978* (1979); Uinseann MacEoin (ed.), *Survivors* (1980); C. Desmond Greaves, *The Irish Transport and General Workers' Union: the formative years 1909–1923* (1982); Margaret Ward, *Unmanageable revolutionaries: women and Irish nationalism* (1983); Mary Jones, *These obstreperous lassies: a history of the Irish Women Workers' Union* (1988); Cliona Murphy, *The women's suffrage movement and Irish society in the early twentieth century* (1989); Donal Nevin, *Trade union century* (1994), 437–8, 444; Pádraig Yeates, *Lockout: Dublin 1913* (2000); Nell Regan, 'Helena Molony (1883–1967)', in Mary Cullen and Maria Luddy (ed.), *Female activists: Irish women and change 1900–1960* (2001), 141–68; information from Nell Regan

Matthew Nathan

1862–1939

Sir Matthew Nathan, soldier and administrator, was born 3 January 1862, second son among nine children of Jonah Nathan and Miriam Nathan (née Jacobs) of London. Both his parents were Jewish; his father—of German origin and a partner in the paper-making firm of Thomas de la Rue—had one son from a previous marriage. Miriam Nathan, 25 years younger than Jonah, exercised a substantial influence on her children's education (they were tutored at home) and their careers. Nathan was commissioned in the Royal Engineers (1880), with an outstanding record as a cadet at the Royal Military Academy, Woolwich. After a period working in the War Office inspectorate-general of fortifications, he served in Africa and India (1884–95) and was appointed secretary of the Colonial Defence Committee. Here he exercised and extended his talent for writing thorough, capable and prosaic memoranda.

Between 1899 and 1909 he served as governor in Sierra Leone and the Gold Coast (1899–1903), Hong Kong (1904–7), and Natal (1907–9). The establishment of the Union of South Africa ended this phase of his career. He was made CMG (1899), KCMG (1902), and GCMG (1908). In 1909 he managed a transfer to the home civil service as secretary of the Post Office (until 1911) and then chairman of the Board of Inland Revenue.

Three years later Nathan was chosen to be under-secretary for Ireland, reaching Dublin in October 1914. The coming of war had altered circumstances in Ireland, but had not affected the policy of preparing for a substantial measure of self-government. Nathan, an exceptionally hard worker, energetically forwarded this programme, building a relationship with John Dillon MP of the Irish party. Although he did sanction the suppression of a number of extreme newspapers, in broad terms he complied with the policy of Augustine Birrell, the chief secretary, to exercise the maximum possible conciliation of the widest possible range of interests in Ireland. The outbreak of the Easter rising in Dublin on 24 April 1916 took Nathan by surprise when he learned of it in his Dublin Castle office (where, characteristically, he was working during a bank holiday). Defective and insufficient intelligence from army and police sources, the order from Eoin MacNeill cancelling the Volunteer manoeuvres, and the very recent success in Munster against a German arms ship, accompanied by the capture of Roger Casement, had together contributed to Nathan's misjudging the underlying reality. During the suppression of the rising and its aftermath, the military forces and their commanders dominated the Irish administration. Birrell and Nathan offered their resignations, which were accepted. The subsequent royal commission of inquiry criticised both men in its report. Nathan's Irish career of one-and-a-half years provided examples both of his kindly disposed and energetic nature and of his inclination to pursue established policies and practices rather than to appraise them stringently and to press for change by advice and advocacy. Doubtless, in part at least, these traits arose from his military and gubernatorial professional formation. Nevertheless, it was Birrell as chief secretary for Ireland since 1907 who set the policy of the Irish government and directed the ways in which it was to be advanced.

Following a dispiriting stint overseeing the defences of London against a hardly credible threat of attack, Nathan was appointed secretary of the newly established war pensions ministry, another rather unhappy experience. In 1920 he became governor of Queensland, Australia, and chancellor of its university (1922–6), serving there until 1925. In 1925 he was awarded an honorary LLD by the university. He retired to the country house in Somerset which he had bought early in the century, and devoted himself to the study of local history, apart from serving on several government committees between 1926 and 1930. He was a fellow of the Royal Historical Society, the Royal Geographical Society, and the Royal Society of Antiquaries. Nathan died 18 April 1939, unmarried, and was buried in the Jewish cemetery, Willesden, London. *The annals of West Coker*, which was not completed at his death, was published in 1957, edited by the historian M. M. Postan.

Michael D. Millerick

Sources

Nathan papers, Bodleian Library, Oxford; Dillon papers, TCD; León Ó Broin, *The chief secretary: Augustine Birrell in Ireland* (1969); León Ó Broin, *Dublin Castle and the 1916 rising* (1970 ed.); Anthony P. Haydon, *Sir Matthew Nathan: British colonial governor and civil servant* (1976); Keith Jeffery (ed. and introd.), *The Sinn Féin rebellion as they saw it* (1999)

Richard O'Carroll

1876–1916

Richard O'Carroll, trade unionist and revolutionary nationalist, was probably the 'Richard Carroll' born 29 February 1876 at 6 Hanover Square, near the north quays, Dublin, son of Richard Carroll, labourer, of that address, and Mary Carroll (née Keogh). A bricklayer by trade, in 1906 (on the crest of a rank-and-file revolt following a divisive lockout of Dublin bricklayers the preceding year) he was elected general secretary of the Ancient Guild of Incorporated Brick and Stonelayers Trade Union. Instilling the body with a renewed vitality, he rebuilt its strength and extended its organisation beyond the Dublin region; by 1913 he had established fourteen branches throughout Ireland, travelling to building sites and provincial offices on a motorcycle provided for his use by the union.

First returned to Dublin City Council, Mansion House ward (1907–16), in a special election to fill a vacancy, he was elected to a full three-year term in 1909, and also served on South Dublin board of poor law guardians. Previously a member of Sinn Féin, he was a founding officer of Dublin Trade Council's labour representation committee (January 1911), subsequently reconstituted as the Dublin Labour Party (DLP). Serving on the Irish Trade Union Congress parliamentary committee (later national executive) (1911–16), he aligned with the committee majority favouring development of an Irish national labour movement separate

from the British movement. Re-elected city councillor in January 1912 as one of five successful DLP candidates (with a sixth soon returned in a by-election), he succeeded James Larkin as party leader on the council when the latter was removed from his seat (September 1912) because of an earlier criminal conviction related to a labour dispute. Able and forthright, though lacking Larkin's charisma, he energetically attacked jobbery and corruption within the corporation bureaucracy, especially in the management of the South Dublin Union. With the labour bloc dwarfed amid the council's eighty members, the party's reform agenda bore little fruit and public enthusiasm waned. After addressing the workers' rally in Croydon Park, Fairview, that preceded the 'Bloody Sunday' police baton charge of a Sackville Street crowd during the Dublin lockout, O'Carroll himself was badly beaten when an evening protest meeting in Inchicore was invaded by police (31 August 1913). He was a Trades Council representative on the Askwith board of enquiry into the lockout, whose recommended bases for negotiation were rejected by employers (September–October). In the January 1915 municipal elections, amid rancorous charges against the DLP arising from the lockout, O'Carroll as party leader avoided revolutionary rhetoric and concentrated on immediate issues: public housing, social services, educational reform. While Labour retained its strength on the council (O'Carroll being returned unopposed), its failure to increase its representation was seen as a setback, attributed largely to the unpopularity of the labour movement's anti-war stand among the numerous working-class Dubliners with relatives in military service.

A member of the Irish Republican Brotherhood and—like many officials of crafts unions—of the Irish Volunteers, during the Easter rising O'Carroll participated in the Camden Street area fighting as a lieutenant of 2nd battalion under the command of Thomas MacDonagh. On Wednesday 26 April, he was flushed out of his position and disarmed by a British army patrol commanded by Captain J. C. Bowen-Colthurst, who earlier the same day had ordered the summary execution of three prisoners, including Francis Sheehy-Skeffington. Held at revolver point and with hands raised, O'Carroll, asked whether he was 'a Sinn Féiner', replied 'From the backbone out!', whereupon Bowen-Colthurst shot him through the chest. Left lying in the street, he was picked up by a passing bread van and brought to Portobello military hospital, where, after nine days of great suffering, he died on 5 May 1916.

O'Carroll resided from 1907 at the Bricklayers' Arms Institute, 49 Cuffe Street. He was survived by his widow Annie and their seven children, the youngest of whom was born two weeks after his death. A monument over his grave in St Paul's cemetery, Glasnevin, was erected in 1935 by the National Graves Association and the bricklayers' union.

Lawrence William White

Sources

GRO; Building and Allied Trades Union records, NAI, file 1097; *Thom* (1907–15); Dublin Corporation, *Diaries* (1908–16); *Catholic Bulletin*, vi, no. 7 (July 1916), 404, 406 (portrait photo.); *Catholic Bulletin*, vi, no. 12 (December 1916), 705; W. P. Ryan, *The Irish labour movement from the 'twenties to our own day* (1919), 198; Desmond Ryan, *The rising: the complete story of Easter week* (1949), 168–9; C. Desmond Greaves, *The life and times of James Connolly* (1961); William O'Brien, *Forth the banners go* (1969); Arthur Mitchell, *Labour in Irish politics 1890–1930: the Irish labour movement in an age of revolution* (1974) (group photo); J. Anthony Gaughan, *Thomas Johnson 1872–1963: first leader of the Labour Party in Dáil Éireann* (1980), esp. 42 (group photo), 71 (biographical note); National Graves Association, *The last post* (1985 ed.), 27, 109; Emmet Larkin, *James Larkin: Irish labour leader, 1876–1947* (1989 ed.); Donal Nevin (ed.), *Trade union century* (1994), 444; Sarah Ward-Perkins (ed.), *Select guide to trade union records in Dublin* (1996), 26–7; Pádraig Yeates, *Lockout: Dublin 1913* (2000)

Elizabeth O'Farrell

1884–1957

Elizabeth O'Farrell, republican and nurse, was born at 42 City Quay, Dublin, the youngest of two daughters of Christopher Farrell, a dock labourer, and his wife Margaret, a housekeeper. She was educated locally by the Sisters of Mercy. The 1911 census recorded her as living at 17 Hastings Street, Ringsend, with her married sister and widowed mother. As a child she formed a lifelong friendship with **Julia (Sighle, Sheila) Grenan** (1884–1972), the second of three children (two boys and a girl) of Patrick Grenan, a joiner; the Grenans lived in Lombard Street, near Elizabeth's childhood home. Julia was also educated by the Sisters of Mercy, and both girls were members of the Sacred Heart and Total Abstinence sodalities. On leaving school, Elizabeth became a midwife, working at Holles Street hospital, while Julia worked as a dressmaker. Both shared strong nationalist beliefs, and often acted in tandem: they joined the Gaelic League and became fluent in Irish, and also joined the Irish Women's Franchise League and the Irish Women Workers' Union. In 1906 they became members of Inghinidhe na hÉireann, the women's nationalist organisation, and joined the Inghinidhe branch of Cumann na mBan soon after its establishment in April 1914 as an auxiliary of the Irish Volunteers. They supported the workers during the 1913 strike in Dublin, and assisted Constance Markievicz in her efforts to prevent recruitment into the British army. Markievicz took a personal interest in both women and trained them in the use of firearms.

On Easter Sunday 1916 (23 April) Markievicz accompanied them to Liberty Hall and told James Connolly they could be trusted completely. With an insurrection planned for the following day, they were assigned to the Irish Citizen Army, with O'Farrell entrusted to deliver dispatches to republican units in Athenry, Spiddal and Galway city, while Grenan was sent to Dundalk and Carrickmacross. On returning to Dublin, they reported for duty to the General Post Office and performed nursing and courier duties over the next few days; they also delivered ammunition from the GPO to the garrison in the College of Surgeons by hiding it under their clothes. After James Connolly's ankle was shattered by a bullet on 27 April, O'Farrell and Grenan volunteered to care for him and stayed in the GPO as it was shelled by British artillery. With the building in flames, they and Connolly's secretary, Winifred Carney, refused to leave until the final evacuation on the evening of Friday, 28 April, and were the last women to leave. They retreated with the garrison to Moore Street, where O'Farrell and Grenan nursed the wounded at No. 16. Here the leaders finally decided to lay down their arms. O'Farrell was chosen by Patrick Pearse to contact the British military on the morning of 29 April to discuss terms of surrender (he feared that a man given this task would be immediately shot down). Given a Red Cross insignia and white flag, she walked out into heavy fire in the Moore Street area and approached an army barricade. She was initially suspected of being a spy but was eventually taken to Brigadier W. H. M. Lowe, who sent her back to Pearse with a demand for unconditional surrender. Accompanied by O'Farrell, Pearse then surrendered in person to Lowe that afternoon (a partly obscured O'Farrell can be seen in a press photograph taken at the moment of surrender). Later that day and on 30 April she volunteered to take the surrender order to Volunteer and Citizen Army units at the Four Courts, the College of Surgeons, Boland's mill and Jacob's factory. It was a dangerous task and she came under fire on several occasions. She also received a suspicious and sometimes hostile reception from garrisons that wanted to fight on, but eventually all were convinced of the authenticity of her orders and laid down their arms.

Grateful for her service in this perilous mission, Lowe assured O'Farrell that she would be released, but after the surrender she was stripped and searched and imprisoned overnight in Ship Street barracks.

On hearing of this, Lowe had her released immediately and apologised for her treatment. Grenan was imprisoned after the surrender in Kilmainham jail until 9 May, and heard the volleys of shots that executed several of the rising's leaders.

After the rising, O'Farrell and Grenan continued to work for Cumann na mBan. They carried dispatches for the IRA during the war of independence, and opposed the 1921 Anglo–Irish treaty. Living together at 27 Lower Mount Street, Dublin, they remained hostile to the Free State, and during and after the civil war collected funds for the families of anti-treatyite prisoners. They regularly attended republican functions and in 1933 followed Mary MacSwiney in resigning from Cumann na mBan when, drifting to the left, the organisation voted to rescind its oath of allegiance to the first and second dáils. Both women supported the 1956–62 IRA border campaign, and in January 1957, following the deaths of the IRA men Sean South and Fergal O'Hanlon, O'Farrell addressed a rally in College Green, Dublin. By that time she was in failing health; she died 25 June 1957 while on holiday in Bray, Co. Wicklow, and was buried in the republican plot in Glasnevin cemetery, Dublin. Julia Grenan died in Dublin on 6 January 1972 and was buried alongside O'Farrell; members of Provisional Sinn Féin provided a guard of honour at her funeral.

In 1967 a memorial plaque to Elizabeth O'Farrell was unveiled at Holles Street hospital and the Nurse Elizabeth O'Farrell Foundation to support nursing postgraduate studies was established. In 2003 another plaque commemorating her was unveiled in City Quay Park, which was renamed Elizabeth O'Farrell Park in 2012.

Frances Clarke and James Quinn

Sources

Eithne Coyle papers (UCD archives, MS P61/4); Elizabeth O'Farrell, 'Events of Easter week', *Catholic Bulletin*, vii (1917), 265–70, 329–34; Julia Grenan, 'Events of Easter week', *Catholic Bulletin*, vii (1917), 396–8; Elizabeth O'Farrell, 'Recollections', *An Phoblacht*, 26 April, 31 May, 7 June 1926; *Irish Press*, 26 June 1957 (incl. photograph of O'Farrell); 7 January 1972; *Irish Times*, 11 January 1972; *An Phoblacht*, iii, no. 2 (February 1972); Margaret Ward, *Unmanageable revolutionaries: women and Irish nationalism* (1983); Donncha O Dúlaing, *Voices of Ireland: conversations with Donncha O Dúlaing* (1984); Ruth Taillon, *The women of 1916: when history was made* (1996); Ann Matthews, *Renegades: Irish republican women 1900–1922* (2010); Ann Matthews, *Dissidents: Irish republican women 1922–1941* (2012); information from Glasnevin Cemeteries Group

Michael O'Hanrahan

1877–1916

Michael O'Hanrahan (Micheál Ó hAnnracháin), nationalist, journalist, and author, was born 16 January 1877 in New Ross, Co. Wexford, one of six sons and three daughters of Richard O'Hanrahan, a cork cutter, and Mary O'Hanrahan (née Williams), both of New Ross. The family were of known Fenian tendencies; his father had supposedly taken part in the 1867 rising. When Michael was young, the family moved to Carlow town, where they lived at 91 Tullow Street. He was educated at Carlow CBS, then attended Carlow College Academy. Joining the Gaelic League in 1898, he founded its first branch in Carlow, becoming its secretary (1899). Proficient in Irish, he taught classes for the league at Carlow's Catholic Institute. He was a delegate of the branch to the second representative congress of the Gaelic League, held in Dublin in 1900. With his brother Henry, he was chief founder of the workers' club on Brown Street, Carlow, the name of which was placed on the building's exterior in both Irish and English. Reputedly deciding against a career in the civil service owing to his distaste at the requisite oath of allegiance to the British crown, in 1901 he started as a cutter in his father's cork business.

Within several years he had moved to Dublin, where he obtained a position as a proofreader at the Cló Cumann printing works, which published magazines and books for the Gaelic League. He was joint secretary with Uaitéar MacCumhaill of the National Council in 1903 during the protests against the visit to Ireland of King Edward VII. In 1905 he became secretary of the chief branch of the Gaelic League, and was a member of Dublin district committee. He attended the first annual convention of the National Council at the Rotunda, Dublin (November 1905), at which Arthur Griffith, speaking to a small audience that also included Patrick Pearse and Patrick McCartan, outlined the proposals of economic self-sufficiency and parliamentary abstentionism that would form the basis of the Sinn Féin movement. Becoming a member of Sinn Féin, in 1909 O'Hanrahan was secretary of the Gaelic League language procession that was held in Dublin, and was an active member of the language week committee.

Joining the IRB, he was a founding member of the Irish Volunteers (November 1913), and was appointed quartermaster general of the 2nd battalion in 1915. Noted for his methodical attention to detail, he was employed full-time on the Volunteer headquarters clerical staff at 2 Dawson Street, Dublin, and stored guns and ammunition in his home at 67 Connaught Street, Phibsborough, where he lived with his mother and several siblings. During the 1916 Easter rising he was third-in-command under Thomas MacDonagh and John MacBride at Jacob's biscuit factory on Bishop Street, Dublin. While foraging in the building for food supplies, O'Hanrahan fell down a flight of stairs and injured his head; despite suffering from concussion, he did not tell MacDonagh of the incident for fear that he would be sent to hospital. After the surrender, O'Hanrahan was court-martialled and sentenced to death. He was executed in Kilmainham jail on 4 May 1916, and was buried in Arbour Hill cemetery, Dublin. His brother Henry, a fellow member of the Volunteers HQ clerical staff and who also fought in the Jacob's factory garrison, was likewise condemned to death, but the sentence was commuted to life imprisonment.

O'Hanrahan had worked as a freelance journalist for several nationalist publications, including *Sinn Féin*, *Nationality*, and the *Irish Volunteer*, using the pseudonyms 'Art' and 'Irish Reader'. His literary works include the historical novel *A swordsman of the brigade* (1914), based on the military exploits of the Irish brigades in France; several hours before his death he wrote a will bequeathing the copyright to his mother and sisters. A posthumous publication, *Irish heroines* (1917), was initially delivered as a lecture by O'Hanrahan to Cumann na mBan during the winter of 1915–16, treating such figures as Rosa O'Doherty and Nuala O'Donnell. *When the Norman came*, a military adventure dealing with Dermot MacMurrough, the twelfth-century king of Leinster, appeared in 1918. The manuscript draft of a third novel entitled 'My sword, my fortune' was destroyed during a raid at O'Hanrahan's home immediately after the rising. Sean O'Sullivan drew a pencil portrait of O'Hanrahan in 1942, and an oil portrait by Leo Whelan was shown at a commemorative exhibition of the 1916 rebellion at the NGI in 1966. Wexford's 1916 roll of honour was dedicated to O'Hanrahan; the rail station in Wexford town is named after him, as is the bridge across the river Barrow at New Ross opened in 1967.

Carmel Doyle

Sources

GRO (birth cert.); *Irish Book Lover*, viii (October–November 1916), 30; *Irish Times*, 5 May 1916; Alice Tracy, 'Michael O'Hanrahan', *Carliovana*, i (December 1963), 12–13, 38–9; Roger McHugh (ed.), *Dublin 1916: an illustrated anthology* (1966), 265; Breandán MacGiolla Choille (ed.), *Intelligence notes 1913–16* (1966); NGI, *Cuimhneachán 1916: a commemorative exhibition of the Irish rebellion 1916* (1966); Martin Shannon, *Sixteen roads to Golgotha* (1966), 169–70; F. X. Martin (ed.), *Leaders and men of the Easter rising: Dublin 1916* (1967); F. X. Martin, '1916: myth, fact and mystery', *Studia Hibernica*, vii (1967), 19; Bernard Browne, *County Wexford connections: a biographical data on famous and infamous Wexford connections which encompasses the whole county* (1985), 8; Piaras F. MacLochlainn (ed.), *Last words: letters and statements of the leaders executed after the rising at Easter 1916* (1990 ed.); *Beathaisnéis*, iii: *1882–1982* (1992); Bernard Browne, *Living by the pen: a biographical dictionary of County Wexford authors* (1997); *1916 rebellion handbook* (1998 ed.); information from Caitriona Murphy, Co. Wexford

Michael J.
O'Rahilly

1875–1916

Michael Joseph O'Rahilly ('The O'Rahilly'), nationalist and journalist, was born at Ballylongford, Co. Kerry, on 22 April 1875, third child and only son of Richard Rahilly, businessman and magistrate, and his wife Ellen (née Mangan); his father claimed collateral descent from the poet Aodhagan Ó Rathaille, his mother from James Clarence Mangan. He was related to the McEllistrim Fianna Fáil political dynasty.

The young Michael Rahilly was educated at Ballylongford girls' national school (1880–82), Ballylongford boys' national school (1882–9), learning Irish after school hours, and Clongowes Wood College, Co. Kildare (1890–93); he started to study medicine at UCD (1894–6) but his studies were interrupted by tuberculosis and he abandoned them altogether to run the family business after his father's death. The business was sold after Rahilly married an Irish-American, Nancy Brown, on 15 April 1899; they were to have six children. After a long honeymoon, the Rahillys settled in Bray, Co. Wicklow, in 1900. 'If I had stayed in Ballylongford I would have taken to drink', he told his children (O'Rahilly (1991)). A family settlement gave him £450 a year; he sometimes mocked himself as a 'licensed loafer'.

At Bray Michael continued to study Irish, genealogy, archaeology and local history; he was a JP for Co. Kerry (1903–7). Experience of Dublin snobbery strengthened his childhood nationalism and Nancy reacted against Dublin after the death of their son Robert in August 1903. They moved to Brighton in 1904, and Michael briefly joined a London branch of the United Irish League. Rahilly may have written to the *United Irishman*, the nationalist paper of Arthur Griffith, as early as 1899, and frequented An Stad, an Irish-Ireland shop in North Frederick Street, Dublin, but he became a regular contributor to the paper only in June 1904. Around this time he coined the title 'The O'Rahilly', though his use of it did not become habitual until *c.*1911, and added the patronymic prefix to his surname. In 1905 the Rahillys moved to Philadelphia to try to salvage the Brown family linen mills and Rahilly temporarily severed his connection with Griffith. He found America 'a vortex of corruption… the stronghold of materialism' (O'Rahilly (1991), 53).

The family returned to Ireland in mid 1909 and settled at Ballsbridge, Dublin. Thereafter nationalism provided this gifted but slightly aimless man with his central purpose in life. Rahilly wrote extensively for Griffith's short-lived daily *Sinn Féin* (1909–10), subscribing £100 to its support and visiting America to seek funds. He joined the Sinn Féin party executive in October 1910 and became its best-known activist after Griffith; one of his first campaigns was to orchestrate opposition to the 1911 royal visit. In 1911–13 he published a circulation-boosting series on Irish family history for the weekly *Sinn Féin*, and painted pedigrees and coats of arms on request. He wrote for the republican monthly *Irish Freedom* under his own name and as 'Rapparee'.

O'Rahilly improved his children's Irish by hiring an Irish-speaking servant and buying a holiday cottage near Dingle, Co. Kerry. He joined the Five Provinces branch of the Gaelic League and became its president; in 1912 he was elected to the league executive. O'Rahilly devised numerous schemes to raise the league's profile. 'Most of the plans were rather fantastic', recalled his friend Desmond FitzGerald, but this was not invariably true: O'Rahilly persuaded the Gaelic League to adopt American-style flag days (hitherto unknown in Ireland); he organised the translation of Dublin street names into Irish and the transcription of ordnance survey material compiled by John O'Donovan; he campaigned to make the post office accept parcels addressed in Irish; and applied his talents as a designer to Irish-language cheque books and a simplified Gaelic type. He was also a motoring enthusiast and founder member of the Irish Aero Club.

In 1913 O'Rahilly revamped the loss-making Gaelic League paper, *An Claidheamh Soluis*. He solicited articles from Eoin MacNeill and Patrick Pearse, which stimulated the formation of the Irish Volunteers; O'Rahilly had already advocated the recruitment of nationalist volunteers and founded a gun club, and he became treasurer of the new movement on its establishment in November 1913. Although he cooperated with the IRB in prompting MacNeill to form the Volunteers, he held the Young Ireland view that secret societies were demoralising and separatists should operate openly. O'Rahilly was central to the Volunteers' gun-running and arms procurement in 1914–15 (even casting bullets in his own house). In April 1915 he published *The secret history of the Irish Volunteers*, in which he accused John Redmond of sabotaging the movement, and in mid 1915 he was served with an order excluding him from Kerry and the south-west.

O'Rahilly apparently favoured a *coup d'état* against Dublin Castle on the outbreak of the first world war, and attempted to organise contacts with Germany during the August 1914 crisis; once this opportunity passed, however, he was aligned with Eoin MacNeill and Bulmer Hobson, who opposed a pre-emptive rising and favoured a defensive strategy. In April 1916, after discovering that the 'Castle document' (which he distributed in Munster) was forged, and hearing of Hobson's kidnapping and the seizure by British forces of the German arms shipment intended for the Volunteers, O'Rahilly played a leading role in persuading MacNeill to call off the rising planned for Easter day. He confronted Pearse with the words 'Anyone who kidnaps me will have to be a quicker shot', and was the courier who took MacNeill's countermanding order to Limerick. Nevertheless, O'Rahilly believed he had a moral duty to stand with men he had recruited and trained. He joined the rebels when they mobilised on Easter Monday: 'I helped to wind up the clock, so I might as well hear it strike.'

At the General Post Office in Dublin he was placed in charge of the roof, food stores, and the prisoners (whom he treated humanely). Desmond FitzGerald, his aide-de-camp, recalled him as cheerful though he was convinced that the rising was doomed; he resisted entreaties to

return home (his wife was pregnant). On Thursday 27 April, during the evacuation of the GPO, O'Rahilly was fatally wounded charging a British barricade in Moore Street. He bled to death slowly in a doorway in Moore Lane (latterly O'Rahilly Place), crying for water and writing his name in blood on a wall; he died on Friday 28 April. The ballad 'The O'Rahilly' by W. B. Yeats celebrates him as an exemplar of existential heroism. His family remained active in republican politics; his sons Richard (1903–84) (calling himself 'The O'Rahilly') and Aodhagan were prominent businessmen.

Patrick Maume

Sources

Michael Joseph O'Rahilly, *The secret history of the Irish Volunteers* (1915); Marcus Bourke, *The O'Rahilly* (1967); Desmond FitzGerald, *The memoirs of Desmond FitzGerald, 1913–1916* (1968); Ruth Dudley Edwards, *Patrick Pearse: the triumph of failure* (1977); Aodhagan O'Rahilly, *Winding the clock: the O'Rahilly and the 1916 rising* (1991)

Patrick Pearse

1879–1916

Patrick Henry Pearse, writer, educationalist, and revolutionary, was born 10 November 1879 at the family home, 27 Great Brunswick Street (latterly Pearse Street), Dublin, the elder son and second of the four children of James Pearse, stone carver and monumental sculptor, originally of London, and his second wife, Margaret, a shop assistant, daughter of Patrick Brady, coal factor, of Dublin.

EDUCATION AND FORMATIVE INFLUENCES

He was educated at Mrs Murphy's private school (1887–91), and the CBS, Westland Row (1891–6). Already convinced of the centrality of the Irish language to a distinctive Irish identity, he joined the Gaelic League in 1896. His father's commercial success allowed him to enrol for a BA (RUI) in Irish, English, and French at UCD, while also taking law courses at King's Inns and TCD (1898–1901). Despite devoting much time to Gaelic League work, he achieved good results in both degrees, reflecting his feel for language and his intense work ethic. Though called to the bar (1901), he would take only one case.

Pearse's vaunting ambition from an early age found expression not only in his founding the New Ireland Literary Society in 1897, but in his publication in 1898 of the three papers he delivered to the society, 'Gaelic prose literature', 'The intellectual future of the Gael', and 'The folk songs of Ireland'—the first two before he was yet 18—as *Three lectures on Gaelic topics*. Impressive in the range of their vocabulary and in the intensity of his reading for his age and his curriculum-constricted education, they provide a rich repository for students of his later years, revealing many of the personality traits of the adult Pearse, however much his views on specific issues might change. Here can be found already the pronounced tendency to speak in absolutes and superlatives, the axiomatic certainty reflected in the use of words like 'undoubtedly' ('among modern nations those which have contributed most to the intellectual welfare of mankind are undoubtedly Italy, England and Germany') (*Collected works: Songs*, 222); the tendency to sanctify the cause of the moment and invoke the blessing of the Deity (as in the climactic exhortation to save the Irish folk song: 'The cause is a holy one—God grant it may succeed!') (*Songs*, 215); the insistence on the glories of ancient Irish literature (*Collected works: Literature*, *passim*); the emphasis on love of nature (*Literature*, 226 ff); the affirmation that 'every great movement that has ever been carried out on this earth has been carried out simply and solely by enthusiasts' (*Literature*, 195–6); the place of Ireland in civilisation, which ought to be 'fascinating not only to men and women of Gaelic race, but to all who have at heart the great causes of civilisation, education and progress' (*Gaelic topics*, 218).

Not the least of his enthusiasms was hero-worship, 'in its highest form...a soul-lifting and an ennobling thing' (*Gaelic topics*, 218). Although his great-aunt Margaret had inculcated in him in childhood particular admiration for Irish heroes, he now ranged as widely as his education permitted, in wondering:

> What would the world be without its heroes? Greece without her Hercules and her Achilles, Rome without her Romulus and her Camillus, England without her Arthur and her Richard, Ireland without her Cuchulainn and her Fionn, Christianity without its Loyolas and its Xaviers (*Gaelic topics*, 228).

Pearse was already a visionary, but in what he dismissed as the political wasteland of 1897 it was in cultural rather than political terms he expounded his vision of a distinctive Irish future:

> The morning will come, and its dawn is not far off. But it will be a morning different from the morning we have looked for. The Gael is not like other men; the spade, and the loom, and the sword are not for him. But a destiny more glorious than that of Rome, more glorious than that of Britain awaits him; to become the saviour of idealism in modern intellectual and social life, the regenerator and rejuvenator of the literature of the world, the instructor of the nations, the preacher of the gospel of nature-worship, hero-worship, God-worship (*Collected works: Political writings*, 221).

Aware of John Henry Newman's vision of a future Ireland as a centre of world scholarship, he salutes the Gael as

> *the* idealist amongst the nations: he loves...painting, sculpture, music, oratory, drama, learning, all those things which delight and ravish the human soul. What the Greek was to the ancient world the Gael will be to the modern; and in no point will the parallel prove more true than in the fervent and noble love of learning (*Collected works: Gaelic topics*, 230).

Anticipating the charge that all this 'is a mere ideal picture', he retorted that he intended it to be, because 'if you wish to accomplish anything great place an ideal before you, and endeavour to live up to that ideal' (*Gaelic topics*, 233).

Pearse's correspondence as secretary of the publications committee of the Gaelic League from June 1900 conveys utter commitment as well as an imaginative approach towards promoting the language, and an inclusive attitude towards the use of the different dialects, which earned him the hostility of those who championed the superiority of their own versions. His work rate made him indispensable to the league, and helped win him the editorship of its bilingual weekly newspaper, *An Claidheamh Soluis* (The sword of light) in 1903. During his editorship (1903–9), he acted on the belief that 'the Gaelic League stands for the intellectual independence of Ireland' (Ó Buachalla, *Letters*, xvii), by striving to make it the cutting edge of 'native thought' (Edwards, 65). An innovative editor, though so expansionist that he had to be quickly reined in for fear of bankrupting the league, his range of interests left him writing most of the paper himself, to a remarkably high level.

With a keen appreciation of the reading market, he was impatient with the purists whose priority was linguistic correctness rather than spreading the word. For all his idealisation of folk culture, he was an active moderniser, insisting that 'a living modern literature *cannot* (and if it could, should not) be built up on the folktale'. Irish literature must of course 'get into contact on the one hand with its own past' but 'on the other with the mind of contemporary Europe—this is the twentieth century, and no literature can take root in the twentieth century which is not of the twentieth century' (*An Claidheamh Soluis*, 26 May 1906).

Pearse practised what he preached, writing several short stories in Irish, of which the best-known was perhaps 'Íosagán', and the best perhaps 'An dearg-daol'. Though of uneven literary quality, his stories helped pioneer modern prose writing in Irish by breaking away from stylised inherited conventions, in that they were partly based on the life and language of Connemara, especially the area around Rosmuc. Here he acquired a cottage in 1907, and here he would spend as much time as he could salvage from the press of affairs in Dublin.

EDUCATIONIST

To promote the role of Irish as a modern language he took an active part in the dispute over the demand that Irish be made mandatory as a matriculation subject for entry to the newly established National University of Ireland. Education remained his abiding passion. If only, he felt, the education system could be inspired with a true love of learning, if only the child could be made the centre of education, a soul might come into Ireland. Nor did he compromise politically at the expense of his educational ideals. He supported the Irish Council bill of 1907, which even John Redmond rejected as a poor substitute for home rule, because it would extend more native control over education. Within education his passion was Irish-language teaching through bilingual techniques. He scoured the international horizon in search of the best bilingual pedagogy; his visit to Belgian schools in 1905 to observe bilingual teaching methods provided him with material for numerous enthusiastic reports in *An Claidheamh Soluis*.

Excited by this concrete Belgian example, he turned towards establishing his own school from 1906, which he eventually realised with the opening of St Enda's in Cullenswood House on Oakley Road, Dublin, in 1908. St Enda's proved a remarkable experiment, above all because of the inspirational personality of Pearse himself and his commitment to a child-centred approach to education to which many of the pupils responded enthusiastically. Although Pearse retained his schoolboy emphasis on the importance of heroic inspiration for inculcating idealism in the young, he advertised St Enda's as offering a modern education, including 'special attention to science and "modern" subjects generally, while not neglecting the classical side' (Edwards, 129). As Pearse explained to an enquiring parent in 1910, St Enda's

> was founded…with the object of providing a secondary education distinctively Irish in complexion, bilingual in method, and of a high modern type generally, for Irish Catholic boys…what I mean by an Irish school is a school that takes Ireland for granted. You need not praise the Irish language—simply speak it; you need not denounce English games—play Irish ones; you need not ignore foreign history, foreign literatures—deal with them from the Irish point of view. An Irish school need no more be a purely Irish-speaking school than an Irish nation need be a purely Irish-speaking nation; but an Irish school, like an Irish nation, must be permeated through and through by Irish culture, the repository of which is the Irish language.

'Nature-Study', he went on, 'forms an essential part of the work…in an attempt to inspire a real interest in and love of beautiful things. Practical gardening and elementary agriculture are taught as part of this scheme'

(Pearse to Mrs Humphreys, 10 May 1910, *Letters*, 152–3). In his mind respect for nature fostered kindness to animals and to children, St Enda's being noted for a reluctance to use corporal punishment in the common British and Irish manner.

His wider reading, once he escaped the straitjacket of the examination-obsessed school curriculum against which he protested so passionately in *The murder machine* (1912), led him to reconsider his earlier antagonism towards modern European literature. By 1913 he had broadened and deepened his schoolboy sense of literary appreciation—reflected at its most uncomprehending in his initially dismissive attitude towards W. B. Yeats—as his sensibilities developed beyond the confines of his education. What was striking was less the narrowness of his original sympathies than his interest in literature at all, and then his developing an awareness of its riches to the extent of inviting Yeats himself to talk at St Enda's. Although continuing to insist on the role of literature in fostering national consciousness, he came to accept that much of the best literature was not explicitly didactic at all, and that it was the first duty of the artist to probe the subject matter unflinchingly from an artistic perspective. This shift in his viewpoint allowed him to come to revere Ibsen, and revise his view of John Millington Synge, overcoming his earlier revulsion at what he saw as the gratuitous romanticisation of violence in the *Playboy of the western world*.

Pearse exalted teaching as a vocation to a level of dedication that few could be expected to achieve. His published papers on education, collected in *The murder machine*, a searing indictment of the English educational system in Ireland, couched as usual in absolutes, consciously extolled the unique virtues of ancient Irish education as a way of boosting the long-battered self-respect of Irish children. The *Irish Review* in February 1913 summarised his educational impact:

> He is an educationalist who is incidentally a poet and a play-wright—but it is in the realm of educational ideas that Mr Pearse has made the most effective innovation. He has estab-lished a secondary school, in which Ireland is taken for granted, and in which, moreover, practical effect is given to

ideas which correspond with the newest discoveries in the method of education

—which the writer identifies as those of Maria Montessori.

A leading authority on the history of education, and on Pearse, reinforces this verdict:

> his educational theories on freedom and inspiration in education, on individual differences, on nature study and school environment, on language teaching and bilingualism, and on the role and status of the teacher, place him securely within the 'New Education' movement. The principles on which he conducted St Enda's, the wide curriculum on offer, his concern for the individual student's needs, the environment of self-motivation and freedom which he created for his pupils' placed him in the front rank of innovative European thinkers on education of his time (Ó Buachalla, *Educationalist*, xxiv).

For all his occasional fulminations against the pretensions of the 'modern', Pearse preached simultaneously a commitment to what he saw as the best of the modern. But that modern was to be honed to achieve the alleged ideals of the Gaelic past. As was his wont, once Pearse had adopted an ideal himself, he proceeded to attribute the reality to the ancient Gaels, living in his imagination of them. If the textbooks and the laboratories would inculcate knowledge, the sagas would teach character. With a keen sense of theatre, Pearse peopled his past with his ideal type characters, from Cuchulainn to Colum Cille, acting as the stage director of Ancient Ireland, as well as paying close attention to the staging of school plays, either in St Enda's itself, or even the Abbey, where Yeats was supportive.

So strident is his invocation of the sagas, of the virtues above all of Cuchulainn, that the unwary can be led into thinking that Pearse dwelt in a perpetual Celtic mist. But the relationship between past and present in his mind was more complicated than that. He regularly invoked the past to legitimise his image of the future. But he ensured the past could be safely summoned to his side. For this past was not the historical past. It was an imaginary past reconstructed in the image of his ideal future. He himself would observe in 1913 that 'Cuchulainn may never have lived and there may never have been a boy corps at Eamhain' (Ó Buachalla, *Educationalist*, 361). Whether Cuchulainn ever existed was not the point. The point, a normal part of the reconstruction of self-respect for defeated peoples, was to endow Ireland with a noble past to enhance its self-respect in the present. Pearse found in the past whatever he needed for his own polemical purposes.

Pearse founded St Ita's School for girls, along the same general lines as St Enda's, in Cullenswood House in 1910, when he turned St Enda's into a boarding school by moving to the Hermitage in Rathfarnham. But it proved an ill-judged move in business terms. The flourishing family firm gradually fell into decay after his father died in 1900; Pearse's devoted younger sculptor brother, Willie, possessed neither the business nor artistic acumen of his father, and the firm went out of business in 1910. As Pearse's educational vision took little account of his overstretched financial resources, he was forced to close St Ita's in 1912, the enlarged St Enda's itself increasingly undermining the precarious financial basis of the enterprise.

POLITICS AND POLITICAL WRITINGS

The struggle to sustain St Enda's may have influenced whatever psychological factors drove Pearse towards an increasingly assertive expression of an Irish right to independence. More certainly, his attitude towards politics began to change as home rule became a possibility from 1911. Although a speech on Robert Emmet that year—Emmet had often visited the Hermitage—anticipated later impulses toward sacrificial rebellion, it is simply unhistorical to deduce from this that Easter 1916 had already sprung fully formed from his mind, and that his every subsequent activity constituted a straight line towards 1916. On the contrary, his move towards politics of any sort, even home rule, much less rebellion, was halting. His insurrectionary impulses could coexist with a range of policy positions. Now forced to consider the potential of a native parliament,

his warning in March 1912 that there would be war in Ireland if the British reneged again on home rule can obscure the fact that he not only supported home rule, but explicitly avowed that he believed a good home rule act could be extracted. He even went so far as to rebuke William O'Brien for claiming that it would not be passed in the present parliament, insisting that 'it *must* be enacted' (Laegh Mac Riangabhra [Pearse] to O'Brien, 30 March 1912, *Letters*, 259).

Although he was still only sporadically active in politics, the calls on Pearse's time were increasing sufficiently to begin diverting his attention from his schools, leading him to warn himself in May 1912 to 'devote your attention to Sgoil Éanna and to Sgoil Íde and disregard political affairs' (Laegh Mac Riangabhra to Pearse, 11 May 1912, *Letters*, 265). Instead it was his own injunction he disregarded, drifting further into politics, initially supporting home rule, and then, as unionist forces in Ulster increasingly barred the way, towards the idea of rebellion. The pledge of Ulster unionists to resist home rule, by rebellion if necessary, in the Solemn League and Covenant of September 1912, proved intoxicating for Pearse. This crucial change in his thinking, which gradually took clearer shape in the light of unfolding events during 1913–14, was induced by his realisation of, and excitement at, the importance of the unionist initiative in challenging British authority as the ultimate determinant of the framework within which Irish public life could be conducted.

Nevertheless, while he had by 1913 begun contemplating the possibility of rebellion, he was still struggling to reconcile his gradualist approach of 1912 with his perception of the growing improbability of home rule. The contradictory impulses can be gleaned from his behaviour throughout the year when he continued to retain hope of home rule while moving, should it founder, to contemplate the alternative of rebellion. This dual-track approach was also in accord with his own instinct to strive for unity among disputatious ideologues, though he could propound his own views vigorously. His earlier response to the incessant conflicts in the Gaelic League had been to insist that fostering the language itself was much the most important national objective, and that internal squabbles simply subverted that prime purpose (Edwards, 36). As his entry into politics exposed him to the ferocious faction fighting along the spectrum of nationalist movements, he proposed in June 1913 that we take *service* as our touchstone, and reject all other touch-stones; and that, without bothering our heads about sorting out, segregating and labelling Irishmen and Irishwomen according to their opinions, we agree to accept as fellow-nationalists all who specifically or virtually recognise this Irish nation as an entity and, being part of it, owe it and give it their service (*Collected works: Political writings*, 144).

In January 1914, in 'The psychology of a Volunteer', he reiterated this plea for unity:

I challenge again the Irish psychology of the man who sets up the Gael and the Palesman as opposing forces, with conflicting outlooks. We are all Irish, Leinster-reared or Connacht-reared...and he who would segregate Irish history and Irish men into two sections—Irish-speaking and English-speaking—is not helping toward achieving Ireland a Nation (*Political writings*, 105–6).

Reading Pearse poses demanding challenges. His style lent itself to ringing declamations, whose apparent finality leaves him particularly vulnerable to being taken out of context. But the martial vigour of Pearse's prose, and his apparently growing impatience for rebellion, can disguise the functional purpose of much of his writing.

As so much of this is heavily tactical, interpretation of his motives on many issues must be necessarily speculative. The written word must be constantly tested against his actual behaviour. Much of his writing, while ostensibly pronouncing immutable truths, was intended for particular audiences. As he came to the conclusion throughout 1913 that a willing-ness to take up arms might be necessary, he sought to establish relations with the main existing organisation committed to the idea of rebellion, the IRB, whose leadership, particularly Tom Clarke, Seán Mac Diarmada, and Bulmer Hobson, would have to be convinced that his prominent support for home rule did not denote lack of true revolutionary fibre. If he wielded a powerful pen, he had neither an organisation behind him, nor a track record of revolutionary ardour. On the other hand, if the IRB had both, they lacked an inspiring voice, whether on paper or platform. Yet, when he claimed in 1915 that he had begun in June 1913 the notable series of articles 'From a hermitage' in *Irish Freedom*, an IRB paper, 'with the deliberate intention, by argument, invective, and satire, of goading those who shared my political views to commit themselves definitely to an armed movement' (*Political writings*, 142), he characteristically overlooked that it was rather the other way round, that it was he who had to persuade them of the genuineness of his commitment. It was they who had to be convinced that he had now moved far enough towards them to allow him become one of them.

In seeking to convince them, Pearse embarked on a strident campaign of persuasion, while at the same time striving to keep options open in case home rule might actually emerge. Yet the metallic certainty of Pearse's hortatory rhetoric can conceal the degree of uncertainty, or at least flexibility, in his thinking. His invocation in June 1913 of Theobald Wolfe Tone's example, 'to set our faces towards the path that lies before us' (*Political writings*, 57), seems clearly to indicate he had now fully adopted the revolutionary route; he seemed to confirm this with a reference to the 'very passionate assertion of nationality' which 'this generation of Irishmen will be called upon to make in the near future'. This surely reads like a call to imminent rebellion—until he qualifies it immediately with the observation that this 'must depend upon many things, more especially upon the passage or non-passage of the present Home Rule bill' (*Political writings*, 147). If it passed, 'the assertion of which I speak will be made by the creation of what we may call a Gaelic party within the Home Rule Parliament, with a strong following behind it in the country' (*Political writings*, 155). However martial his rhetoric, he was still groping his way along a two-stage path, imagining independence emerging through home rule rather than as an alternative to it.

In December 1913, the same month in which he was finally admitted to the IRB, he made the type of ringing declaration of the right to rebellion that appears to leave no doubt of his commitment to insurrection as the only route to independence:

> unarmed men cannot make good their claim to anything
> which armed men choose to deny them...surely it is a sin

against national faith to expect national freedom without adopting the necessary means to win and keep it. And I know of no other way than the way of the sword: history records no other, reason and experience suggest no other.

That appears to demolish the two-stage interpretation—until he immediately proceeds, in characteristic fashion, to the qualification 'when I say the sword I do not mean necessarily the actual use of the sword: I mean readiness and ability to use the sword'.

A month later, he expresses this two-stage approach in more concrete terms, arguing that an armed Volunteer movement 'would make home rule, now about to be abandoned in deference to an armed Ulster, almost a certainty', while adding 'should home rule miscarry, it would give us a policy to fall back upon' (*Political writings*, 203). Nor did the potential uses of home rule vanish from his mind even while he was planning rebellion. As late as May 1915, one of his hypothetical cases of 'Why we want recruits' was if a Tory or coalition government, then imminent, were to 'repudiate the Home Rule Act' (*Political writings*, 123). This too could be read tactically. But even as late as his penultimate pamphlet, *The spiritual nation*, published in February 1916, Pearse did not shrink from reaffirming his earlier belief in the stepping-stone approach in the then circumstances. In vigorously defending Thomas Davis against the charge that he was not a separatist, he drew the analogy with himself:

> The fact that he would have accepted and worked on Repeal in no wise derogates from his status as a separatist, any more than the fact that many of us would have accepted home rule (or even devolution) and worked on with it derogates from our status as separatists. Home rule to us would have been a means to an end: Repeal to Davis would have been a means to an end (*Political writings*, 319).

REVOLUTIONARY

In 1913, however, as he strove to convince the IRB leaders of the genuineness of his revolutionary aspirations, he embarked on a publication campaign which could at times strike strident notes. A classic example was *The coming revolution* in November 1913, in which he announced the shift from cultural to political in his priorities, now disingenuously presenting his Gaelic League years as having been intended from the beginning as merely an apprenticeship for the political struggle. In order to dispel the image of him as a 'harmless' cultural nationalist, he virtually set about reinventing himself in a manner likely to appeal to the 'hard men' of the IRB. He exulted at the sight of arms in Orange hands, taking up the theme of Eoin MacNeill's phrase that 'the North began' when the UVF began to challenge the monopoly of British gun power in Ireland earlier in the year. But he went far beyond MacNeill in extolling bloodshed as a spiritual value in itself, in some of the most sanguinary phrases in his entire work:

> I am glad that the Orangemen have armed, for it is a goodly thing to see arms in Irish hands. I should like to see the A.O.H. armed. I should like to see the Transport Workers armed. I should like to see any and every body of Irish citizens armed. We must accustom ourselves to the thought of arms, to the sight of arms, to the use of arms. We may make mistakes in the beginning and shoot the wrong people; but bloodshed is a cleansing and a sanctifying thing, and the nation which regards it as the final horror has lost its manhood. There are many things more horrible than bloodshed; and slavery is one of them (*Political writings*, 98).

If the conclusion here echoes standard 'western' ideology, the spiritual value attributed to bloodshed as a value in itself reflects a distinctly minority rhetorical tradition.

Pearse's heightened political profile throughout 1913 enabled him to seize the opening offered by the broader nationalist response to the UVF. He acquired his first organisational foothold on becoming director of organisation of the Irish Volunteers established under the leadership of Eoin MacNeill in November 1913. Though heavily infiltrated by the IRB, the Volunteers were intended to reinforce the campaign for home rule, not to subvert it. However, his acceptance into the IRB in December marked a significant shift in his perception of the possibilities of political action. Henceforth, open though he would remain to alternative scenarios, his propensity for highly charged rhetoric became ever more pronounced, culminating in his inspirational address over the Fenian grave of Jeremiah O'Donovan Rossa in August 1915.

Nevertheless, joining the IRB, however important in institutional terms, was not a crossing of an ideological Rubicon. It was still the growing financial plight of St Enda's that dominated Pearse's purpose when he went on a fund-raising trip to America from March to June 1914. The American visit may have proved conducive to the drift of his thinking towards rebellion, and he honed his rhetoric in America to appeal to insurrectionary impulses among his potential donors. But when he returned from America it was still with the intention of returning in 1914–15 to continue his fund-raising for St Enda's.

Events closer to home gradually brought a shift of approach. The Curragh mutiny in March 1914, and the Ulster unionist gun-running at Larne in April, made partition in some shape highly likely, given superior unionist gun power. Redmond seized control of the Volunteers in June, marginalising the potential rebels. Events now moved quickly beyond Irish control. If the UVF provided focus, the Bachelor's Walk killing of civilians by the British army, following the landing of the relatively small number of guns for the Volunteers from the Howth gun-running in July, roused Pearse to a pitch of excitement at the thought of blood spilt—however involuntarily—for Ireland. Then when the British decision to declare war on Germany on 4 August seemed to offer a fresh opportunity to foment rebellion, Pearse was seized with excitement at the beckoning prospects: 'A European war has brought about a crisis which may contain, as yet hidden within it, the moment for which the generations have been waiting' (*Political writings*, 87). Redmond's call to join the British army split the Volunteers. Pearse remained with the small minority of about 12,000 under Eoin MacNeill who retained the title of Irish Volunteers, while about 170,000 joined Redmond's new National Volunteers. This might have seemed a decisive defeat for the minority, but in fact it strengthened their position. If the Volunteers who followed MacNeill left Pearse with far fewer numbers to organise, these were also far more committed to the idea of rebellion. The figures are deceptive. There was no correlation between numbers and energy. Indeed, fewer than 30,000 of the National Volunteers appear to have actually joined the British army as Redmond's recommended route to home rule, and the organisation virtually imploded.

Pearse, whose platform persona concealed his formidable skills as a committee man, quickly used the new opportunities opened by the war, which made plausible the prospect of substantial aid from Germany, to improve his position. In October 1914 he was appointed press secretary of the Irish Volunteers, a useful position for enhancing his profile. In December he became director of military organisation, enhancing his value for the IRB, for it would be through his ability to mobilise the Volunteers that the much smaller IRB could hope to mount a credible insurrection. In March 1915 he presided over a meeting of the four commandants of the Dublin Volunteer battalions to discuss a possible rising in September. His appointment as director of military organisation in the three-man military committee that the IRB itself established in May 1915 confirmed that he had made himself a pivotal figure in the planning process. It was a meteoric rise. A member for only a year and a half, he had enjoyed virtually vertical ascent in an organisation that had hesitated to admit him at all.

When the rebellion, which the IRB decided in September 1914 to mount before the war ended, might actually occur, depended heavily on the supply of guns—as well on the war not ending before they got around to a rising. Pearse now focused on getting guns. While Easter 1916 would be heavily invested with resurrectionary symbolism, the contemplated September 1915 rising might have occurred had the tentative plans for securing German guns materialised at that stage. The protracted search for arms obliges revision of the image of Easter 1916 as simply a blood sacrifice. There are passages in Pearse glorifying both blood and sacrifice, not least with regard to the world war. When he wrote in December 1915 that 'War is a terrible thing, but war is not an evil thing. It is the things that make war necessary that are evil' (*Political writings*, 216), he was simply reiterating the standard position of the belligerents. But in his intoxication with the idea of bloodshed for love of 'fatherland' in general, he went beyond conventional war rhetoric in actually celebrating the bloodshed:

It is good for the world that such things should be done. The old heart of the earth needed to be warmed with the red wine of the battlefields. Such august homage was never offered to God as this, the homage of lives given gladly for love of country.

There was one conspicuous exception to this celebration of the purifying power of bloodshed. He bitterly denounced Redmond for sacrificing the blood of allegedly 50,000 Irish war dead.

The passages in Pearse that exalt the idea of sacrificial bloodshed have made it tempting, and easy, to depict him as hysterically blood-crazy. That dimension is there. But the publication of his *Letters* in 1980 by Séamas Ó Buachalla compelled attention to a very different side of his personality. As F. S. L. Lyons put it in his foreword:

> Here it is enough to point to their most outstanding feature…the rigorous exclusion of the poet and dreamer from a scene dominated by the able organiser…future biographers will have to weigh this pragmatic correspondence against the flamboyance, sometimes even the barely suppressed hysteria of Pearse's published writings from 1914 onwards. In doing so, perhaps they will come at last to a balanced view (Ó Buachalla, *Letters*, foreword, vii, ix).

The evidence for interpreting the rising as solely a blood sacrifice in Pearse's mind has been regularly cited, above all the climactic quote from MacDara, in his 1915 play *The singer*: 'One man can save a people, as one man redeemed the world. I will take no pike. I will go into battle with bare hands. I will stand up before the Gall as Christ hung naked before men on the tree!' This capacity for self-identification with Christ on the cross provides a striking insight into one part of Pearse's psychology. It would partly resurface at his trial. But it has to be set against other more prosaic evidence. For Pearse was desperately trying for two years to get as many weapons as possible 'to act with tremendous effect', as he told his American contacts in October 1914 (Pearse to J. McGarrity, 19 October

1914, *Letters*, 332). Even the commitment to rebellion has to be set against a much less quoted but quite explicit defence of Thomas Davis in February 1916 against the criticism that he was not committed to revolt:

> That Davis would have achieved Irish nationhood by peaceful means if he could, is undoubted. Let it not be a reproach against Davis. Obviously if a nation can obtain its freedom without bloodshed, it is its duty so to obtain it. Those of us who believe that, in the circumstances of Ireland, it is not possible to obtain our freedom without bloodshed, will admit thus much. If England, after due pressure, were to say to us, 'Here, take Ireland', no one would be so foolish as to answer, 'No, we'd rather fight you for it.' But things like that do not happen. One must fight, or at least be ready to fight ('The spiritual nation', *Political writings*, 323–4).

Pearse's sacrificial impulses, however powerful, were not his sole driving force towards rebellion. A blood-sacrifice rising did not require the elaborate planning necessary to give it military credibility. Pearse the dreamer might hang as MacDara on his cross, but the Pearse of the military council of the IRB worked on the ground. The main IRB reason, with Pearse to the fore, for dissuading James Connolly from rising in January 1916 with his tiny Citizen Army was precisely because such a rising would have been pure blood sacrifice, and they needed to wait until the planned arrival of the guns from Germany at Easter to mount a serious revolt.

That the Easter rising was obviously doomed has led to an understandable fascination with the blood-sacrifice passages in Pearse, to the relative neglect of other emphases. Those passages form a legitimate part of any critique. But interpreting everything said and done over previous years through the distorting prism of the Easter rising exposes the danger of reading history backwards, the negation of thinking historically. The prism is distorting because it is so easy to forget that neither Pearse nor anyone else planned the actual rising that occurred. It was the rising no one planned. It cannot be made the basis for inferences about intentions.

Historians are not at liberty to scour earlier sources for premonitory signs for a type of rising none foresaw, exhuming every word pointing in one direction only, and dismissing the rest.

THE RISING

The military council of the IRB planned a rising to begin on Easter Sunday, 23 April, under cover of a mobilisation order by Pearse for Volunteer manoeuvres, which the IRB intended to turn into rebellion. About ten times as many Volunteers were to be involved, with far greater firepower, as was in fact the case on Easter Monday. The intended rising, if still highly likely to be crushed, was to have been a far more formidable military effort than the actual rising.

A sequence of unforeseen events at the last moment subverted the plans. The decisive one was the confusion that resulted in the *Aud*, the ship carrying 20,000 rifles from Germany, being captured by the British navy off the coast of Kerry on Good Friday. This led Eoin MacNeill, the head of the Volunteers, who had been kept in the dark about the plans for a rising, to publish a countermand in the *Sunday Independent*, throwing the plans into chaos. It was only when the plans imploded that the leaders sought to salvage what they could by mounting a rising on Easter Monday, 24 April. We do not know what transpired at the crisis meeting of the leaders on Sunday morning following the publication of MacNeill's cancellation order, but Tom Clarke seems to have been the only one who wanted to proceed on Sunday.

Pearse was chosen as the president of the Irish Republic they intended to proclaim. How that happened remains unclear. Clarke, the senior figure among them, was the first signatory of the proclamation of the Republic, and the presumptive president. Pearse's appointment may have been due to the belief that public relations would be crucial during a rising whose duration, even then, no one could foresee, and that Pearse was the supreme communicator among the signatories, whereas Clarke's talents lay more in conspiracy than in communication. The following day, Pearse duly read out the proclamation of the Republic after the rebels seized the General Post Office, which became their HQ. Mainly his own composition, the proclamation stands as the final published statement of his ideals. Part of it was no more than war propaganda. The reference to the support of 'gallant allies in Europe', was natural in the light of the promised guns from Germany, even if they would now never arrive. But at his trial, Pearse exposed the hollowness of that piece of propaganda when emphasising its purely functional purpose, for 'Germany is no more to me than England is' (Edwards, 318). To him 'German domination was as odious as British' (Edwards, 223). Phrases to the effect that the rebels were 'striking in full confidence of victory', after 'patiently waiting for the right moment to reveal itself', were also patently war propaganda.

If the abrupt change of plans affected the war propaganda sections of the proclamation, the bulk of the text, the core justification of Ireland's right to independence, and the outline of the basic values of the Republic, were timeless arguments. The commitment to 'equal rights and equal opportunities' for all may have been influenced by the socialist James Connolly. If so, Connolly was pushing an open door. There was no necessary contradiction between the thinking of Pearse and Connolly at this level. The opening salutation, 'Irishmen and Irishwomen', expressed Pearse's life-long commitment to equality for women, as did the promise of universal suffrage 'for all her men and women'. The manner in which Pearse came more specifically under Connolly's influence was in formulating the last of the four underlying propositions of the proclamation, contained in *The sovereign people*, his final pamphlet, published on 31 March 1916 (*Political writings*, 337):

> (1) The end of freedom is human happiness. (2) The end of national freedom is individual freedom; therefore individual happiness. (3) National freedom implies national sovereignty. (4) National sovereignty implies control of all the moral and material resources of the nation.

The proclamation was hopelessly out of touch with reality in its view of Ulster unionist resistance to home rule, which Pearse romanticised just as he did so much else in Irish history. The issue is brushed aside, enveloped in the guarantee that the Republic was committed to 'cherishing all the children of the nation equally, and oblivious of the differences carefully fostered by an alien government, which have divided a minority from the majority in the past'. The rebels might be 'oblivious of the differences', unionists were not. The proclamation contains no trace of blood-sacrifice doctrine. When it speaks of 'having waited patiently for the right moment to reveal itself' for the rebellion, the 'right moment' purported to be for 'victory'. That the proclamation committed the rebels to Ireland's 'exaltation among the nations' is quintessential Pearse.

PRESIDENT

Whatever the motives behind his selection as president, Pearse seemed intoxicated with the sense of having achieved this unique status. It was as if he indeed now incarnated Ireland, as broodingly intimated in his poem 'Mise Éire'. He issued bulletins redolent of his pre-eminence. Typical war bulletins, they exuded expectations of victory even in the face of inevitable defeat, announcing imminent success until close to the end. Even at the end Pearse eschewed the sacrificial theme, claiming the rebels would have won but for MacNeill's countermanding order. Nevertheless, he also characteristically exonerated MacNeill from blame, acknowledging that he too had acted in the best interests of Ireland, thus facilitating a subsequent closing of Volunteer ranks. It must be doubtful if Clarke, bitterly critical of MacNeill during the week, could have employed so conciliatory a tone.

DEATH

Clarke too might have been slower to contemplate surrender. After he had hesitated about surrendering initially, the sight of the shedding of innocent blood seems to have revolted Pearse as much as the rhetoric of blood had excited him. Earlier in the week, however appalled by the looting, he refused to follow his own injunction to shoot captured looters. Now, after seeing three civilians with a white flag shot down, Pearse surrendered, in the hope of saving civilians and his followers, on 29 April. Sentenced to death on 2 May after a trial in which his bearing won the admiration of the presiding English officer, he played out his presidential role to the full, summoning shades of MacDara in proposing himself as the sole sacrifice.

He was executed at 3.30 a.m. on 3 May. He used the short respite to snatch a final propaganda victory in composing a poem to the beauty of nature and farewell letters to his brother Willie, himself shortly to be executed, and to his mother, all of which would contribute to the beatific public profile he would soon come to enjoy.

LEGACY

The task of rescuing Pearse from the clutches of his idolaters and demonisers continues. 'The balanced view', for which F. S. L. Lyons argued, has yet fully to emerge. As an interim verdict on Pearse's political significance, it may be surmised that there would have been a rising without him. But in terms of public image there could not have been *the rising* without him. It may even be ventured, remembering that Pearse republished in 1916 *The murder machine*, and *An mháthair agus sgéalta eile*, as if intent on reasserting the continuing centrality of education, and of the Irish language, to his thinking, that in the longer run his cultural legacy will prove at least as significant as his political.

J. J. Lee

Sources

NLI: Pearse papers and letters (MS 5049), Seán T. O'Kelly papers (MSS 8469; 10,192), J. J. Doyle papers (letters from Pearse); Pádraic H. Pearse, *Collected works*, i: *Plays, stories, poems* (1917); ii: *Songs of the Irish rebels; Specimens from an Irish anthology; Some aspects of Irish literature; Three lectures on Gaelic topics* [1917/18] (repr. 1924); iii: *Political writings and speeches* (1922; 1966); Raymond J. Porter, *P. H. Pearse* (1973); Ruth Dudley Edwards, *Patrick Pearse: the triumph of failure* (1977); Cathal Ó Háinle (eag.), *Gearrscéalta an Phiarsaigh* (1979); Séamas Ó Buachalla (ed.), *The letters of P. H. Pearse* (1980), with a foreword by F. S. L. Lyons; Séamas Ó Buachalla (ed.), *A significant Irish educationalist: the educational writings of P. H. Pearse* (1980); Brian P. Murphy, *Patrick Pearse and the lost republican ideal* (1991); Liam de Paor, *On the Easter proclamation and other declarations* (1997); Elaine Sisson, *Pearse's patriots: St Enda's and the cult of boyhood* (2004); Regina Uí Chollatáin, *An Claidheamh Soluis agus Fáinne an Lae 1899–1932; Anailís ar phríomhnuachtán Gaeilge ré na hAthbheochana* (2004)

William Pearse

1881–1916

William ('Willie') Pearse, revolutionary and sculptor, was born 15
November 1881 at 27 Great Brunswick Street (Pearse Street), Dublin,
second son among two sons and two daughters of James Pearse, a monumental sculptor originally from London, and his second wife, Margaret
Pearse (née Brady), a shop assistant from Dublin. From childhood Willie
was devoted to his older brother, Patrick. In 1891 the Pearse brothers
entered CBS, Westland Row. Willie possessed limited academic ability
and was frequently physically chastised in school, contributing to his
brother's distaste for corporal punishment. He was considered artistic-
ally talented, however, and natural heir to the family business. From
1897 he attended the Metropolitan School of Art, where he studied
sculpture under Oliver Sheppard. He followed Patrick into the New
Ireland Literary Society and the Gaelic League, providing Irish classes
for his fellow art students. He was a member of the executive of the
Wolfe Tone and United Irishmen Memorial Committee (1898), often
wore a kilt, and played Gaelic sports, being a mediocre hurler but a good
handball player.

On his father's death in 1900, Willie did not take immediate control
of the family business. He left Patrick in charge and continued his studies

in South Kensington and Paris, acquiring a more cosmopolitan awareness. On returning to Ireland he showcased work in RHA and Oireachtas exhibitions between 1906 and 1913. In 1907 he exhibited, with other members of the Irish Art Companions, at the Irish International Exhibition. He maintained a frequent correspondence with, and fondness for, Mabel Gorman, a young girl who was his favourite model—she posed for such pieces as 'Memories' and 'Éire Óg'—although the relationship became strained before her death in 1914. Pearse & Sons continued to carry out commissioned work on churches (St Mary's cathedral, Limerick) and for nationalist bodies (Father Murphy memorial, Wexford); Willie's favourite piece was the 'Mater Dolorosa' in St Andrew's church, Westland Row, Dublin. The business declined, however, and closed in 1910.

By then Willie was teaching art and English at his brother's school, St Enda's, and at its companion school for girls, St Ita's. He was effectively assistant headmaster at St Enda's, giving Patrick more time for political activity. He shared with Patrick a fondness for dressing up, and nurtured acting ambitions. With Thomas MacDonagh, he ensured that drama was given a prominent position on the school's curriculum. With mixed success he played Pilate in Patrick's 'Passion play' at the Abbey (1911) and Ciaran in Patrick's 'The master' when it was staged at the Irish Theatre, Hardwicke Street (1915). He rejected an offer to join Sir Frank Benson's professional touring company, but did establish the Leinster Stage Society with his sister, Mary Brigid. In 1912 the society staged a season at Cork Opera House which was a critical and financial disaster.

His brother's closest confidant, Willie too joined the Irish Volunteers in November 1913, but was not intimately involved in the planning stages of the 1916 rising. During the rebellion (24–9 April) he was a captain on the headquarters staff and occasionally (if Patrick was indisposed) acting chief of staff. In reality he had no authority and 'on no plausible definition could he have been called a ringleader' (Townshend, 282). On surrender he was court-martialled and, contrary to expectations, executed in Kilmainham jail a day after his brother (4 May 1916). Many suspected that he was executed simply because of his relationship to Patrick, although he was among the first to be tried and the only prisoner to plead guilty, and these factors may have contributed. In unsuccessfully pleading for the return of his body to his family, John Dillon described him as 'a most inoffensive creature' (Edwards, 329). The shooting of such an innocuous figure, who had played a minor part in the rising, did much to discredit the executions in the eyes of many moderate nationalists.

William Murphy

Sources

Desmond Ryan, *The man called Pearse* (1923), 50, 60–76; Mary Brigid Pearse, *The home life of Patrick Pearse* (1934), 17, 28; Louis N. Le Roux, *Patrick H. Pearse* (1932); Milo McGarry, 'Memories of Sgoil Eanna', *Capuchin Annual 1930*; Margaret M. Pearse, 'St Enda's', *Capuchin Annual 1942*, 227–30; Desmond Ryan, 'Margaret Pearse', *Capuchin Annual 1942*, 312–18; Margaret M. Pearse, 'Patrick and Willie Pearse', *Capuchin Annual 1943*, 86–8; *Cuimhní na bPiarsiach*, i, ii, iii (n.d.); *Studies*, lv (1966); Ruth Dudley Edwards, *Patrick Pearse: the triumph of failure* (1977); Séamas Ó Buachalla (ed.), *The letters of P. H. Pearse* (1980); *Irish Times*, 17 January 1984; Henry Boylan, *A dictionary of Irish biography* (1998 ed.); Theo Snoddy, *Dictionary of Irish artists, 20th century* (2002 ed.); Turlough Breathnach, 'Willie Pearse and his world', *Ireland of the Welcomes*, xlviii, no. 4 (1999); Elaine Sisson, *Pearse's patriots: St Enda's and the cult of boyhood* (2004); Charles Townshend, *Easter 1916: the Irish rebellion* (2005)

Mary
Perolz

1874–1950

Mary (Máire, Marie) Perolz, republican and trade unionist, was born 7 May 1874 in Market Alley, Limerick city, daughter of Richard Perolz, a Dublin-born, Protestant printer of French Huguenot origin, and Bridget Perolz (née Carter), a Catholic. The family moved to Tralee, Co. Kerry, and then to Cork city, where her father worked on the *Cork Examiner*. Reared a Catholic, Mary was educated by the Mercy sisters in Tralee, and the Presentation sisters in Cork and in Dublin, where she completed her schooling at George's Hill Convent. Strongly nationalist under the influence of the Presentation nuns, she joined the Gaelic League, and was a colleague of William Rooney in the Celtic Literary Society during the 1890s. An early member of Inghinidhe na hÉireann, the nationalist women's organisation founded by Maud Gonne in 1900, she taught Inghinidhe classes in history and Irish by lantern-light in the loft of loaned premises on Dublin's Strand Street, playfully insisting that such conditions rendered the activity 'more fun'. She acted in several joint theatricals of Inghinidhe and the Celtic Literary Society, appearing in a programme of *tableaux vivants* illustrating episodes from ancient Irish saga, and in the initial Dublin production of 'Eilís agus bhean déirce', by Peadar Mac Fhionnlaoich, the first Irish-language play staged in the city (December 1902).

A close friend to Countess Markievicz and James Connolly, by 1916 she was prominent in both Cumann na mBan and the Irish Citizen Army

(ICA), and was registered owner of the *Spark*, a nationalist weekly printed by Connolly in Liberty Hall. She helped procure arms for the ICA, and in the weeks before the Easter rising served as a courier of messages between leaders of the planned insurrection within Dublin and to Volunteer commandants in the country. When Markievicz was excluded under the defence of the realm act from addressing the Fianna Éireann festival in Tralee, and was ordered by Connolly not to defy the ban and risk arrest with the Easter rising impending, Perolz, who physically resembled Markievicz, and had a suitably nimble tongue, stood in as a replacement. Posing as Markievicz up to the moment of her address, she was shadowed by detectives on the train to Tralee and interrogated about her supposed 'Russian citizenship'. She electrified the festival audience by reading out the exclusion order, conveying regrets from Markievicz for not appearing, and delivering the text of the latter's lecture on the 1867 Fenian rising (26 March 1916).

Dispatched as a courier to Cork city on Easter Monday morning (24 April) bearing the remobilisation order issued by Patrick Pearse in the wake of the countermand by Eoin Mac Neill, Perolz failed to make direct contact with local Volunteer commandant Tomás MacCurtain, who was elsewhere in the county. Arrested in Dublin shortly after the insurgents' surrender, she was one of five women internees deported to England (20 June), all of whom, in common with Markievicz (who was imprisoned in England on a life sentence), were ICA members. Released the next month on appeal, Perolz was for a time the most prominent republican woman free to circulate actively in Dublin. Her incarceration so scandalised some members of her family, that they changed their surname to 'Prole' to avoid association with her.

Perolz was prominent in the revival after the rising of the Irish Women Workers' Union (IWWU). Representing the union at the first post-rising convocation of the Irish Trade Union Congress and Labour Party (Sligo; 7 August 1916), she was notable in moving amendments to resolutions, partly to assure that the phrasing included reference to 'working women' as well as to 'working men', partly to assure that resolutions addressed the particular needs of women workers, and the industries in which they predominated. Especially important was her amendment to the draft national labour programme, advocating strategies to improve the health of working-class women and children, including maternity centres and medical inspection of schoolchildren. Perolz was elected acting president of the IWWU (February 1917), substituting for the still imprisoned Markievicz, who was elected honorary president. She travelled to England with Helena Molony and Kathleen Lynn to welcome the male republican internees on their release (June 1917); hearing that Markievicz was also to be freed, they remained to accompany her home to a tumultuous reception in Ireland. Perolz joined Sinn Féin and canvassed for the party in the 1918 general election. Amid disappointment at the paucity of women candidates fielded in the election, she was mentioned as a possible candidate for Dublin Corporation (January 1920). For over thirty years she was an inspector under the 1908 children's act with the Dublin board of public assistance.

At age 45 she married in the Roman Catholic pro-cathedral (21 April 1919) James Michael Flanagan (sometimes styled O'Flanagan), a clerk known widely by the sobriquet 'Citizen Flanagan'. They lived with members of his family at 127 Botanic Road, Glasnevin, and subsequently at St Lawrence Cottage, Strand Road, Sutton, Co. Dublin; it is not recorded that they had children. Perolz remained an outspoken champion of the rights of women in industry and in the labour movement. She died in the early days of December 1950 and was buried at Mount Jerome cemetery, Dublin. A memorial was unveiled over her grave by Senator Margaret Pearse in August 1955.

Lawrence William White

Sources

GRO (birth, marriage certs.); R. M. Fox, *History of the Irish Citizen Army* (1943), 132–3, 141–2, 184–5; Marie Perolz, witness statement (9 May 1949), Bureau of Military History (WS 246); *Irish Press*, 5 December 1950; 29 August 1955; *Irish Times*, 27 August 1955; *Irish Independent*, 29 August 1955; Jacqueline Van Voris, *Constance de Markievicz: in the cause of Ireland* (1967); Lily Conlon, *Cumann na mBan and the women of Ireland 1913–25* (1969), 22–3; Margaret Ward, *Unmanageable revolutionaries: women and Irish nationalism* (1983); Diana Norman, *Terrible beauty: a life of Countess Markievicz* (1987); Mary Jones, *These obstreperous lassies: a history of the Irish Women Workers' Union* (1988); Margaret Ward, *Maud Gonne: Ireland's Joan of Arc* (1990); Kathleen Clarke, *Revolutionary woman: an autobiography 1878–1972* (1991); W. K. Anderson, *James Connolly and the Irish left* (1994); Margaret Ward, *In their own voice: women and Irish nationalism* (1995), 21, 84; Ruth Taillon, *The women of 1916: when history was made* (1996); Sinéad McCoole, *Guns and chiffon: women revolutionaries and Kilmainham gaol: 1916–1923* (1997), 31; Sinéad McCoole, *No ordinary women: Irish female activists in the revolutionary years, 1900–1923* (2003) (photo)

Joseph Mary Plunkett

1887–1916

Joseph Mary Plunkett, poet, journalist, and revolutionary, was born 21 November 1887 at 26 Upper Fitzwilliam Street, Dublin, second child and eldest son among three sons and four daughters of George Noble Plunkett (1851–1948), man of letters, barrister, art historian, nationalist, and papal count, and Mary Josephine Plunkett (née Cranny) (1858–1944). Born into the Catholic branch of a family prominent in Ireland for some six centuries—the martyred bishop Oliver Plunkett, co-operativist Sir Horace Plunkett, and writer Lord Dunsany were all noteworthy kinsmen— Plunkett enjoyed the most moneyed background of the eventual leaders of the 1916 rebellion. His paternal grandfather, Patrick Plunkett (1817–1918), born on a small farm adjoining the demesne of his relatives, the Plunketts of Killeen castle, Co. Meath, entered business in Dublin in the 1840s, first in the leather trade, then in building. He and Joseph Plunkett's maternal grandfather, Patrick Cranny (1820–88), likewise a self-made builder, from Borris, Co. Carlow, between them developed much of the south city suburbs; the two men's wives were first cousins, and Joseph's parents were second cousins.

Plunkett was reared in his parents' Dublin home and in two rented properties in the south county: Charleville, Templeogue (briefly in 1897), and Kilternan Abbey, near Enniskerry, Co. Wicklow (1900–08). He matured into an eccentric, nervous personality in a household dominated by his mother's erratic, capricious character, alternately neglectful and abusive, alongside his father's benign detachment from domestic life. Owing to his chronically poor health from early childhood—he suffered from glandular tuberculosis, and frequent bouts of pleurisy and pneumonia—Plunkett's formal education, chiefly at a series of Jesuit institutions, was peripatetic. After primary education at the Catholic University School, Leeson Street, he briefly attended a Marist school in Paris, before entering Belvedere College, and also had private home tutors. He studied philosophy for two years at the Jesuits' Stonyhurst College, Lancashire, which made a deep and lasting impression. Highly imaginative and verbally agile, dexterous in languages, and autodidactic, he was intellectually inquisitive across a diverse range of subjects, both abstruse and practical. While deeply immersed in scholastic philosophy and Catholic mystical writing, he pursued interests in physics, chemistry, aeronautics, photography, and wireless telegraphy, and contemplated a career in science or medicine.

His close and formative friendship with teacher and poet Thomas MacDonagh, who encouraged his interest in poetry, began in 1910 when he sought a tutor in Irish to prepare for the matriculation examination of the NUI (which he failed). Though the two were contrasting personalities—Plunkett, quiet and delicate, MacDonagh vivacious and assertive—their friendship nurtured Plunkett's sense of intellectual self-confidence. Religion was a recurrent topic of friendly disputation between Plunkett, the believer, and MacDonagh, the sceptic. While attending an Irish summer school at Gortahork, Co. Donegal (1910), Plunkett pursued a doomed romance with a medical student, Columba O'Carroll, the subject of much of his poetry. Though he passed the matriculation examination at the RCSI (1911), ill health precluded his attendance. Seeking a gentler winter climate than Ireland's, he travelled in the eastern Mediterranean, spending the early months of 1911 with his mother in Italy, Sicily, and Malta, and the winter of 1911–12 in Algiers, where he studied Arabic language and literature, and cultivated an interest in orientalism. With MacDonagh's energetic, critical and practical assistance, he produced a slim volume of verse, *The circle and the sword*, published during his absence (1911). On returning to Ireland (spring 1912), he fell seriously ill with influenza; suffering lung haemorrhages, he was hospitalised for several months, after which he set up house with his sister Geraldine in a family property at 17 Marlborough Road, Donnybrook.

POLITICAL COMMITMENTS

Purchasing a financially unstable literary and topical magazine, the *Irish Review* (June 1913), Plunkett assumed the editorial chair, and was soon working with MacDonagh to alter radically the periodical's policy of political non-partisanship to reflect his own new-found political interests. Engaging for the first time in public affairs, he was joint honorary secretary with his future brother-in-law Thomas Dillon of the Dublin Industrial Peace Committee, organised by Thomas Kettle to mobilise intellectuals and clergy behind independent mediation efforts during the 1913 lockout. His intervention varied sharply with that of his mother, who stridently opposed the trade unions' initiative to send children of locked-out workers on respite visits to families in Britain. Trade-union leader James Larkin refused a subscription from Plunkett as tainted money, owing to the fact that Countess Plunkett, unbeknownst to her family, had recently purchased slum tenements in the city centre.

Though his physical infirmities precluded active soldiering, Plunkett offered his services to Eoin MacNeill on the launch of the Irish Volunteers, and attended the inaugural public meeting at the Rotunda (25 November 1913). Elected to the provisional committee, he utilised the *Irish Review* to propagandise for the movement; the consequent alienation of the journal's traditional readership base (consisting mainly of civil servants) contributed to its demise. When, during a general wartime crackdown on the separatist press, police in London seized a quantity of copies of the November 1914 number, which included the provocative 'Twenty plain facts for Irishmen', the financial consequences proved fatal to the publication. In 1914 Plunkett became co-partner with MacDonagh and Edward Martyn in management of the newly launched Irish Theatre, conceived as a vehicle for original plays and translations of continental drama. He supplied the company's premises in the Hardwicke Hall, a property owned by his mother and also housing the Dun Emer Guild, but seems eventually to have differed with his partners over the nature of their agreement, and to have withdrawn from the venture by March 1916.

Though Plunkett supported, in the interests of unity, the co-option to the Volunteers' provisional committee of nominees of Irish parliamentary party leader John Redmond (June 1914), he adamantly opposed Redmond's declaration at Woodenbridge, Co. Wicklow, pledging the support of the Volunteer movement for Britain in the first world war (September 1914). He attended the secret meeting of advanced nationalists summoned by Thomas Clarke and Seán Mac Diarmada at the Gaelic League headquarters, Parnell Square, that determined to stage an armed rising against British rule during the course of the war (9 September 1914). Increasingly more prominent within the rump movement of anti-Redmondite Irish Volunteers, at the body's first convention (October 1914) he was named to the twelve-member central executive; in December 1914 he was appointed to the newly formed headquarters staff as director of military operations with the rank of commandant.

Planning the rising

At the behest of the advisory committee established at the secret 9 September meeting, Plunkett indulged a long-held amateur interest in military strategy and tactics (nurtured by schoolboy participation in the Stonyhurst officers' training corps), by drafting an embryonic plan for military operations in the Dublin area. Inducted into the Irish Republican Brotherhood (IRB), and admitted into the small band of revolutionary conspirators headed by Clarke and Mac Diarmada, Plunkett became the chief strategist in the planning for the rising, working in concert with Patrick Pearse and Éamonn Ceannt on expanding the plans to include the entire country, and on devising the detail. It is probable that Plunkett thus originated the strategy of concentrating the insurrection in Dublin on the seizure and defence of large city-centre buildings.

In March–June 1915 Plunkett travelled by a circuitous route to Berlin—his previous valetudinarian journeys supplying a plausible cover that allowed him to slip through wartime security strictures—to negotiate with the German foreign office for assistance in the planned rising. There he joined Roger Casement—already seeking German support for an Irish rebellion, sponsored by the American-based Clan na Gael—in drafting a lengthy memorandum, styled the 'Ireland report', outlining an ambitious operation involving a Volunteer rising in Dublin and the west, coordinated with a German invasion up the Shannon estuary. Though the Germans ultimately rejected the plan, Plunkett—who disagreed with Casement's insistence on the necessity of an invading German expeditionary force—secured a tentative German undertaking to land a shipment of small arms and ammunition on the eve of an Irish rising, sometime in spring 1916 (a date necessitating postponement of the rising from its initial designation for autumn 1915).

While Plunkett was absent on this mission, the planning group, comprising him, Pearse, and Ceannt, was formally constituted by Clarke, without the knowledge of the IRB supreme council in its entirety, as a military committee (May 1915), subsequently styled the military council. Plunkett travelled to New York to brief Clan na Gael leader John Devoy on the progress of the German negotiations and the status of preparations for the rising within Ireland (September–October 1915). He played a decisive role in persuading the socialist revolutionary James Connolly to cooperate with the IRB conspirators; highly impressed with Plunkett's plan, after co-option to the military council (January 1916) Connolly was Plunkett's chief associate in finalising preparations.

REBELLION, MARRIAGE, AND EXECUTION

From summer 1915 Plunkett resided at Larkfield, a rambling rural property recently purchased by his mother in Kimmage, Co. Dublin, and used by the Volunteers as a weapons store, explosives factory, training base, and quarters for enlistees returning from overseas. Over the winter he became engaged to Grace Gifford (1888–1955)— illustrator, caricaturist, and MacDonagh's sister-in-law—drawn to her by their deep mutual interest in the Catholic religion, to which she converted (7 April 1916). Suffering a serious breakdown in health, in the first week of April 1916 Plunkett underwent surgery on tubercular glands in his neck, convalescing thereafter in a nursing home on Mountjoy Square, but attending to military council business on several daytime visits to Larkfield. He was instrumental in the genesis of the 'castle document', a seeming government order for sweeping arrests of nationalist leaders; long thought to have been an outright forgery accomplished by Plunkett and his cohorts, it was likely an authentic, leaked contingency plan, which Plunkett altered to appear more extensive in scope and imminent in intent. Its circulation was intended to galvanise sentiment within the Volunteers towards intensified military preparedness and probable armed resistance.

On Good Friday (21 April) Plunkett moved to the Metropole hotel, close by Dublin's General Post Office. He participated in the final pre-rising deliberations attending MacNeill's countermand of the Volunteers' Easter Sunday manoeuvres. As a member of the military council he signed the proclamation of the Republic and served on the provisional government. Pallid and wan, his neck swathed in bandages, but attired in elaborate military costume, and charged with 'a hectic energy' (MacDonagh (1945), 588), throughout the week-long rebellion he served with the headquarters garrison in the GPO, where his aide-de-camp was Michael Collins. Court-martialled and sentenced to death, on the evening of 3 May, hours before his execution, Plunkett married Grace Gifford in the chapel of Kilmainham jail. Separated immediately after the service, the couple were allowed a ten-minute visit in Plunkett's cell later in the night. Plunkett was executed by firing squad on 4 May 1916. The pathos of his last hours contributed to the sway of public opinion toward sympathy for the insurgents. According to Plunkett's sister Geraldine, Gifford was pregnant at the marriage, and miscarried some weeks later while living at Larkfield. Active in the republican movement throughout the war of independence and civil war, thereafter she worked as a magazine illustrator and cartoonist, commercial artist, and theatrical costume designer.

ASSESSMENT: POETRY, POLITICS, AND CHARACTER

A sequence of poems entitled 'Occulta', completed by Plunkett in July 1915 and intended as a separate volume, was included with earlier and later verse in a posthumous collection, *The poems of Joseph Mary*

Plunkett (1916); edited by Geraldine Plunkett, the volume enjoyed brisk sales for a time, going through four printings within three years. In subject and technique Plunkett's poetry bespeaks his deep devotion to Christian and neoplatonic mysticism, and his later dabbling with orientalism. Influenced by William Blake, Francis Thompson, and George Russell ('Æ'), and by such mystical writers as SS John of the Cross and Teresa of Avila, his verse is compact, rhapsodic, and strongly rhythmic. Flawed too frequently by vagueness, strained imagery, and tortured syntax—the work of an apprentice who never achieved mature poetic articulation—his poems are most powerful when expressing an intense inner conflict, arising from consciousness of 'the gulf between human capacity and human aspiration' (Kennelly, 56), and anguish over the intimate duality between good and evil at war within the human heart. A common theme is mystic union with a suffering other—the poet's beloved, the crucified Christ, the feminine personification of the Irish nation—as the tragically necessary crucible of renewal and rebirth.

Though party to the declaration of an Irish Republic, Plunkett ideologically was more a Catholic nationalist, who mooted within conspiratorial circles the post-war advisability of an independent Irish kingdom under a German Catholic prince. Serious and intellectual in disposition, he expressed a taste for the theatrical in flamboyant, exotic clothing and jewellery. His characteristically nervous manner could, at times of heightened emotion, border on the histrionic. Despite his physical frailty, he was mentally robust and possessed of a steely inner resolution.

FAMILY

Several of Plunkett's immediate family were involved in the Easter rising and the subsequent republican movement. His father, Count Plunkett, in early April 1916 dispatched from Berne a message to Casement in Berlin, then proceeded to Rome where he discussed the Irish nationalist case with Pope Benedict XV. Imprisoned briefly in Dublin after the rising, he and Countess Plunkett were deported for nine months to Oxford. Winning a parliamentary by-election (February 1917), and aligning with Sinn Féin, he opposed both the 1921 treaty and the 1926 launch of Fianna Fáil, remaining committed to republican abstentionism as a member of the legitimist second dáil. Joseph Plunkett's elder sister, Philomena ('Mimi') Plunkett (1886–1926), served as courier in 1916 between the IRB military council and Clan na Gael leaders in New York, and afterwards was secretary of Cumann na mBan. She married Diarmuid O'Leary, a London-based IRB man, and later an ITGWU official. A younger sister, Mary Josephine ('Moya') Plunkett (1889–1928), largely apolitical, joined a Catholic religious order for eight years without professing, then worked as a qualified midwife in Africa. Geraldine Plunkett (1891–1986), who studied science at UCD, married Thomas Dillon, UCD lecturer and later professor of chemistry at UCG, on Easter Sunday 1916, and witnessed the occupation of the GPO from their bridal room in the Imperial hotel; an intended double wedding with her brother and Grace Gifford had been obviated by Plunkett's illness and the timing of the rising. Their children included writer Eilís Dillon and journalist Michael Dillon. The youngest sister, Josephine Mary ('Fiona') Plunkett (1896–1976), long active in Cumann na mBan, was imprisoned during the civil war and on occasions in the 1920s and 1930s; she was among thirteen women interned in Mountjoy jail under the emergency legislation of 1940.

The second of the Plunkett brothers, George Oliver Michael Plunkett (1894–1944), commanded the so-called 'Kimmage garrison' of Irish Volunteers quartered prior to the Easter rising on the family's Larkfield property. During Easter week he was attached with fifty-six men of his command to the headquarters garrison in the GPO. After evacuation of the building on Friday 28 April, he rescued a wounded British soldier stranded between the lines on Moore Street, then braved hostile fire to retrieve the man's rifle. Though he was court-martialled and sentenced to death, the sentence was commuted to ten-years' penal servitude. Included in the general prisoner release of June 1917, he fought in the war of independence and in the anti-treaty Four Courts garrison, after which he was imprisoned for the duration of the civil war. Prominent throughout the 1920s–30s in the militarist wing of the IRA, which shunned any political activity, he served on the army council that launched the 1939 British bombing campaign, during which he was interned. The youngest sibling, John ('Jack') Plunkett (1897–1960) also fought in Easter week in the GPO and with the anti-treaty Four Courts garrison at the outset of the civil war. A one-time UCD engineering student, who worked as an engineer in the ESB, throughout lengthy membership of the IRA he specialised in production of explosive devices and in radio transmission. Arrested in a December 1939 police raid on an IRA wireless broadcasting station, while interned in the Curragh he survived a forty-day hunger strike.

Lawrence William White

Sources

GRO (b. cert.); *Catholic Bulletin*, vi, no. 7 (July 1916), 397; Padraic Colum (ed.), introduction to *Poems of the Irish revolutionary brotherhood* (1916), ix–xxxvi; Geraldine Plunkett (ed.), foreword to *The poems of Joseph Mary Plunkett* (1916), vii–xvi; Donagh MacDonagh, 'Joseph Plunkett', *An Cosantóir*, v, no. 11 (November 1945), 581–8; Diarmuid Lynch, *The IRB and the 1916 insurrection* (1957); F. X. Martin (ed.), *The Irish Volunteers 1913–1915: recollections and documents* (1963), 31, 96–7, 155, 162, 195, 199, 201–2; Max Caulfield, *The Easter rebellion* (1964); Brendan Kennelly, 'The poetry of Joseph Plunkett,' *Dublin Magazine*, v, no. 1 (spring 1966), 56–62; Geraldine Dillon, 'Joseph Plunkett,' *Dublin Magazine*, v, no. 1 (spring 1966), 63–5; *Irish Times*, Easter rising supplement, 7 April 1966; Breandán Mac Giolla Choille (ed.), *Intelligence notes 1913–16* (1966); Martin Shannon, *Sixteen roads to Golgotha* (c.1966); F. X. Martin (ed.), *Leaders and men of the Easter rising: Dublin 1916* (1967); Edd Winfield Parks and Aileen Wells Parks, *Thomas MacDonagh: the man, the patriot, the writer* (1967); *Memoirs of Desmond Fitzgerald: 1913–1916* (1968); Kevin B. Nowlan, *The making of 1916: studies in the history of the rising* (1969), 164–6, 172–4, 177–9, 182–3, 194, 219, 223–5, 245–9, 257–9, 303; Piaras F. Mac Lochlainn, *Last words: letters and statements of the leaders executed after the rising at Easter 1916* (1971); Sydney Czira, *The years flew by* (1974); *Irish Times*, 30 December 1974, p. 10; León Ó Broin, *Revolutionary underground: the story of the Irish Republican Brotherhood 1858–1924* (1976); Johann A. Norstedt, *Thomas MacDonagh: a critical biography* (1980); Roger McHugh and Maurice Harmon, *A short history of Anglo-Irish literature* (1982); Conor Foley, *Legion of the rearguard: the IRA and the modern Irish state* (1992); Moira Laffan, *Count Plunkett and his times* (1992); Uinseann MacEoin, *The IRA in the twilight years* (1997); *1916 rebellion handbook* (1998 ed.); Michael Foy and Brian Barton, *The Easter rising* (1999); Michael Laffan, *The resurrection of Ireland: the Sinn Féin party, 1916–1923* (1999); Patrick Maume, *The long gestation: Irish nationalist life 1891–1918* (1999); Marie O'Neill, *Grace Gifford Plunkett and Irish freedom: tragic bride of 1916* (2000); Pádraig Yeates, *Lockout: Dublin 1913* (2000); Brian Barton, *From behind a closed door: secret court martial records of the 1916 Easter rising* (2002); Charles Townshend, *Easter 1916: the Irish rebellion* (2005); Geraldine Plunkett Dillon, *All in the blood: a memoir* (2006)

John
Redmond

1856–1918

John Edward Redmond, Parnellite and leader of the Irish parliamentary
party (1900–18), was born 1 September 1856 in Dublin, third child
among two daughters and two sons of William Archer Redmond, a
member of a Catholic gentry family in Co. Wexford, and Mary Redmond
(née Hoey), who belonged to a Protestant and unionist family from Co.
Wicklow. He lived for part of his youth in Ballytrent House, near
Rosslare, Co. Wexford. His great-uncle John Edward Redmond had been
MP for Wexford borough (1859–65), and his father held the same seat
(1872–80). Politics was in his blood. As a schoolboy in Clongowes,
Redmond acquired a love of literature and he excelled as a debater. He
then proceeded to TCD, an unusual move for a Catholic at that time, but
he was a mediocre student and he left after only two years. In 1876 he
went to London to help his father in the house of commons, and he
worked for a short time as a clerk in the vote office.

PARNELLITE MP, 1881–91

When his father died in 1880 Redmond hoped to inherit the family seat,
but instead C. S. Parnell offered it to his protégé T. M. Healy. Redmond
was not kept waiting for long; after a delay of some weeks he was returned
unopposed for New Ross in February 1881. He was then aged 24. With

slight exaggeration he would later boast that he took his seat, made his maiden speech, and was expelled from the house of commons, all on the same evening. He was appointed a party whip, and his oratorical skills were exploited not merely in parliament, but also in making speeches throughout Ireland and Britain. In 1883–4 he and his younger brother, Willie, who was always a close ally and confidant, made a fifteen-month tour of Australia, New Zealand, and the US. They raised large sums of money for the party, and this experience gave Redmond a lifelong belief that Ireland should play a full role in developing the empire. In Sydney he met and married Johanna Dalton, who belonged to a prominent Irish-Australian family. Over the decades he made frequent visits to America.

Redmond was a junior member of the committee that chose home rule candidates for the 1885 general election. In the debates on the first home rule bill a year later he rejected the idea that Ulster differed significantly from the rest of Ireland. He had studied law intermittently, and for some years after he was called to the bar in 1887 he defended nationalists in court. He supported the Plan of Campaign led by John Dillon and William O'Brien, hoping not merely to achieve rent reductions for Irish tenants but also to lure the Conservative government into using coercive measures. In 1888 he was accused of using intimidating language and was sentenced to five weeks in jail—where one of his fellow inmates was his brother, by now the home rule MP for Fermanagh North. A prison sentence was a badge of honour, almost a requirement for a home rule politician. The following year his happy home life was devastated when his wife died suddenly, leaving him with three young children.

Parnellite leader, 1891–1900

Redmond did not belong to Parnell's inner circle, but by the end of the 1880s his oratorical skills and his ability in managing party business ensured that he was prominent among the second rank of home rule MPs. He became the leading figure among the minority who remained loyal to Parnell in the split of 1890–91—a decision that was at odds with his instinctive conservatism, but was partly explicable by personal and class loyalties. He refused to 'sell' the leader of the party, arguing that to do so would destroy its independence. Healy, scourge of the Parnellites, conceded that Redmond avoided rancour but described him nonetheless as callous, calculating, cool-headed, able, and astute (Callanan, *Parnell split*, 151). He was clearly a formidable opponent. After the split he sought compromise and reunification, and in January 1891 he participated in the Boulogne negotiations with William O'Brien.

When Parnell died the following October, Redmond played the main role in organising an elaborate funeral in Dublin, and immediately afterwards he was elected as leader of the minority faction. Despite a series of defeats in the course of the previous year, he and his colleagues decided to continue the fight, and he resigned his Wexford seat to contest the vacancy in Cork city created by Parnell's death. The result was humiliating and he obtained less than a third of the vote. However, only weeks later, in December 1891, he defeated Michael Davitt and was elected for Waterford city—a seat which he held for the rest of his life.

The Parnellites were routed in the 1892 general election and they won only nine seats to their opponents' seventy-two. Redmond welcomed the second home rule bill in 1893, although he described it as a compromise. He dismissed once again the danger of agitation in Ulster, and he forecast, wrongly, that the Conservatives would reform the house of lords. In the following years he made his mark as a skilled parliamentarian, revealing qualities unsuspected during the 1880s, and he became one of the finest orators in the house of commons. He was a heavy man of imposing appearance, 'with the face and figure of a Roman emperor' (Gwynn, *John Redmond*, 25), and in later years Prime Minister Asquith's nickname for him was 'Leviathan'. His physical presence reinforced his eloquence. Occasionally he indulged in personal abuse, but he was normally dignified in his battles with the anti-Parnellites, and he was often ready to collaborate with them, with unionists and landlords, and even with Fenians. He sought an amnesty for imprisoned dynamiters, and for a while he became one of the republicans' favourite Irish politicians.

In 1896 he sat on the recess committee, whose recommendations led to the creation of the Department of Agriculture and Technical Instruction. He supported the land act of that year, and he also facilitated the financial relations commission, which concluded that Ireland had been over-taxed. He welcomed the local government act of 1898 as an important step towards self-government. Unlike Dillon, who was by now leader of the anti-Parnellites, he believed that as the Irish people became more prosperous and acquired more responsibilities their determination to achieve home rule would increase rather than diminish.

By this stage he had settled into a routine that would vary little in future years. He divided his time between London and Aughavanagh, a former military barracks in the Wicklow hills which had once been Parnell's hunting lodge. It now became Redmond's Irish refuge. The building had no telephone and in winter it was sometimes cut off by snow-drifts; this was to his taste because, like Parnell, he often chose to be out of his colleagues' reach. He enjoyed the life of a country squire, taking long walks and shooting grouse. His second marriage (1899), to Ada Beesley from Warwickshire, brought him private contentment. Although he enjoyed the company of friends and family he was basically a solitary man who disliked social occasions. He was serious, formal, kindly and courteous, but he had little personal contact with most of his fellow MPs.

Over the years Redmond remained hostile to the Liberals, as befitted a Parnellite who had been conditioned by the experiences of 1890–91, and he was wary of an alignment with British radicals. He was convinced that since the Liberals would never regain power without Irish support there was little or no need to conciliate them, and that since the house of lords' power of veto could not be surmounted, home rulers would have to strike deals with the Conservatives. He hoped to ease class conflict and, if possible, to win over the Irish gentry; in local elections he urged nationalists to vote for worthy Protestants, unionists, and landlords—generous and far-sighted advice which was usually ignored.

United party chairman, 1900–10

In January 1900 the home rule movement was reunited—appropriately at a meeting in Committee Room 15, where the split had been finalised nine years earlier. The sparring politicians were influenced by public disgust at their incessant bickering and by widespread Irish hostility to the British war in South Africa. Another incentive was the spread of William O'Brien's new United Irish League (UIL) whose aims included the imposition of unity and discipline on the home rule movement from outside and from below the ranks of its feuding MPs. This encouraged them to end their disputes. The anti-Parnellites were themselves bitterly divided, and this helped explain their magnanimity in consenting to a leader from among their opponents.

For different reasons the three leading anti-Parnellites were prepared to accept Redmond as the chairman of the reunified party. Despite their long-standing mutual dislike and distrust, Redmond and Healy had drawn (briefly) closer together. The UIL had undermined Parnellite support, particularly in Connacht, and this led O'Brien to believe that he could control Redmond. And although Dillon was unenthusiastic and would have preferred another Parnellite leader, he feared isolation and gave way grudgingly.

Redmond was astonished by his unanimous election as chairman, but any appearance of unity was deceptive; soon the party was embroiled in new quarrels between rival factions. Redmond and O'Brien struggled for control of the UIL, and in a compromise settlement in June 1900 the league became the national organisation of the Irish parliamentary party. Redmond was elected its chairman (later president). But as leader of the home rule movement his powers were limited and—unlike Parnell—he was obliged to consult with party colleagues; he would be a chairman, not a chief. He adjusted rapidly to the views of the Dillonite majority and drifted away from cooperation with unionists. In December 1900 he yielded to pressure from Dillon and O'Brien by acquiescing reluctantly in Healy's expulsion from the party. He remained concerned to prevent any further divisions within the movement till home rule had been achieved—after which, he believed, it would break up and be replaced by new parties.

Redmond was sceptical towards the proposal for a conference between representatives of landlords and tenants, but he and O'Brien supported the plan once it received the endorsement of George Wyndham, the chief secretary. They were among the tenants' representatives at the ensuing negotiations, and the two sides soon recommended unanimously an ambitious scheme of land purchase which would be aided by the state. A bill along these lines was introduced in parliament in March 1903 and Redmond secured amendments in favour of the tenants. Dillon remained aloof and hostile, seeing the bill as a trap and fearing that home rule might lose its appeal if the land question were to be solved. But Redmond's enthusiasm was fully vindicated, and over the next few years the Wyndham act allowed over 200,000 tenant farmers to buy their holdings on most attractive terms.

In his first years as party chairman Redmond was placed awkwardly between Dillon and O'Brien. Conscious of the balance of power in the party, he chose not to defend O'Brien against Dillon's attacks on the policy of conciliation—till O'Brien resigned suddenly from the UIL directory and from parliament in November 1903. Despite his difficult temperament he had become a useful ally, and his departure left Redmond exposed and more dependent on Dillon's wing of the party—a faction that welcomed conflict and confrontation.

Another setback soon followed. Initially Redmond supported the abortive devolution scheme of 1904–5 proposed by Antony MacDonnell, the under-secretary. He believed it would strengthen the demand for a national parliament in Dublin and that, because it was a 'Conservative' initiative, it might escape the house of lords' veto. Dillon and the unionists opposed it, for conflicting reasons, and the result was a humiliating defeat for the policy of conciliation. The Conservative and unionist onslaught on Wyndham inaugurated a new polarisation of Irish political life, and it provided a powerful argument against further compromise.

All Redmond's confident expectations were disproved by the massive Liberal victory in the 1906 elections, giving the new government a large overall majority and enabling it to dispense with Irish support. He was attracted by the Liberals' proposals for a limited form of devolution in the Irish Council bill, which envisaged a partly elected body with limited administrative functions but no legislative powers, and he endorsed them warily. He believed that, however inadequate it might be, this measure could be a stepping stone towards the ultimate objective of an Irish parliament. But he yielded to internal opposition and was forced to insist that nothing less than home rule would be acceptable to the party; there would be no gradual or incremental approach. Once again he gave way to his more intransigent colleagues and followers.

O'Brien and Healy rejoined the party, left it once more, and then carried on a vendetta against its leaders (who now included Joe Devlin). Personal feuds and fluctuating alliances were among the home rulers' most striking characteristics.

Although the Liberals were unwilling to concede the nationalists' principal demand, Redmond had grounds for satisfaction in these years. He was able to facilitate legislation such as the Irish labourers act, which provided money to build rural labourers' cottages. He cooperated eagerly with the Liberals in drafting the Irish universities bill. He welcomed the 1909 land act which introduced the principle of compulsory purchase. But he remained instinctively conservative and he was suspicious of some aspects of the Liberals' welfare policies. He regarded old age pensions as an extravagance because of the future burdens they would impose on Irish finance, and (like the government) he opposed women's suffrage. He also remained aloof from a new round of agrarian conflict which characterised the ranch war of 1906–8.

The constitutional crisis of 1909–11 enabled Redmond to distance himself from agitation at home and to concentrate on events in Westminster. With considerable unease he acquiesced in the 'people's budget' of 1909, although its increase in liquor licences and taxes on spirits made it deeply unpopular in Ireland. This was a dangerous strategy, but it succeeded. The result was the rejection of the budget by the house of lords, a commitment by the Liberals to introduce a home rule bill, an early general election in January 1910, and political deadlock in which the Liberals and Conservatives gained almost exactly the same number of seats. This development surpassed all Redmond's expectations and placed him in the position that home rulers had always sought: with his seventy-one seats he held the parliamentary balance of power. In theory he could make and unmake governments, although in practice he would have no reason to restore the anti-home-rule Conservatives to office.

He seized the opportunity provided by the lords' folly and demanded an end to their power of veto. In these unexpected circumstances he was happy to abandon the policy of conciliation which, with some wavering, he had followed (or tried to follow) since the 1890s. He urged the government to break the power of the lords and then to introduce a home rule bill which could no longer be blocked by the upper house. Since the unionists had chosen an uncompromising path they would no longer be reassured and conciliated; instead, as Dillon and his followers had always wished, they would be confronted and defeated.

For a short while some cabinet ministers contemplated resignation in preference to renewed dependence on Irish support. Redmond was unyielding, insisting 'no veto, no budget', and the government committed itself to abolishing the lords' veto power before he in turn agreed to vote for the budget. The hatred that he aroused among Conservatives and unionists in the following years confirmed the extent of his achievement. He was excluded from negotiations between the main British parties from June to November 1910, but when these failed to result in a compromise—to his great relief—a second election was called in December. It confirmed the verdict of January, after which the government proceeded to abolish the lords' veto and replace it with the ability to delay 'ordinary' (non-budget) bills for two parliamentary sessions.

THE HOME RULE CRISIS, 1912–14

This measure was followed in April 1912 by the introduction of a third home rule bill, which was expected to come into effect in summer 1914. In many respects its terms were disappointing for Irish nationalists. A wide range of powers would be retained by London, and the number of Irish MPs in Westminster would be reduced from 103 to forty-two. Ireland would be treated as an entity, although to Redmond's dismay Asquith warned privately that at a later stage concessions might have to be made to the Ulster unionists. However, it seemed certain that this bill would be enacted, unlike its two Gladstonean predecessors, and Redmond gave it his full support. He claimed that it would be a final settlement of the quarrel between the two islands.

Like Asquith, Redmond rejected proposals whereby Ulster counties could vote on whether they wished for inclusion or exclusion. But for him this was a new problem; in the past his concern had been to win over southern landlords, rather than the unionist majority in Ulster. While prepared to offer inducements, such as the over-representation of Ulster in a home rule parliament, he was adamant in his rejection of partition. He and Asquith realised that at this stage the Conservatives and unionists were determined on confrontation, and although the prime minister was aware of the danger of civil war he chose to delay any compromise proposals. Both men hoped that as the final enactment of home rule grew nearer the unionists would become desperate, and that therefore they would be satisfied with fewer concessions.

This strategy has been much criticised, and with the benefit of hind-sight it seems clear that the government's position in 1914 would have been strengthened if it had shown greater generosity towards unionist Ulster in drafting the home rule bill. But in 1912 Redmond did not foresee the ferocity of later Conservative and unionist resistance—and since Asquith's principal concern was to prevent a breach with Irish national-ists, thereby endangering his government, his immediate aim was to postpone rather than resolve the Irish crisis (Fanning, *Fatal path*, 67).

Redmond was genuinely shocked when his opponents, led by Edward Carson, threatened and planned an Ulster rebellion, and he dismissed their threats as bluff. He had always believed in constitutional methods and parliamentary procedures, and he felt that now the unionists were changing or breaking the rules. In 1910 his first biographer had written: 'Redmond is more for times of peace: Parnell for times of war' (Redmond-Howard, *Redmond*, 138). Unexpectedly 'times of war' now lay ahead, and he was ill-equipped for the challenge. He was determined not to follow the unionists' example and to form a nationalist paramilitary force; to do so would be to abandon his hard-earned image of a responsible statesman to whom power could safely be entrusted, throwing away his partial triumph over British prejudices against the Irish. He was aware that Carson and the unionists had a freedom of manoeuvre (and also a sense of desperation) which nationalists did not share.

But the formation of the Ulster Volunteers was emulated by other, more radical nationalists, and Redmond was embarrassed when they created a rival volunteer force in November 1913. He was being under-mined from within at a time when he believed that it was imperative to display unity under his leadership. His problems were compounded by the Dublin lockout of 1913–14, which he saw as a distraction from the struggle for home rule—exactly the sort of internal division that he had always deprecated. His (and his party's) sympathy with tenant farmers did not extend to urban workers.

He urged the government to remain firm, but from November 1913 onwards he encountered pressure to compromise and to accept the exclu-sion of certain Ulster counties from the home rule area. He remained convinced that 'mutilation' would be unacceptable to his followers. Asquith warned that there was a danger of civil war and a possibility that the king might dismiss the government in an effort to avert such a disaster. The dissolution of parliament would ensure that, at best, the whole home rule debate would start all over again—an unwelcome and unlikely prospect.

The following March Redmond made a series of concessions, finally agreeing that individual Ulster counties would be allowed to opt out of home rule for a period of six years. This would give the Conservatives two opportunities to gain power in general elections, in which case they could be expected to make exclusion permanent. On the one hand, Carson rejected this suggestion as a sentence of death with a stay of execution, while on the other, many nationalists were appalled by Redmond's acquiescence in partition.

Subsequent events—the Curragh 'incident' and the Larne gun-running—made violence more probable, but Redmond advised against any provocative response such as prosecuting the gun-runners. Instead he decided to neutralise potential opposition within Irish nationalism. In June 1914 he confronted the standing committee of the Irish Volunteers, pointing out that its members held their positions through self-appointment and that they were all Dublin-based. He demanded that his party should nominate half of the standing committee, and he threatened to disrupt the Volunteers if his terms were not accepted. A majority of the members gave way, with an understandable ill grace. Belatedly and unwillingly he had followed Carson's example.

In late July 1914 Redmond and Dillon joined leaders of the Liberals, Conservatives, and unionists in the Buckingham Palace conference, a last attempt to reach a compromise over Ulster. They failed predictably to agree on the 'excluded' areas. The unionists were implacably opposed to county option, but they were now prepared to accept six- rather than nine-county exclusion. They demanded Fermanagh and Tyrone, which had small nationalist majorities. Tension grew with the approach of the parliamentary deadline, the date by which the home rule bill would have to be passed, amended by agreement, or abandoned. It was heightened further by the Howth gun-running and the subsequent killings at Bachelor's Walk. Then, just as the crisis was due to be resolved in one form or another, the first world war broke out.

From the very beginning Redmond supported the British war effort. In his speech in the house of commons on 3 August 1914 he urged that all British troops should be withdrawn from Ireland and that the hitherto rival Volunteer forces would defend the island. This would have the attraction of bringing the two communities together and would therefore help to maintain a united Ireland. He consulted only a few colleagues before making this statement, and Dillon and other nationalists were later to be deeply critical of his action, but any other response would have been uncharacteristic and probably ill-judged. Home rule had not yet been enacted, and he still needed the Liberal government's goodwill. A European war provided the opportunity for Irish nationalists to prove their claim that home rule would not threaten British strategic interests. And Redmond believed that Germany was responsible for the war.

His public support was unconditional, but in private he continued his pressure on Asquith. This soon produced results. Home rule became law on 18 September 1914, although it would not be implemented till a date not later than the end of the war, and not till special amending legislation had been passed for Ulster. After decades of effort, patience, and disappointment, home rule was on the statute book at last, and nationalist Ireland celebrated its triumph. But the enactment (and simultaneous postponement) of home rule turned out to be a pyrrhic victory, and the events of the next few years would show that the unionists had greater cause for rejoicing.

Two days later Redmond addressed a group of Irish Volunteers who were drilling at Woodenbridge, Co. Wicklow, encouraging them to join the British army and to fight as far as the firing line extended. The Volunteers' standing committee, which he had recently packed with his own supporters, was ignored. As in his support for Parnell, Redmond 'committed himself sparingly but completely…The code of honour behind this commitment can be seen as self-indulgent or heroic' (Maume, *Long gestation*, 119). Eoin MacNeill and the other original Volunteer leaders did not wish their followers to join the British army, and these remarks precipitated a split in the force. The vast majority supported Redmond rather than MacNeill; the ratio was 15:1 in his favour. However Dillon and other colleagues were dismayed by what they saw as his excessive enthusiasm for the war effort.

Like most other observers Redmond expected the war to end quickly, and in that event his gamble would probably have succeeded. But early enthusiasm vanished as the conflict dragged on interminably and as the death toll rose steadily. The war's unpopularity rubbed off on those, like Redmond, who encouraged Irishmen to enlist and were seen as recruiting sergeants. He became increasingly out of touch with nationalist opinion, rarely visiting Ireland except to relax in Aughavanagh, and he lost valuable financial support from Irish-American groups who opposed any involvement in 'England's war'. He also encountered suspicion and obstruction from those whom he wished to help. The War Office was hostile to his romantic idea of an 'Irish brigade' or division, it ignored the Irish Volunteers in its recruiting campaign, and it indulged in gratuitous snubs towards nationalists. By contrast, Carson and his followers received preferential treatment, and in political terms the 36th division was more thoroughly 'Ulster' than the 16th was 'Irish'.

When a coalition government was formed in May 1915 Redmond was offered a cabinet post, but he followed the party's traditional policy and declined. He did not propose what he felt *should* have been offered: a cabinet seat without portfolio and without a salary. His refusal was in accordance with traditional party policy, but in the circumstances it was probably a mistake—and the fact that his rival Carson entered the cabinet as attorney-general put Irish nationalists at a disadvantage.

Throughout the early years of the war Redmond had virtually no input into Irish policy. One important exception was his achievement in ensuring that Ireland would be exempt when conscription was imposed on the rest of the UK in January 1916; Irishmen would be spared when the English, Scots, and Welsh were dispatched to the battlefields. Another was his—ultimately self-destructive—advice to Dublin Castle to show patience and restraint towards the provocations of republican extremists. (Later he blamed himself for having reassured the chief secretary that there was no danger of a rebellion in Ireland.) Preparations began for a transfer of limited powers after the war, and he was briefed on his future responsibilities, but it was revealing that while he had struggled constantly to achieve home rule he seems to have made no detailed plans for using it.

With the enactment of home rule the party no longer had a goal, and its machinery, already rusty through disuse, fell into further neglect. Yet although voters were apathetic it still maintained a wide if shallow support base, and home rulers won all the six by-elections they contested between the outbreak of war and late 1916. Redmond remained optimistic about his prospects once the conflict would come to an end.

The Easter rising was, if only incidentally, an assault on him and all that he stood for. He expressed his detestation and horror at the insurrection and claimed that the Germans had plotted, organised, and paid for it. Nonetheless he appealed to Asquith, both in private and public, for leniency towards those who had not been involved in planning the rebellion—even threatening to resign as party leader. As the executions continued he became more depressed and more desperate, aware of the damage they would cause to moderate nationalism. He shared Dillon's views that the British were 'washing out our whole life work in a sea of blood' (Lyons, *Dillon*, 381). In private he talked about retirement.

But the rising also provided him with an unexpected opportunity. Asquith decided on a new initiative to resolve Irish problems during wartime, and he delegated Lloyd George to negotiate with nationalists and unionists—separately, rather than face-to-face as had been the pattern in July 1914. These discussions, characterised by 'creative ambiguity and well-intentioned elision' (Jackson, *Home rule*, 170), lasted two months, from May to July, and Redmond was led to believe that home rule would be granted during the war. However, his position had been seriously weakened, and from the beginning it was taken for granted that six counties rather than four were to be excluded from the home rule area. There would be no county plebiscites, and the nationalists would have to abandon Tyrone and Fermanagh. Lloyd George was deliberately vague about the duration of 'exclusion', but in private both sets of leaders realised that a temporary arrangement was unlikely to be reversed. The number of Irish MPs in Westminster would remain unchanged. Against expectations Redmond won the support of a nationalist convention in Belfast, although he was obliged to threaten his own resignation if the plan were rejected.

Southern unionists were horrified by the prospect of imminent home rule for most of Ireland and they feared that nationalism would fall into the hands of republican supporters of the Easter rebels. Assisted by allies in the Conservative party they undermined Redmond and the moderate nationalists who, even at this late stage, might have offered them a more attractive future. They schemed successfully against the plan, imposing terms impossible for home rulers to accept: a reduction in the number of Irish MPs at Westminster and public recognition that partition would be permanent. He broke off the negotiations, protesting that he and his colleagues had been deceived.

The result was disastrous. Redmond's morale was shattered and he was widely blamed for the failure to build on an opportunity presented to him by the Easter rebels. The immediate implementation of home rule, even in the aftermath of a failed rebellion, might possibly have revitalised moderate nationalism, but the failure of the negotiations made the party seem naïve, incompetent, and futile. It stagnated, and public opinion drifted away from the cause of home rule. Redmond made no public appearance for months.

Decline, 1917–18

The following January, after a decisive defeat in the Roscommon North by-election, Redmond alarmed his colleagues by planning to announce that the party was ready to make way for other, younger men if the people so wished. Throughout 1917 the home rule movement was overshadowed by the new mass Sinn Féin party.

However, in June he was presented with what he saw as yet another chance to reach a settlement. Lloyd George, by now prime minister, offered him immediate home rule for the twenty-six counties or, alternatively, an Irish convention representative of all sections of Irish opinion. He guaranteed the enactment of any 'substantial agreement'. Unwisely Redmond chose the latter option, unable to resist the temptation to negotiate, and the result was a long, incompetently managed series of meetings in TCD. The omens for the convention were poor, Sinn Féin boycotted it, and both Dillon and O'Brien refused to have any involvement. Redmond soon suffered a personal blow when his brother Willie was killed in the battle of Messines.

But depression and declining health did not prevent him from throwing his weight behind this last effort to reach a compromise settlement. Nationalists sought to expand the degree of autonomy which they would exercise under home rule, while Ulster unionists, whose position had already been secured, objected to the prospect of tariff barriers being raised against Britain. Convention members observed confidentiality, and this repeated the problems posed during the 1916 negotiations: Redmond was once again effectively silenced and invisible to the Irish public, but now at a time when his republican opponents were active. He concentrated on reaching an agreement with the southern unionists who were, like his own party, weak and demoralised. Eventually a coalition of Catholic bishops and nationalist politicians sabotaged his proposals on the grounds that he was giving too much away. One of his parliamentary colleagues recalled Redmond's reaction: 'everything, in his judgment, was wrecked; he saw nothing ahead for his country but ruin and chaos' (Gwynn, *Last years*, 325).

It was a miserable end to his career, although at least he was spared the final disaster. After an operation for gallstones in London he died of heart failure on 6 March 1918. Within weeks the Irish convention failed to reach 'substantive agreement' and the British decided to impose conscription on Ireland, thereby radicalising nationalists and propelling large numbers into the ranks of Sinn Féin. In the general election of December 1918 the home rule party was wiped out in southern Ireland, winning only six seats to seventy-three for Sinn Féin.

More clearly than is the case with most politicians, Redmond's career ended in failure. Had he died four years earlier, in sight of the promised land, his life would be seen very differently. He had been a great orator and parliamentarian. For years he had attempted to win over and conciliate his opponents, although he was unable to persuade enough of his followers to share his views; unionist fears that he was not representative of his party were sometimes justified. He was an ideal advocate of Irish nationalism in Britain, and particularly in Westminster, but he became increasingly out of touch with Irish opinion. Like all politicians he sometimes stooped and trimmed. He was courageous and adaptable, and under changed circumstances the critic of the Liberal alliance in the 1890s had become its principal advocate by the 1910s. Over many years he persevered in the fight for home rule, coping with hostility from the Conservatives and indifference from the Liberals.

He responded with varying success to the rapidly changing fortunes of his final years. He showed skill and determination in exploiting the opportunities provided by a first upheaval, the political crisis initiated by the house of lords. But his background and temperament left him unable to respond effectively to a second 'revolution': the abandonment of normal constitutional procedures by Conservatives and unionists, and the ensuing militarisation of Irish public life. He was widely seen as being too anxious to trust the promises and assurances of British ministers, and he was outmanoeuvred by Asquith. He was spectacularly unlucky in the timing of the first world war and—like very many others—he miscalculated its duration. Ultimately he and his party fell victim to the rival extremes of Ulster unionism and Irish republicanism.

Nonetheless he was a worthy and noble representative of the Irish political tradition, he proved that patience, negotiation and compromise could bring about important reforms, he helped to embed parliamentary procedures in the habits and instincts of Irish nationalists, and he played a significant role in transforming Ireland in the decades before the first world war. The miscalculations and failures of his later years have obscured his many achievements.

Michael Laffan

Sources

NLI, Redmond papers; TCD, John Dillon papers; L. G. Redmond-Howard, *John Redmond: the man and the demand* (1910); S. Gwynn, *John Redmond's last years* (1919); D. Gwynn, *The life of John Redmond* (1932); F. S. L. Lyons, *John Dillon* (1969); J. O'Brien, *William O'Brien and the course of Irish politics, 1881–1918* (1976); P. Jalland, *The Liberals and Ireland: the Ulster question in British politics to 1914* (1980); P. Bew, *Conflict and conciliation in Ireland, 1890–1910: Parnellites and radical agrarians* (1987); A. Gailey, *Ireland and the death of kindness: the experience of constructive unionism, 1890–1905* (1987); N. Mansergh, *The unresolved question: the Anglo–Irish settlement and its undoing* (1991); F. Callanan, *The Parnell split, 1890–91* (1992); P. Bew, *Ideology and the Irish question: Ulster unionism and Irish nationalism, 1912–1916* (1996); F. Callanan, *T. M. Healy* (1996); P. Maume, *The long gestation: Irish nationalist life, 1891–1918* (1999); A. Jackson, *Home rule: an irish history, 1800–2000* (2003); J. Finnan, *John Redmond and Irish unity, 1912–1918* (2004); D. Meleady, *Redmond: the Parnellite* (2008); R. Fanning, *Fatal path: British government and Irish revolution* (2013); D. Meleady, *John Redmond: the national leader* (2013)

Desmond
Ryan

1893–1964

Desmond Ryan, journalist, historian and republican socialist, was born 27 August 1893 in Dulwich, London, one of at least two children of William Patrick Ryan, journalist and radical, native of Templemore, Co. Tipperary, and Elizabeth Ryan (née Boyd). The family moved to Navan, Co. Meath, in 1906 during his father's brief and controversial editorship of the *Irish Peasant*, and lived thereafter in Dublin. Educated initially at Christian Brothers' schools in Dulwich and Westland Row, Dublin, Desmond was deeply influenced by his father's literary interests and courageous espousal of a post-Parnellite, anticlerical, pro-labour brand of nationalism. He was one of the initial forty students (1908) of St Enda's, the progressive, Irish-language school founded by Patrick Pearse, where his interests in the Irish language and Irish studies generally intensified. While reading Irish, English, and French at UCD (after his family's return to London in 1910) he continued to reside in the St Enda's premises at The Hermitage, Rathfarnham, where he taught classes and served as Pearse's secretary. He formed a deep and abiding devotion to his mentor, who on the eve of the Easter 1916 rising designated Ryan as his literary executor. Recruited into the Fianna Éireann circle of the Irish Republican Brotherhood, in preparation for the rising he helped manufacture explosive devices in the St Enda's grounds. During Easter week he served under Pearse in the GPO in E company, 4th battalion, of the Irish Volunteers, after which he was interned for several months in Stafford detention barracks, Wormwood Scrubs prison, and Frongoch internment camp.

On release he sat his university examinations, obtaining an arts degree (BA, NUI (1916)), then joined the *Freeman's Journal* as a reporter. In a series of books and articles he contributed to the general public reappraisal of the Easter rising, propagating the ideas of Pearse and other 1916 leaders, and helping to forge the potent myth of their heroic and self-sacrificing idealism. In fulfilment of the author's express pre-execution wish, he edited Pearse's magazine articles chronicling the history of St Enda's, republished as *The story of a success* (1917), for which Ryan composed a concluding chapter. His biographical memoir, *The man called Pearse* (1919), the first book-length treatment of the subject, established the legacy of Pearse as chief leader of the 1916 rising, and propagated the hagiographic image of 'a perfect man, whose faults were the mere defects of his straight and rigid virtues' (Ryan (1919), 3). The two titles were incorporated into Ryan's five-volume compilation of Pearse's *Collected works*, published in a comprehensive edition by Phoenix in 1924. Ryan wrote the first biography (1924) of James Connolly, whose republican socialism was exerting a growing and defining hold over his own politics.

Thus engaged as journalist and author, Ryan seems not to have played an active part in the troubles of 1919–21. Though supporting the Anglo–Irish treaty as a potential step toward a Connollyite cooperative workers' commonwealth, he was deeply disillusioned by the internecine divisions of the civil war, and moved to London as a practising journalist. He translated a biography of Pearse from the French of Louis Le Roux (1932), whom he had advised on the original work. In an autobiography, *Remembering Sion* (1934), most impressive for its passages of lyrical impressionist reminiscence, he modified his youthful assessment of Pearse, acknowledging defects of character and judgement, while still asserting the man's ultimate greatness. He wrote an historical novel, *The invisible army: a story of Michael Collins* (1932) (posthumously reissued as *Michael Collins and the invisible army* (1968)), and *Saint Eustace and the albatross* (1935), a Swiftian satirical allegory of London intellectual bohemia. In a body of historical works he pursued a study of Irish separatism through

biographical treatment of certain of its principal figures. *Unique dictator: a study of Eamon de Valera* (1936), a balanced critique that identified both the flaws and achievements of de Valera's style of political leadership, was notable as a rare contemporary attempt at objective assessment. There followed *The phoenix flame: a study of Fenianism and John Devoy* (1937); *The sword of light: from the four masters to Douglas Hyde 1636–1938* (1939), a study of the submergence of Gaelic civilisation and its ultimate revival; and *Sean Treacy and the 3rd Tipperary Brigade* (1945). In writing *The rising: the complete story of Easter week* (1949), Ryan supplemented vast personal knowledge with extensive research, and coined the phrase 'the triumph of failure' to describe the legacy of the insurrection; the book retains interest largely for its sketches of personalities, both major and minor, and its record of the wealth of individual experience within a climactic historic event.

Returning to Ireland at the onset of the second world war, Ryan had a small poultry farm and apple orchard in Swords, Co. Dublin (1943–56), and in later years resided at 3 Charleston Road, Rathmines. Versed in socialist history, biography and ideological currents worldwide—the subjects of much of his extensive journalism and lecturing—he was long active on the left wing of the Labour party. He edited *Torch*, the feisty journal of the party's Dublin region organisation (early 1940s), and was involved in the 1913 Club (1957–8), a discussion group that anticipated Labour's leftist swing of the 1960s. He edited and annotated three volumes of selections from the writings of Connolly: *Socialism and nationalism* (1948), *Labour and Easter week* (1949), and *The workers' republic* (1951); in his introduction to the first title, and in the copious annotation throughout all three, he disputed the assimilation of Connolly into nationalist martyrology at the neglect of his socialism, and asserted his place in the working-class movement internationally. In his most significant contribution to Irish historiography, Ryan collaborated with labour leader William O'Brien, a close personal friend, in editing the two volumes of *Devoy's post bag* (1948, 1953), compiled from the voluminous correspondence of John Devoy, which remains a valuable research guide to the Fenian movement in Ireland and America. His last works were a selection from *The 1916 poets* (1963), and the posthumous *The*

Fenian chief: a biography of James Stephens (1967), re-establishing the historic importance of a neglected revolutionary conspirator.

Ryan's biographic approach to historical writing encouraged a 'great men' perspective, paradoxically inconsistent with his socialist commitment. While the bulk of his work has been superseded by the primary research of subsequent academic historians, it nonetheless holds an important place in the development of modern Irish historiography, being among the first attempts at an extensive, interpretative, and dispassionate study of the separatist movement. While his own ideological perspective often intrudes, his appetite for accuracy in detail and fairness in assessment was notable for one working so close to, and as an actual actor in, wrenching, divisive, and emotive events. Writing for a popular audience, in his mature work he revised certain of the shibboleths and sentimentality of official nationalist myth that his own earlier work had helped to generate. A gentle, erudite man, whose favourite recreation was bookshop prowling, he was generous in his assistance to fellow researchers. Ryan married (1933) Sarah Hartley, from northern England; they had no children. He died after a long illness at Baggot Street hospital, Dublin, on 23 December 1964. His papers are deposited in UCD archives.

Lawrence William White

Sources

Desmond Ryan, *The man called Pearse* (1919); Louis N. Le Roux, *Patrick H. Pearse* (1932); Desmond Ryan, *Remembering Sion* (1934); F. X. Martin (ed.), *The Irish Volunteers 1913–1915: recollections and documents* (1963), 21; Max Caulfield, *The Easter rebellion* (1964); *Irish Independent*, 24 December 1964 (obit., photo); *Irish Times*, 24 December 1964 (obit., photo); GRO (death cert.); F. X. Martin (ed.), *The Easter rising and University College, Dublin* (1966); John M. Heuston, *Headquarters Battalion Easter week 1916* (1966), 63; Patrick Lynch, introduction to Desmond Ryan, *The Fenian chief* (1967), pp xi–xxv; F. X. Martin (ed.), *Leaders and men of the Easter rising: Dublin 1916* (1967); F. X. Martin, '1916 – myth, fact, and mystery', *Studia Hibernica*, vii (1967), 28–9; Piaras F. Mac Lochlainn, *Last words: letters and statements of the leaders executed after the rising at Easter 1916* (1971), 24–6, 30; Ruth Dudley Edwards, *Patrick Pearse: the triumph of failure* (1977); Michael Gallagher, *The Irish Labour Party in transition, 1957–82* (1982); Sean O'Mahony, *Frongoch: university of revolution* (1987); W. K. Anderson, *James Connolly and the Irish left* (1994); *1916 rebellion handbook* (1998 ed.); information from NUI archive

Francis Shaw

1907–70

Francis Shaw, Jesuit priest, Celtic scholar and historical polemicist, was born 26 March 1907 in Mullingar, Co. Westmeath, the fourth child among four sons and two daughters of Patrick Walter Shaw (1872–1940), merchant, and his wife Mary 'Minnie' (née Galligan). The Shaws were a leading Mullingar business dynasty; Patrick Walter Shaw owned several premises in the town (and a number of racehorses) and sat on a number of public bodies, including Mullingar town commissioners and Westmeath County Council; he chaired Westmeath County Board of Health. In local politics, the Shaw family formed a distinctive faction independent of both the local Redmondite organisation and the radical dissident group led by Laurence Ginnell. P. W. Shaw, however, endorsed the support expressed by John Redmond for the Allies in the first world war and addressed several recruiting meetings. He was a Cumann na nGaedheal TD for Longford–Westmeath (1923–33).

From an early age Francis Shaw took a strong interest in the Irish language, and was awarded fifteen prizes and medals at local and national feiseanna. He was educated at Mullingar Christian Brothers' School and Terenure College, Dublin. The latter school was chosen because its Carmelite proprietors were willing to make allowances for his frail health by letting him sleep in a single room rather than a dormitory. Shaw's health problems were chronic; late in life he stated he had hardly ever had a pain-free day.

On 1 September 1924 Shaw entered the Jesuit novitiate at Tullabeg, Rahan, Co. Offaly, and after his first profession (21 November 1926) undertook his juniorate studies at the Jesuit residence in Rathfarnham Castle, Dublin, where Fr Lambert McKenna encouraged him to pursue a career in Celtic studies. In 1929 Shaw graduated from UCD with first-class honours in Celtic studies, winning a postgraduate scholarship and a Mansion House Fund scholarship in Irish language and literature; at UCD he wrote for the college magazine, the *National Student*. In 1930 he won a travelling scholarship in Celtic studies, and in 1931 graduated MA with first-class honours (his principal areas of study being Irish history and the Welsh language). He studied philosophy at the Ignatius Kolleg (the German Jesuit house of studies) at Valkenburg (near Limburg) in the Netherlands (1930–32), where his mentors included Osborn Bergin; Eoin MacNeill, whose lectures Shaw recalled as 'unorthodox and unpredictable...they taught in action the way of research' (Martin and Byrne (1973), 303); Rudolf Thurneysen, under whom he also studied at the University of Bonn (1932–3; he returned to Ireland prematurely because of ill health); and T. F. O'Rahilly.

Shaw's presence in Germany during the Nazi seizure of power contributed to his abiding distaste for that movement. In 1935 he sparked public controversy by suggesting at a meeting in UCD that advocates of Irish-medium education for English-speaking children displayed a narrow nationalism comparable to Nazism; in April 1936 he published an article in the *National Student* denouncing Nazi persecution of Catholicism, the regime's general lawlessness, and the writings of Nazi ideologue Alfred Rosenberg (1893–1946):

> this farrago of impiety, stupidity and ludicrous ignorance of history...a religion of race and racial hatreds, founded on pseudo-scientific theories which are discredited by all serious historians and ethnologists.

Shaw undertook further study at UCD (1933–6); in 1934 he produced a highly praised edition of the Old Irish text *Aisling Oengusso*. During his studies at UCD he regularly presented papers to the Irish-language student society Cumann Liteardha na Gaeilge and taught at the Irish-language summer college in Ballingeary, Co. Cork. He studied theology at the Jesuit faculty in Milltown Park, Dublin (1936–40), where he was ordained priest on 31 July 1939. He was allowed to substitute a long retreat for tertianship studies because of his ill health, and became a professed Jesuit on 24 December 1945. From autumn 1940 until his death Shaw lived in the Jesuit community at 35 Lower Leeson Street, Dublin, of which he was superior (1945–51); he annually constructed the Christmas crib in its chapel. He was also a consultor of the Irish Jesuit province (1947–53).

Shaw initially expected to spend some years on research after ordination. In March 1941, however, he was appointed professor of early and mediaeval Irish at UCD in succession to Bergin through the influence of D. A. Binchy, and held this post for the remainder of his life. Later in 1941 he was appointed to the board of the Institute for Advanced Studies, and in 1942 was elected MRIA. Shaw was a painstaking teacher, and assisted foreign students with evening tuition, often in their own languages. His sense of humour and combative argumentation brightened his lectures and survives in such published remarks as his dismissal of the wilder theories of the archaeologist R. A. S. Macalister regarding cross-cultural parallels:

> The swastika in Dublin is associated with laundrying [a reference to the well-known Swastika Laundry]. Therefore the Nazi movement is the cult of hygiene and Hitler is a soap-and-water god! (*Studies* (June 1935), 320).

Shaw's devotion to teaching, combined with his poor health, meant that his research interests (mediaeval Irish medical tracts, whose significance in pioneering a simplified Irish free from the inflated rhetoric of the bardic schools he held to be greatly undervalued; ancient Irish clothing, houses and social life generally; the history of Celtic scholarship) found expression only in occasional publications, including articles and book reviews, in the Jesuit journal *Studies* and similar outlets. Shaw remarked that whenever he set about reducing his collection of typewritten transcripts of medieval medical texts to coherence he had to go to hospital.

Shaw was an outspoken opponent of T. F. O'Rahilly's thesis on the existence of two St Patricks, both on scholarly and devotional grounds: he held that mediaeval miracle tales and scholarly positivism alike hindered recognition of the deep interior spirituality found in the 'Confession' and 'Letter to Coroticus'. He was scathing about scholars who (unlike his hero MacNeill) relied on printed editions (often outdated) rather than reading manuscripts. A recurring theme is that vague and ignorant romanticisation hinders the Irish nation from recognising authentic heroes such as George Petrie, Eugene O'Curry and Johann Kaspar Zeuss.

Shaw held the view, common among social historians, that history paid too much attention to the powerful and articulate and should explore the experience of the common people. He was encouraged in this by love of country sports and the fields and rivers of his native lake country; he praised his fellow Westmeath man Fr Paul Walsh for supporting his topographical studies by walking the land, and claimed that MacNeill, as an Antrim 'countryman', understood Ireland better than did the urban Patrick Pearse and James Connolly. As he grew older, he felt his own lifetime had witnessed the end of an immemorial rural Irish way of life, whose traces, he hoped, would at least be preserved in the records of the Folklore Commission. He thought that popular commercial culture, particularly from America, was debasing public taste, and lamented that the authentic romance and heroism found in lives of saints and missionaries were being eclipsed by the synthetic Hollywood varieties. In 1942 he published a pamphlet criticising the novel and film *Gone with the wind* for excessive 'realism' in their depictions of sexuality and childbirth and for superficiality in their depictions of Catholicism. His rousing defence of literary censorship against 'long-haired intellectuals' appealed to readers to keep the faith even if the European war subjected Ireland to the same devastation as that suffered by the defeated states of the American south.

Shaw attributed the totalitarian movements of the twentieth century to the efforts of ideologues to force common humanity into utopian projects. His scepticism of state power was influenced by contemporary Catholic social thought, and he saw Irish identity as essentially Catholic; but, though this forms a subtext in his 1963 article on the essentially Roman nature of early Irish spirituality and his analysis of the 'Celtic twilight' of W. B. Yeats as owing more to Macpherson's Ossian (mediated through Arnold and Renan), the rhetorical inflation of Standish James O'Grady, and 'the charlatan Blavatsky and Brahman philosophers' than to the authentic past as revealed by Celtic scholarship, Shaw was not a bigot. Throughout his career he lauded Protestant scholars such as Edmund Curtis, John Gwynn, and Douglas Hyde; he admired Pope John XXIII and welcomed his attempt to open the Catholic church to the world.

Shaw took a strong interest in radio for religious purposes and popular education; he gave several 'retreats for the sick' on Radio Éireann, encouraging listeners to mentally re-enact, in Ignatian style, the life of Jesus, and he contributed to the Thomas Davis lecture series on early Ireland. He also wrote on spiritual and other matters for the Jesuit devotional magazine, the *Sacred Heart Messenger*, and was active in An Rioghacht (the League of the Kingship of Christ) and the Sodality of the Sacred Heart. His illness gave him a particular interest in ministry to the sick; he was a frequent hospital visitor, and directed the sodality of the nursing staff at St Vincent's Hospital (1944–59). He was popular as a confessor and spiritual adviser, and frequently mediated family disputes in local households.

Dean of the faculty of Celtic studies in UCD (1964–70), he served in the NUI senate (1963–70), and was spoken of as a possible successor to Michael Tierney as president of UCD; he served as interim president after Tierney's resignation in 1964, but did not seek the post. During the 'gentle revolution' protests of the late 1960s, Shaw supported the 'establishment' group around President J. J. Hogan, and his defeat in UCD governing body elections in December 1969 strengthened advocates of greater student participation in university governance. After a year's illness, Shaw died in a Dublin nursing home on 23 December 1970, and was buried in the Jesuit plot in Glasnevin cemetery.

Shaw's posthumous fame rests on an article published two years after his death. He had been invited to contribute an essay to the spring 1966 issue of *Studies* (commemorating the 1916 rising), but his 10,000-word article, 'Cast a cold eye...prelude to a commemoration of 1916', was turned down by the journal's editor (Fr Burke Savage) and the Jesuit provincial as over-long and inopportune. Shaw acquiesced, but prepared a 20,000-word version which circulated in typescript. In 1971 a copy was acquired by the New Ulster Movement (precursor of the Alliance party), which saw the piece as directly relevant to the developing Northern Ireland troubles, and gave it further informal circulation. Under these circumstances, Fr Troddyn (editor of *Studies*) and the provincial decided that official publication would reassert their copyright and assist understanding of Irish current affairs; the article appeared in the summer 1972 issue of *Studies* (vol. lxi, no. 242, pp 113–53) under the title (chosen by Troddyn) 'The canon of Irish history: a challenge'.

In 'The canon of Irish history', Shaw attacks the four last pamphlets produced by Patrick Pearse in 1915–16 to justify the forthcoming Easter rising. The pamphlets, Shaw contends, equate the Gaelic tradition with physical-force separatism as the 'gospel of Irish nationality', with Wolfe Tone, Thomas Davis, James Fintan Lalor, and John Mitchel as its 'four evangelists'; claim that John Redmond and his political allies committed national apostasy in accepting home rule rather than full independence as a final settlement; and equate the rebels, precipitating war and their own deaths to redeem a corrupted Ireland, with Jesus crucified to redeem sinful humanity. Shaw argues that Pearse projected Standish James O'Grady's essentially pagan concept of heroism and a modern republican ideology essentially alien to Irish society onto the Gaelic past; that Pearse and his allies denied and betrayed the concrete achievements and genuine patriotism of others, particularly Redmond and MacNeill; that Pearse, and by extension the whole physical-force republican tradition, engaged in blasphemous self-deification to justify imposing their will on the majority in a manner reminiscent of twentieth-century fascism and communism; and that the independent Irish state owes more to an older and broader popular sense of Irish nationality, which Redmond and MacNeill represented, than the irreligious and destructive mindset of Tone and Pearse.

'The canon' sums up the concerns of Shaw's lifetime. Its critique of Pearse resembles his 1930s critique of Yeats; its invocation of the horrors

of twentieth-century European history reflects his longstanding sensitivity to those horrors; its vaguely defined but essentially Catholic and rural-populist version of Irish identity reflects Shaw's lifelong self-presentation as spokesman and servant of the plain people of Ireland; and Redmond and MacNeill are cast, like Zeuss and Petrie, as heroes unjustly forgotten by those enjoying the fruits of their labours.

In 1966 Shaw had concluded his essay by hoping that recent moves towards north-south reconciliation indicated that both parts of Ireland, north and south, as well as Ireland and Britain, might recognise their commonalities and join in preserving the best in their cultures from American commercial cosmopolitanism. The essay's publication six years later, at the height of the Northern Ireland troubles, coincided with intensive debate (associated with such figures as Conor Cruise O'Brien (1917–2008)) about whether traditional Irish nationalist self-images had contributed to the conflict in Northern Ireland and threatened to unleash similar conflict in the Republic; this context gave the essay an explosive impact. An *Irish Times* editorial (11 September 1972) noted that Shaw's view of Pearse as a destructive ideologue comparable to Rosenberg raised awkward questions about numerous eulogies of Pearse as a model Christian patriot: 'Has every other cleric been wrong and only Father Shaw been right?' The Jesuits were accused by Cruise O'Brien of opportunism in suppressing Shaw's piece until it became convenient to distance the Catholic church from militant nationalism (*New York Review of Books*, 25 January 1973), and by an *Irish Press* editorialist (1 September 1972) of re-enacting previous clericalist betrayals of Irish nationalism: 'The name of Pearse will easily survive this modern Shavian broadside.'

Shaw's essay has been subjected to extensive critique (Lyons, Lee, Ó Snodaigh) over its failures to place Pearse in context and to address the place of Irish Protestants and unionists in Irish nationality; its dismissive attitude to republicanism and socialism; and its over-simplistic view that pre-1916 Ireland was a democracy. (Shaw also unduly minimises the political differences between Redmond and MacNeill.) It is still, however, regularly cited in debates about the relationship between nationalism and Irish historiography; when *Studies* marked its centenary by publishing a selection of essays from past issues, Shaw's essay was singled out by former Taoiseach John Bruton as 'the most startling essay in the volume'. Some who praised Shaw's critique of Pearse's sacrificial politics were advocates of a secularist liberalism which would have horrified Shaw, and the essay survived, when the man behind it was virtually forgotten, into an Ireland whose social and political attitudes he would have found unrecognisable.

Shaw's papers are held at the Irish Jesuit Archives, 35 Lower Leeson Street (reference J451), which also has files concerning the 1972 publication of 'The canon of Irish history" (CM/LEES/359, 383). A miniature plaster side-portrait by the sculptor Gary Trimble is held in the same building.

Patrick Maume

Sources

Westmeath Examiner, 24 October, 8 November 1931; 28 July 1934; 16 March, 21 September 1940; 15 March 1941; *Irish Times*, 10 September, 2 October 1964; 11 December 1969; 11 September 1972 (includes F. S. L. Lyons, 'The shadow of the past', p. 12, on Shaw's 'The canon'); Marian Keaney, *Westmeath authors: a bibliographical and biographical study* (1969), 174–6; *Irish Independent*, 25–8 December 1970; obituary, by Fr Francis Finnegan, *Irish Province News* (1971), 76–8; M. Proinséas Ní Catháin, 'The academic and other writings of Rev. Professor Francis Shaw, SJ', *Studies*, lx, no. 238 (summer 1971), 203–7 [list is incomplete]; *Studia Celtica*, vii (1972), 177; Francis Shaw, 'MacNeill the person', in F. X. Martin and F. J. Byrne (ed.), *The scholar revolutionary: Eoin MacNeill, 1867–1945, and the making of the new Ireland* (1973), 299–311 (includes note on contributor, p. 300); *Lochlann*, vi (1974) [supplement to *Norsk Tidsskrift for Sprogvidenskap*, xi], 180–81; Pádraig Ó Snodaigh, *Two godfathers of revisionism: 1916 in the revisionist canon* (1991); Diarmuid Breathnach and Máire Ní Mhurchú, *1882–1982: Beathaisnéis*, iii (1992), 152–3; J. J. Lee, '"The canon of Irish history: a challenge" reconsidered', in Toner Quinn (ed.) *Desmond Fennell: his life and work* (2001), 57–82; Philip O'Leary, *Gaelic prose in the Irish Free State 1922–1939* (2004), 52; Michael Wheatley, *Nationalism and the Irish party: provincial Ireland 1910–1916* (2005); Bryan Fanning (ed.), *An Irish century:* Studies *1912–2012* (2012); John Bruton, remarks at launch of Bryan Fanning (ed.), *An Irish century*, 21 March 2012, www.john-bruton.com/2012/03/irish-century-studies-1912-2012.html (accessed 27 June 2012)

Francis Sheehy-Skeffington

1878–1916

Francis Sheehy-Skeffington, radical, was born Francis Skeffington on 23 December 1878, in Bailieborough, Co. Cavan, only child of Joseph Bartholomew Skeffington, inspector of schools, and his wife Rose (née Magorian). He was brought up in Downpatrick, Co. Down. Educated privately by his father, he was emotionally closer to his mother, who came from a poor farming family and was eighteen years older than the forceful husband whose condescension she endured. J. B. Skeffington believed education, logic and discipline solved all problems, and his son brought these characteristics into conflict with some of his father's beliefs. From the time he was eleven years old, W. T. Stead's *Review of Reviews* became the boy's 'bible'. Through Stead, he adopted J. S. Mill's feminism and the belief that women's suffrage was vital for the triumph of social reform and public probity. Many of his opinions and exhibitionist tactics derived from Stead, who perished in 1912 on the *Titanic*.

Skeffington studied modern languages at UCD from 1896 to 1902, graduating BA (1900) and MA (1902). He arrived in college as a non-smoking teetotaller, vegetarian and anti-vivisectionist, pacifist and feminist. His nonconformity was marked by his refusal to shave and his distinctive garb: a rough tweed suit with knee-breeches, a collarless shirt, long stockings and large boots. College contemporaries were amused and intimidated by his tendency to take casual remarks as expressions of heartfelt opinion, engaging the speaker in fierce argument or pressing him to defend his views in public.

Skeffington took a leading role in reviving the college Literary and Historical Society, becoming auditor for 1897–8, having beaten James Fitzgerald-Kenney by one vote. Through it he befriended both James Joyce, who portrayed him as McCann in *Stephen Hero* and *A portrait of the artist as a young man*, and Tom Kettle. He clashed with Joyce on sex, on W. B. Yeats's *Countess Cathleen* (which Skeffington thought an insult to Ireland), and on Stead's petition in support of the Hague peace conference. Joyce called Skeffington the second most intelligent man in college, but saw his worldview, like those of Catholics and ultra-nationalists, as distorting individual lives in the name of abstract heroism. Joyce and Skeffington issued in pamphlet form (1901) articles that were refused publication in the student magazine, *St Stephen's*.

A keen mountain climber, walker and swimmer, Skeffington believed that vigorous physical exercise was preferable to 'unnatural' stimuli. These exercises were undertaken to maintain sexual continence, not only from religious motives (he was an increasingly sceptical Catholic who became an atheist *c*.1902), but also because of his firm belief in personal responsibility. With J. S. Mill he held the view that the world was overpopulated and the emancipation of women would remedy this by turning them from concentration on reproduction to a broader range of interests. He thought intellectual development reduced the sexual drive and disapproved of artificial contraception on 'aesthetic' grounds and because he believed it facilitated irresponsibility and exploitation. However, he opposed a 1911 campaign against risqué English newspapers as a clericalist attack on free speech.

At college Skeffington also made the acquaintance of Hanna Sheehy, daughter of David Sheehy, MP. They reinforced each other's feminist beliefs, became engaged in 1900 and married on 27 June 1903, assuming each other's surnames to become Sheehy-Skeffington. Their partnership was based on deep intellectual and emotional ties and soon after their marriage Hanna adopted her husband's atheism, trying to persuade her siblings to follow suit.

After teaching at St Kieran's College, Kilkenny, Skeffington became the first lay registrar of UCD in 1902. He resigned in 1904 after publicly criticising the college's reluctance to admit women on equal terms with men. Thereafter he and Hanna supported themselves precariously on his freelance journalism and her teaching. He was Irish correspondent for the *Manchester Guardian*, *L'Humanité* and the *Daily Herald*, and wrote non-political articles for the *Freeman's Journal*. He also wrote undistinguished fiction—notably an historical novel, *In dark and evil days*, under the pseudonym 'Christopher Francis'.

The couple had one son, Owen Sheehy-Skeffington, born 19 May 1909. Hanna suffered severe medical problems during the pregnancy, which, she recorded before the birth, was the result of a deliberate decision to which she fully consented. They raised their son without religious education and also refused to have him vaccinated. Conor Cruise O'Brien later expressed horror at reminiscences of how Francis locked Owen in a dark room as a 'humane' substitute for corporal punishment; in fact he believed corporal punishment acceptable in early childhood and it was Hanna who opposed it.

Despite strong links with British radicals, Sheehy-Skeffington refused to consider a career abroad, believing that his duty lay in Ireland. He saw Irish nationalism as inherently democratic, challenging a bureaucratic *ancien régime* which he regarded as the natural ally of 'clericalism'. Michael Davitt was one of his heroes, and he opposed the conciliationist policy of William O'Brien as appeasing aristocrats. He co-founded the Young Ireland branch (YIB) of the United Irish League (UIL) in 1904, and in 1906 was assistant editor of the short-lived weekly *Nationist*, intended as a mouthpiece for the YIB and rival to D. P. Moran's *Leader*. Here he first published 'dialogues of the day', commenting on public affairs. These continued in pamphlet form, in the short-lived *National Democrat* (1907), which he co-founded to continue Davitt's campaign for secular education, in the *Irish Peasant* of W. P. Ryan in 1907, and in the *Irish Nation*, also run by Ryan from 1908 to 1910. Sheehy-Skeffington published a biography of Davitt in 1908, stressing Davitt's clashes with the clergy and his commitment to a principled radicalism not confined by national chauvinism. He was refused access to Davitt's papers and produced a selective and idealised portrait. Arthur Griffith accurately criticised his claim that Davitt had never departed from fairness and dignity in his attacks on Charles Stewart Parnell in 1890 and 1891. Sheehy-Skeffington, however, distrusted cultural nationalism as reactionary, and opposed the Gaelic League as he thought Irish was inferior to Esperanto.

The Sheehy-Skeffingtons were co-founders in 1908 of the Irish Women's Franchise League (IWFL) and regularly addressed meetings in the Phoenix Park, Francis adding a 'Votes for Women' badge to his characteristic costume. He joined the Socialist Party of Ireland in 1909, but retained membership of the UIL until May 1912, when he resigned in protest at the Irish party's refusal to include women's suffrage in the home rule bill. Later that month, he and Hanna co-founded the suffragist weekly *Irish Citizen*, becoming sole proprietors early in 1913. The IWFL adopted militant tactics: Hanna was imprisoned twice, while Francis adopted disguises to heckle Asquith and Bonar Law on their visits to Dublin. The AOH retaliated for denunciations of John Redmond by beating up suffragists and dispersing their meetings; when participants in a Phoenix Park meeting were chased into the zoo, the *Leader* published a widely circulated verse, 'Skeffy in the zoo', accompanied by a cartoon of Sheehy-Skeffington at the chimpanzees' tea party.

He came into renewed conflict with the AOH during the 1913 lockout for his vehement support of the strikers. He attacked clerical claims that a proposal to send strikers' children to Liverpool was a form of proselytisation, and he was stripped and beaten by Hibernians while smuggling children onto a train at Kingsbridge (later Heuston) station in Dublin. He participated in the formation of the Irish Citizen Army as a workers' self-defence force, though he resigned early in 1914 over its increasing militarisation and ties with the nationalist Irish Volunteers.

As a nationalist, a pacifist and a radical, he opposed war in 1914. He feared that an Allied victory would strengthen the autocratic tsarist empire at the expense of a relatively advanced Germany, and a triumphant Britain would become aggressively imperialist and repress Ireland. The war added to his financial problems by cutting off freelance work, while his anti-war stance alienated political donors. Imprisoned on 29 May 1915 for making anti-recruiting speeches, he went on hunger and thirst strike after his conviction on 9 June, and even the *Leader* called for all possible action to save his life. After his release on 16 June under the 'cat and mouse act', to evade re-arrest he went to England and thence to the USA. From August to December 1915 he worked with feminist and separatist groups there, trying unsuccessfully to raise funds for the *Irish Citizen*.

Although Sheehy-Skeffington's pacifism did not imply absolute non-resistance (he believed sections of officialdom contemplated 'a military pogrom', which the Volunteers would be justified in resisting), he feared the Volunteers were developing militarist tendencies and preferred to encourage passive resistance through a campaign against wartime taxation. During the 1916 rising he attempted to organise a civilian defence force to prevent looting, and showed great bravery, on one occasion attempting to rescue a wounded British officer under fire. As he was returning home on the night of 25 April 1916, the military arrested him and took him to Portobello (later Cathal Brugha) barracks, Rathmines, Dublin. Here he fell into the hands of Captain John Bowen-Colthurst, an unstable officer who took him as a hostage on a raid. On the morning of 26 April 1916, Sheehy-Skeffington and two other civilians were shot by firing squad on Bowen-Colthurst's orders. One of the last persons to see him alive was Monk Gibbon, who had imagined him an eccentric but was lastingly impressed by his 'greatness' and 'conscious dignity'. Sheehy-Skeffington had insured his life for £500 in 1915, which covered his debts, and the *Irish Citizen* continued after his death.

Bowen-Colthurst subsequently raided the Sheehy-Skeffingtons' house, seeking evidence to justify his actions. A court martial found him guilty but insane, and after a brief confinement he emigrated to Canada. Bowen-Colthurst may have genuinely suffered from temporary insanity, but official inquiries were highly inadequate and their attempts to minimise the crime consolidated Sheehy-Skeffington's fame as a nationalist martyr. His career is overshadowed by his death and disputes about whether Hanna's subsequent political development continued or betrayed his legacy. A distinctively Edwardian rationalist radical, he himself agreed that he was a crank—'a small instrument that makes revolutions'.

Patrick Maume

Sources

Francis Sheehy-Skeffington, *In dark and evil days* (1916), with a biographical preface by Hanna Sheehy-Skeffington; Richard Ellmann, *James Joyce* (1982, rev. ed.); Leah Levenson, *With wooden sword: a portrait of Francis Sheehy-Skeffington, militant pacifist* (1983); Margaret Ward, *Hanna Sheehy Skeffington: a life* (1997); Conor Cruise O'Brien, *Memoir: my life and themes* (1999); James Meenan (ed.), *Centenary history of the Literary and Historical Society* (2005 ed.)

Margaret Skinnider

1893–1971

Margaret Skinnider, republican, teacher, and trade unionist, was born in Glasgow, Scotland, to immigrant parents from Co. Monaghan. Qualifying as a teacher at Craiglockhart, she taught mathematics in Glasgow's Hillhead district. Active in the women's suffrage movement, she joined the Glasgow branches of both the Irish Volunteers and Cumann na mBan (c.1914). At the outbreak of the first world war, she joined a women's rifle club, becoming an expert shot. Invited to Dublin at Christmas 1915 by Countess Markievicz, who had heard of her Glasgow activities, she smuggled detonators concealed in her hat, then tested them with Markievicz in the Dublin mountains. Joining the Irish Citizen Army (ICA), she participated in raids for explosives and exercised her mathematical skills by drawing from observation detailed maps to scale of Beggars Bush and Portobello military barracks for use by the republican insurgents. Declaring that she could pass for a boy 'even if it came to wrestling or whistling' (Skinnider, 20), she proved the assertion by accompanying a troop of Fianna Éireann cadets about the city, dressed in their uniform.

Alerted by Markievicz to the imminence of the rising, she returned to Dublin from Glasgow at the commencement of her Easter 1916 school holidays. She manufactured cartridges in Liberty Hall, and conveyed a message to Belfast (Thursday 20 April), accompanying family members

of James Connolly to Dublin the following morning. During Easter week she served in the ICA's St Stephen's Green contingent under the command of Michael Mallin, with Markievicz second-in-command; an advance scout, she was the first of the contingent on the Green. Detailed as dispatch rider, she travelled by bicycle dressed in women's clothing to arouse less suspicion (though often drawing hostile fire), but changed into ICA uniform breeches while taking turns on sniper duty in the Royal College of Surgeons. When Mallin rejected her plan to hurl a bomb from a passing bicycle into the British-occupied Shelbourne Hotel as too risky for a woman, she argued that, as women were equal with men under the Irish Republic, they had an equal right to risk their lives. While engaged in a sortie attempting to fire a building in Harcourt Street to cut off the retreat of a British sniping party, she was shot and critically wounded (Wednesday 26 April). Attended in the College of Surgeons for four days with her life in the balance, she was removed to St Vincent's Hospital immediately before the garrison's surrender. The most serious woman casualty among the insurgents, she spent seven weeks recovering in hospital; arrested briefly and questioned, she was released through the intervention of the hospital's head doctor. Deceiving the authorities with her Scottish accent, she obtained a travel permit to Glasgow.

While speaking in America on a Cumann na mBan propaganda tour (1917–18), she wrote an account of her part in the rising, *Doing my bit for Ireland* (1917). Back in Ireland, she trained Volunteer recruits and was otherwise active with Cumann na mBan through the war of independence (1918–21). An opponent of the Anglo–Irish treaty, she was IRA paymaster general until her arrest, whereupon she was incarcerated in Mountjoy jail and North Dublin Union (1922–3). Her republican activities notwith-standing, she obtained a teaching position, which she held until retirement, in the Irish Sisters of Charity national school, King's Inns Street, Dublin (c.1923–61). Increasingly active in the Irish National Teachers' Organisation (INTO), she campaigned over many years for equal pay and status for women teachers. During the six-month 1946 teachers' strike, she served on the strike executive committee, then on the salaries and arbitration committee established in the aftermath. Her efforts were instrumental in securing common incremental salary scales for women and single men (1949). She served INTO as central executive committee member (1949–61), vice-president (1955–6) and president (1956–7), in the latter office representing Ireland at the world conference of the Organisation of the Teaching Profession (Manila, Philippines). On her retirement from teaching, she served on the Irish Congress of Trade Unions executive council (1961–3).

Skinnider was unmarried. She resided at 3 Sion Road, Glenageary, Co. Dublin. She died on 11 October 1971, and was buried beside Countess Markievicz in the republican plot, Glasnevin cemetery.

Lawrence William White

Sources

Margaret Skinnider, *Doing my bit for Ireland* (1917) (portrait frontispiece); R. M. Fox, *History of the Irish Citizen Army* (1943), 136, 158, 164, 230; Max Caulfield, *The Easter rebellion* (1964); *Irish Press*, supplement, 9 April 1966 (photo); T. J. O'Connell, *History of the Irish National Teachers' Organisation 1868–1968* (1968) (photo opposite 208, 232); *Irish Times*, 12 October 1971 (obit.); Frank Robbins, *Under the starry plough: recollections of the Irish Citizen Army* (1977); Uinseann MacEoin (ed.), *Survivors* (1980); Margaret Ward, *Unmanageable revolutionaries: women and Irish nationalism* (1983); Andrée Sheehy Skeffington, *Skeff: the life of Owen Sheehy Skeffington 1909–1970* (1991); Donal Nevin (ed.), *Trade union century* (1994), 445; Margaret Ward, *In their own voice: women and Irish nationalism* (1995), 68–70; Kit and Cyril Ó Céirin, *Women of Ireland: a biographic dictionary* (1996); Ruth Taillon, *The women of 1916: when history was made* (1996)

Survivors: the afterlife of the Easter rising in the lives of its participants

Simply by taking place, the Easter rising irrevocably altered the political situation. The transformation of the young **Ernie O'Malley** (1897–1957) from unreflective interest in the British effort in the world war to amateur Easter week sniper, beginning his transmutation into a career as guerrilla and soldier-intellectual, reflects a wider pattern. Issues that had been deferred were forced back onto the agenda, and the revelation of how far they were from solution led to further radicalisation on all sides. Individuals and movements that had seemed in the mainstream were soon hopelessly marginalised, while previously marginal figures rose to prominence. In later years, Conor Cruise O'Brien (descended in the maternal line from the prominent Sheehy dynasty of home-rulers) famously recalled a discussion with his wife, Máire MacEntee, about whether the Easter rising had been justified, which ended with the comment that if there had been no rising his family would have been a central part of the new governing class and hers would not.

The rising seemed to change everything and to make everything possible. Just as the home-rulers-cum-land-agitators of the 1880s had swept aside a previous generation of nationalists of varying hues, the survivors of that 1880s generation were themselves swept aside. When the revolutionary wars eventually came to an end in the early 1920s, new states were in existence north and south, and elements of the social and political fabric (some dating back centuries, such as the offices of lord lieutenant and lord chancellor of Ireland) had vanished. At the same time, it was inevitable that the expectations of millennial transformation aroused by the rising would be disappointed. Much of the administrative and social machinery created under the nineteenth-century liberal state remained in place for good or ill, with a certain amount of rationalisation and refurbishment. (When the Cosgrave government in 1924 dissolved Dublin Corporation for a mixture of political and administrative reasons, Augustine Birrell, the former chief secretary, commented that he would have loved to do the same thing but nationalist opinion would never have tolerated it from British administrators.)

How far the survival of the nineteenth-century state model, with its limited powers, emphasis on low taxation and expenditure, and consignment of various social functions to private (usually religious) bodies, was an inevitable product of the dominant mindset of a Catholic-nationalist people dominated by small farmers—a mindset concealed by the rhetoric of national resurrection—and how far it reflected the hijacking or the defeat of the revolution's original aspirations by the forces of conservatism, remains a matter of dispute. Certainly, the playing out of the revolution recapitulated a generational pattern visible at intervals throughout the history of nineteenth-century Irish nationalism: the new generation, after some brief years of struggle and dominance, replicated some of their predecessors' experiences—the split, the factional disputes, the experience of remaining in place as national leaders until they had grown old and the experiences that had formed them were unknown to the restless young. There was one critical difference—namely, that the generation who came to prominence from 1916 actually achieved control of an Irish state, and it was this achievement that underlay their long survival in power.

Those who participated in the suppression of the Easter rising or in the subsequent punishment of the rebels generally were not prominent in Irish public life thereafter, although **John Lymbrick Esmonde** (1893–1958), a Redmondite MP elected in 1915 and army recruit stationed in Dublin during the rising, later became a prominent barrister and Fine Gael TD for Wexford. He was briefly considered as a possible taoiseach of the first inter-party government in 1948. The fact that this proposal was made by Seán MacBride, son of the executed John MacBride, who would have socialised with Esmonde as a fellow barrister, and who found the old Redmondite more acceptable than the Fine Gael leader and 1916 veteran Richard Mulcahy—because Esmonde was not implicated in the civil war executions of republicans and had served as defence counsel for IRA men in several trials of the 1930s and 1940s—illustrates how later divisions blurred those visible in Easter week of 1916. The persistence of a tradition of Redmondite politics and apologetics should not, however, disguise the speed with which large sections of the Catholic professional classes, and the institutions that formed them, adapted to the changed gallery of national heroes; within fifteen years, Clongowes went from celebrating Catholic contributions to the British empire to setting pupils to write panegyrics on the idealists of 1916.

Sections of the southern unionist community made similar adaptations. **William Evelyn Wylie** (1881–1964), who saw action in Easter week as a member of the TCD Officer Training Corps and acted as prosecutor during post-rising courts martial (he later claimed to have interceded in favour of some defendants, including Éamon de Valera and W. T. Cosgrave), advocated constitutional compromise as a legal adviser to the British administration during the war of independence, and enjoyed a long and distinguished career under the new regime as land judge and leading administrator of the Royal Dublin Society. Wylie left a fragmentary memoir, published in 1989 by the old IRA combatant and veteran civil servant Léon Ó Broin; it gives valuable insights into the aftermath of the

rising, but has provoked controversy over such details as Wylie's claim (probably incorrect) that Constance Markievicz broke down at her trial and pleaded 'you cannot shoot a woman'.

Unreconciled diehard unionists were less articulate, but there were exceptions. The fantasy novelist and army officer **Lord Dunsany** (1878–1957), who, as a captain in the Inniskilling Fusiliers, was wounded and captured on the first day of the rising and spent the rest of the week in Jervis Street hospital speculating whether the flames from O'Connell Street would reach it, lampooned the cult of the GPO (and many other nationalist pieties) in his 1935 novel *Up in the hills*, in which nondescript peasant guerrillas complain (since they burnt their village post office): 'We ought to get pensions too.'

DIVIDED VICTORS

In the late 1930s, W. B. Yeats speculated that after some generations of leisure and affluence a new Irish governing class would 'date their origins from the Post Office as American families date theirs from the Mayflower'. Yeats himself did much to shape retrospectively the image of the rising as a poets' rebellion deriving from the cultural revival which he himself had shaped from the 1890s (though his biographer Roy Foster has examined how the phrasing and publication context of Yeats's poems on the rising contain ambiguities, and allow for possible alternative outcomes in ways that contradict the aura of inevitability later associated with the *fait accompli*).

Of the first four heads of post-treaty Irish governments, three had fought in the Easter rising: W. T. Cosgrave in the South Dublin Union as Éamonn Ceannt's second-in-command, Éamon de Valera as commandant in Boland's Mills, and Seán Lemass in the GPO. To these might be added **Michael Collins** (1890–1922), chairman of the provisional government elected under the terms of the treaty by the parliament of Southern Ireland (regarded as subordinate, in all but technical and IRB matters, to the Dáil Éireann government under Arthur Griffith). Collins was in the GPO as Joseph Plunkett's aide-de-camp, and rose to prominence in the post-1916 leadership by his activities in the Frongoch internment camp and (after

release) the deployment of his considerable administrative and organisational skills in the Irish National Aid and Volunteers' Dependants' Fund.
These same skills were further deployed when he exercised both civilian
and military authority as minister of finance and director of intelligence
throughout the war of independence. Collins's unfavourable contrast
(privately expressed) of the poet-leaders of the 1916 rising with the professional revolutionaries Clarke and Mac Diarmada—encapsulated in his
remark at the funeral of Thomas Ashe that the rifle volley just heard was
the only appropriate speech at the grave of a Fenian—anticipated both
the development of the independence struggle and one of the lasting historiographical disputes over the essence of the rising.

The image of **William T. Cosgrave** (1880–1965) as national leader—
he was president of the Irish Free State's executive council (1922–32)
—was largely that of the administrator he had been before the rising (as
a Sinn Féin councillor he had taken an interest in the South Dublin Union
buildings, and his knowledge of their lay-out proved useful to the rebel
garrison). His government's self-projection as tough-minded technocrats
(like Cosgrave's own carefully nurtured persona as a Dublin-accented,
ordinary man of the people) was part of their claim to be inheritors of
the rising, promising to fulfil all the hopes aroused by 1916 once they had
repaired the damage inflicted by the Black and Tans and the anti-
treatyites. They portrayed themselves as a native government responsible
to the people, sweeping away the rubble of the ancient regime in the same
manner in which they oversaw the reconstruction of O'Connell Street,
and undertaking modernising infrastructural projects—notably the
Shannon scheme, opposed by prominent ex-unionists—that would never
have been undertaken by a penny-pinching Dublin Castle. Their opponents saw these technocratic pretensions as a façade—like the new
O'Connell Street that concealed the persistence of the slums—and
compared the draconian security policies of the Cosgrave regime to older
unionist rhetoric about 'resolute government', suggesting that, despite
their rebel pasts, Cosgrave and his colleagues were political and social
puppets of 'masonic' ex-unionist vested interests.

After displacing Cosgrave in 1932, **Éamon de Valera** (1882–1975)
presented himself, as did his Fianna Fáil party, as the embodiment of the

1916 rising, and his dismantling of the treaty settlement in the 1930s, culminating in wartime neutrality as the ultimate assertion of sovereignty, as the fulfilment of the traditional genealogy of Irish nationality summed up by Pearse in *The spiritual nation*. With Douglas Hyde, as the first president of Ireland, presented as 'the successor of our rightful princes', de Valera himself featured at various public commemorations as the culmination of Irish history, 'the last surviving commandant of 1916'. Opposition politicians were allowed to speak at such events only if they refrained from 'political' utterances—that is from criticising de Valera and suggesting he was not in fact the culmination of Irish history and his government the only legitimate heir of the 1916 leaders.

De Valera's long tenure of power began as leader of the revived Sinn Féin movement from 1917 until the treaty debacle of 1922. After his decade-long interregnum as political chief of anti-treaty abstentionism and then (from 1926) founder-leader of the 'slightly constitutional' Fianna Fáil, he held power as head of government for most of the period from 1932 until his retirement to the presidency in 1959, where he remained as ceremonial figurehead for a further fourteen years. Such an extended grasp of power was based on much more than his personal record. It reflected a subtle political intelligence, significant leadership skills, and an ability to present himself not only as the embodiment of the plain people of Ireland—selectively recalling his childhood in a labourer's cottage in Bruree—but also as a romantic and exotic figure with the Spanish name and heavy cloak, and as an authority figure with a certain air of the priest he had almost become. Nevertheless, he would not have had the opportunity to make use of those skills had he, a young mathematics teacher, not been drawn into the Volunteer movement from 1914, had he not risen to the rank of commandant and been placed in charge of the Boland's Bakery garrison during Easter week (when some of his outposts inflicted heavy casualties on British troops coming up from the south and trying to cross the Grand Canal at Mount Street Bridge), had he not had a chance to assert his leadership among the prisoners—not only by rank, but through age, education, tactical skill and even physical stature—and then to emerge from prison in 1917 to win parliamentary election for East Clare and selection as leader of Sinn Féin.

De Valera's ability to command fervent support was matched by his capacity to provoke bitter enmity, often from people who had previously revered him. Some of this enmity found expression in inquiring whether his 1916 record might be less heroic than his eulogists claimed. How far had he been complicit in the attempts to save him from execution after the rising by pointing out that his American birth entitled him to American citizenship (a fact often cited, with varying degrees of crudity, to dispute his pretensions to represent quintessential Irishness)? There is evidence that de Valera escaped execution because he was regarded by officialdom as relatively insignificant, but the fact that the British and American governments habitually denounced as murder the deaths of American citizens travelling on belligerent vessels sunk by German submarines may have contributed to his survival. Why did de Valera not reinforce the small number of defenders at Mount Street Bridge? Rather, he held his main force in reserve to defend against a direct attack that never came, as British commanders chose to bypass outlying garrisons and strike at the rebel nerve centre in central Dublin. Did de Valera's inaction derive from a nervous breakdown when faced with the realities of warfare and the prospect of commanding troops in action, as some garrison members claimed in accounts made public after his death? Was he even, in fact, the last surviving commandant of the rising? In 1917 an appeal to American opinion was signed by de Valera, Thomas Ashe and Thomas Hunter (more usually described as vice-commandant to MacDonagh) on the grounds that they were the three surviving commandants; the title was also disputed by the chronically discontented W. J. Brennan-Whitmore, who after de Valera's death took to describing himself as 'last surviving commandant'—though whatever his actual rank, he had not commanded a major garrison as de Valera had.

When in 1953 the *Irish Weekly Independent* published a series of reflections on three decades of Irish independence under a masthead juxtaposing images of the burning GPO and of the newly constructed Busáras (the office wing of which was officially called Áras Mhic Dhiarmada), the association of neo-classical Dublin with an ancient regime displaced by the rising and of international-style modernism with the independent Irish state was visible in embryo. The modernising project of the independent

state is conventionally associated with the Ireland of the 1960s; the connecting link is **Seán Lemass** (1899–1971), de Valera's long-serving industry and commerce minister and his successor as taoiseach (1959–66), whose deployment of modernist architecture in the service of bureaucratic activism and economic renewal is symbolised by the design and the sculpted industrial iconography of the 1930s Department of Industry and Commerce building in Dublin's Kildare Street, and whose willingness to use state intervention to promote economic development (even when this involved abandoning the protectionism most national-ists—and the earlier Lemass—had seen as intrinsic to the national project) contrasts with the Gladstonianism of the immediate post-independence governments. The move from nineteenth-century liberal to twentieth-century social-democratic state model with which Lemass is associated is arguably as epochal as the achievement of political independence.

The historian J. J. Lee, who regarded Lemass as the decisive visionary who made twentieth-century Ireland, remarked in his magnum opus, *Ireland 1912–1985*, that it was sobering to think how profoundly Irish history might have been altered if the teenaged Lemass had been killed by a stray bullet in the GPO, and to wonder what contributions for good or ill might have been made by some unknowns who actually were killed. The scope for speculation of this sort is endless; for example, Lemass's future party rival, the Belfast-born engineer and litterateur **Sean MacEntee** (1889–1984), who had previously been a member of Connolly's Socialist Party of Ireland and was a published poet, was with a group of Volunteers from Dundalk who while making their way to Dublin killed a policeman at Castlebellingham. For this he was sentenced to death; had he been executed, might he now be cited as an example of a promising young radical whose death helped to account for the economic and cultural conservatism of the southern state, rather than being remembered for his election-time deployment of red scares against Labour, Clann na Talmhan and Clann na Poblachta, his Gladstonian fiscal (though not cultural) conservatism as minister for finance (1932–9, 1951–4), and his criticisms of the Beveridge report as 'state socialism' while minister with responsi-bility for health in 1941–6. (He was also minister for industry and commerce (1939–41) and minister for health (1957–65).)

A long list might be made of future revolutionaries and political or social leaders who were out in 1916: **Seán T. O'Kelly** (1882–1966), a future Fianna Fáil minister and president (1945–59), whose duties included pasting up copies of the proclamation around the city and who called himself bill-poster to the Republic; the Cork entrepreneur and Sinn Féin activist **J. J. Walsh** (1880–1948), who led the Hibernian Rifles (military wing of the separatist Irish-American alliance faction of the AOH) into action in Dublin at the GPO, who became Sinn Féin TD for Cork, then Free State postmaster general and party fixer, broke with Cumann na nGaedheal because he advocated protectionism, and in his last years was a successful businessman and employers' lobbyist and reluctant Fianna Fáil supporter; Dr **James Ryan** (1891–1970), medical officer at the GPO and hero-worshipper of Seán Mac Diarmada, from a prominent Wexford nationalist dynasty, who became an anti-treaty and Fianna Fáil TD for Wexford (1923–65), serving as a pragmatic minister for agriculture (1932–47), health (1947–8, 1951–4) and finance (1957–65), and having a son and grandson who also became public representatives.

The dichotomy between revolutionary martyrdom and survivors' governmental responsibility is illustrated by the trajectory of the brothers **Harry** (1887–1922) and **Gerald ('Gerry') Boland** (1885–1973), from an IRB family background (their father is alleged to have begun his career as a lookout at the 1867 Manchester rescue of Fenian prisoners, and to have died as a result of being hit on the head when he joined a Parnellite crowd fighting to remove anti-Parnellite staff from a newspaper office at the outbreak of the Parnell split), and themselves heavily involved in those social and political networks. In 1916 Gerry was in Jacob's factory and Harry in the GPO. The latter subsequently emerged as a leading revolutionary organiser in association with Michael Collins, working in the United States as diplomat, gun-runner and coordinator of de Valera's propaganda tour, before returning to Ireland to oppose the treaty and become a republican martyr shot under suspicious circumstances in the early days of the civil war. Gerry, a prominent Dublin IRA leader in the war of independence, succeeded Harry as a TD while still interned, became a leading Fianna Fáil organiser, and held several cabinet positions, but is chiefly remembered as a hammer of the IRA as minister for justice in 1939–48. His later years were increasingly preoccupied with the memory of Harry, and in 1970 he resigned from Fianna Fáil in solidarity with his son Kevin's view that Jack Lynch's government had betrayed republican principles by suppressing the conspiracy to arm northern nationalists. After his father's death, Kevin Boland acidly commented that it was not surprising that de Valera, who supported Lynch's actions, had proved less steadfast than the Bolands, since his republican pedigree only went back to 1916, but theirs to 'the smashing of the van' at Manchester!

The most prominent leaders of the rising outside Dublin also illustrate this dichotomy. **Thomas Ashe** (1885–1917), the talented Irish Irelander from Kerry with an extensive record of Gaelic League and separatist activity in north County Dublin (where he worked as a schoolteacher), led a column of Fingal Volunteers in a series of attacks on communications in counties Dublin, Louth and Meath during Easter week, culminating in the defeat of an RIC column at Ashbourne. In prison he emerged as a leader, playing a major role in the decision that separatists should contest elections (initially opposed by de Valera), and on release in mid 1917 became IRB president and a skilful election organiser. He might have become a major political leader; instead, he was assimilated to the developing martyr-cult of the 1916 leaders when he went on hunger strike after being imprisoned for seditious speech, and was subjected to violent force-feeding by an unskilled doctor, leading to his death in September 1917. Ashe's funeral became a major display of public support for Sinn Féin, and the inquest into his death inflicted further political damage on the Dublin Castle administration and on Redmondism. Ashe's image as martyr was reinforced by the posthumous publication of his poem 'Let me carry your cross for Ireland, Lord', with its assimilation of Ashe's anticipated death for the separatist cause to the sacrificial death of Jesus. The deep resonances of Ashe's Pearse-like invocation of Christian imagery are shown by the fact that his poem subsequently found its way into the Church of Ireland standard hymnal and is known to have been sung at least once at the dedication of an Orange banner. Even Roddy Doyle's novel *A star called Henry* (1999), in which the fictitious Sinn Féin propagandist Henry Smart is shown fabricating the poem under highly ribald circumstances, bears witness to its residual aura; one does not desecrate that which has no influence.

Richard Mulcahy (1886–1971), second-in-command and strategic brain of Ashe's north Dublin column, and also a Gaelic Leaguer, had perhaps the most prominent post-rising career of anyone who fought outside Dublin, as chief of staff of the IRA in the war of independence, and then of the Irish Free State army, cabinet member under Cosgrave (albeit out of office in 1924–7 after disputes over his handling, as defence minister, of the army mutiny), Fine Gael leader in succession to Cosgrave, broker of the 1948 inter-party government by his willingness to stand aside as taoiseach, and a somewhat nondescript minister of education under John A. Costello (1948–51, 1954–7). In his last decades, Mulcahy set about recording the reminiscences of the revolutionary generation, one of his aims being to dispute the claims of de Valera and his allies to exclusive ownership of the revolutionary heritage. Though brothers-in-law, he and Seán O'Kelly were never reconciled after the civil war; Mulcahy habitually pointed out that O'Kelly had spent most of the war of independence as a diplomat abroad, and when O'Kelly as Irish president unveiled a monument to the battle of Ashbourne, Mulcahy, the senior surviving participant, refused to attend.

The future diplomat **Robert Brennan** (1881–1964) was also a participant outside Dublin, memorialising the rebel occupation of Enniscorthy in his memoir *Allegiance* (1950). The shared roots and future divisions of those who participated in the rising are exemplified by two other Enniscorthy participants. **William Sears** (1868–1929) and **Sean Etchingham** (1870–1923) had worked together on the separatist and feminist local paper, the *Enniscorthy Echo*. They went to prison together and served in the second dáil together, but Etchingham, already dying of tuberculosis contracted in prison, delivered some of the bitterest denunciations of the treaty in the debate over its ratification, while Sears (who had sent his son David to study under Pearse at St Enda's) became a prominent though discontented Cumann na nGaedheal backbencher in the 1920s.

DISSIDENTS

The view that the post-independence state represented the true spirit of Easter week 1916 was disputed by some who had participated in it and who saw themselves as true to its spirit. Such included Marxists and social radicals, like the 'boy commandant' **Sean McLoughlin** (1895–1960), who had been present in the last stages of the retreat from the GPO and the garrison's attempted escape via Moore Street, and was later a communist activist in Ireland and Britain; or like **Liam Mellows** (1892–1922), who gathered a Volunteer force in Galway during Easter week (though it dispersed after some days having seen little in the way of fighting), and who as a prisoner during the civil war shortly before his execution expressed his views on the treaty as yet another betrayal by the men of property in terms sufficiently radical for later socialist republicans to look to him as an exemplar.

Feminists also had cause for discontent. **Kathleen Clarke** (1878–1972), widow of the executed 1916 leader Tom Clarke (whom she had met through the Fenian activism of her own father and uncle), had herself been a founding member of Cumann na mBan in 1914 and prominent in preparations for the Easter rising. The tensions between her and de Valera, which included disputes over the political and economic status of women and which ended in her political marginalisation, later led historian Owen Dudley Edwards to joke that, while Stalin had merely threatened to appoint someone other than Nadezhda Krupskaya to the post of Lenin's widow, de Valera had actually done so by replacing Mrs Clarke with Pearse's sister Margaret as party mascot embodying the Fianna Fáil claim to represent the executed leaders. Mrs Clarke's experience resembled that of some other feminists with less revolutionary pedigrees (including some whose biographies appear in this volume) who had been drawn to separatism as part of their participation in a wider counterculture defining itself against the restrictions and deferences of Edwardian Ireland, but then found the post-independence state a deep disappointment.

Other participants had fallen out with de Valera well before Clarke broke with him in the 1940s. One interpretation of the political sources of ultra-republicanism in the treaty and civil war era is that it was driven by older and marginalised 'political' Sinn Féiners anxious to compensate for military inaction in Easter week. This might be true of the hapless **Austin Stack** (1879–1929), leader of the Tralee Volunteers, who, failing to make contact with the gun-running *Aud*, made enquiries at Tralee police station after the arrest of Roger Casement, resulting in his own arrest; he remained prominent till his death in abstentionist Sinn Féin and the legitimist 'republican government' under the second dáil. A variant might be represented by the athlete, travelling salesman and Gaelic Leaguer **Cathal Brugha** (1874–1922) (like Pearse, his English name—Burgess—reflected mixed ancestry with which he was sometimes taunted, though Brugha's Protestant father had been an advanced nationalist). During the South Dublin Union fighting, Brugha was wounded several times and left behind by the retreating garrison, but held off a large number of British soldiers single-handedly while propped against a wall. This achievement, coupled with his previous Irish-Ireland record, brought him fame, a leading role in post-rising Sinn Féin, and several wounds that left him in permanent pain. As minister for defence (1919–22) he saw himself as a soldier, worked openly from his offices, and resented the encroachment of Michael Collins on military affairs. Admirers of Collins subsequently claimed that Brugha played little part in the actual war effort; Brugha's allies disputed this and suggested that Collins's fame was partly produced by public relations. Brugha was also genuinely morally concerned about the readiness of Collins and other guerrilla leaders to kill civilians on suspicion of espionage. The bitterness between Collins and Brugha spilled over into the treaty debates, where Brugha took a hardline republican position; when the civil war broke out, Brugha joined the fighting in O'Connell Street and recapitulated his actions of 1916, fighting a rearguard action, coming out with guns blazing after allowing other garrison members to surrender, and being wounded, this time fatally.

The same pattern of an old Easter week soldier, his strategies and opinions already formed, being less at ease amid post-1916 guerrillas and politicians, can be applied to the Meath-born rhymester **Brian O'Higgins** (1882–1963). A veteran of the GPO garrison, O'Higgins promptly recorded his experiences in a memoir, *The soldier's story of Easter week* (1925), and from 1918 to 1927 was de Valera's colleague as TD for Clare constituencies, but when de Valera abandoned Sinn Féin O'Higgins broke with him. To the end of his life, this diehard 'second dáil republican' maintained that the independence movement had in fact been defeated and betrayed. His repackaging of the traditional separatist view of Irish history in his widely read *Wolfe Tone Annual* (1938–62) was still sufficiently influential in the early 1960s for F. X. Martin, when calling for historical reassessment of the Easter rising, to speak of the 'Pearse–O'Higgins' view as epitomising the romanticisation which he saw as the principal obstruction to objective reconsideration.

OUT OF LIVING MEMORY

The 1966 commemorations, marking the rising's fiftieth anniversary, can be seen as the last hurrah of the revolutionary generation, a final desire to place their story on record, to honour their memories, and to proclaim them as steadfastly faithful to the ideals and aspirations of 1916. Within the next decade, nearly all the remaining survivors of 1916 who had attained prominence in the public life of the nation had passed away.

In that same decade, however, debate over the legacy of the rising was urgently renewed as new claimants to the legitimate lineage of descent from Easter week exploded upon the scene. The tone of the 1966 celebrations, extolling as exemplars the men and women who were out in 1916, contrasted sharply with the official downplaying of the physical-force tradition a few years later in response to the Northern Ireland troubles. The divisions within Ulster had helped to light the fuse for the 1916 rising, but the subjugation of northern nationalists was the great flaw of the settlement that grew out of Easter week. The Northern Ireland conflict that broke out after 1969 in reaction against that subjugation placed 1916 in a new light, and for decades thereafter discussion of the Easter rising was dominated by debate over the morality and efficacy of physical force, and haunted by the possibility that—just as the 1916 rising had doomed home rule, and the northern turmoil of the late 1960s had dispelled the pretensions of technocratic, reforming unionism—sparks from the northern troubles might ignite the social tensions and irrational attitudes lurking in the Republic.

But these fears and the disputes over the interpretation of Easter 1916 largely relate to the rising as symbol; as living memory, the rising died with the generation who experienced it.

Patrick Maume

LIST OF ABBREVIATIONS

AOH	Ancient Order of Hibernians
b.	born
BA	Bachelor of Arts
Burke, *Landed gentry*	John Burke, *A genealogical and heraldic history of the commons of Great Britain and Ireland, enjoying territorial possessions* (3 vols, London, 1833–8; reissued 1837–8 as *A genealogical and heraldic history of the landed gentry...*; variant titles in later editions)
Burke, *LGI*	Sir [John] Bernard Burke, *A genealogical and heraldic history of the landed gentry of Ireland...* (London, 1899; 4th ed. (1958) published as *Burke's genealogical and heraldic history of the landed gentry of Ireland*)
Burke, *Peerage*	J[ohn] Burke, *A general and heraldic history of the peerage and baronetage...* (London, 1826; 6th ed. (1839) published as *A genealogical and heraldic dictionary of the peerage and baronetage...*; variant titles in later editions)
c.	about (*circa*)
CBS	Christian Brothers' School
C-in-C	commander in chief
CMG	companion of the Order of St Michael and St George
d.	died
DIAS	Dublin Institute for Advanced Studies
DIB	*Dictionary of Irish Biography*
DMP	Dublin Metropolitan Police

DNB	*The dictionary of national biography*, ed. Sir Leslie Stephen and Sir Sidney Lee (66 vols, London, 1885–1901; reprint with corrections, 22 vols, London, 1908–9; supplementary vols for 1901 and after)
DNB, MP	*The dictionary of national biography: missing persons*, ed. C. S. Nicholls (Oxford and New York, 1993)
ed.	edited by, edition, editor(s)
FRCSI	fellow of the Royal College of Surgeons in Ireland
GCMG	knight or dame grand cross of the Order of St Michael and St George
GOC	general officer commanding
GPO	General Post Office
GRO	General Register Office (Dublin)
HMC	Historical Manuscripts Commission
IBL	*The Irish Book Lover* (Dublin, 1909–57, 32 vols)
ICA	Irish Citizen Army
IHS	*Irish Historical Studies: the joint journal of the Irish Historical Society and the Ulster Society for Irish Historical Studies* (Dublin, 1938–)
IRB	Irish Republican Brotherhood
ITGWU	Irish Transport and General Workers' Union
JP	Justice of the Peace
KCMG	knight commander of the Order of St Michael and St George
MA	Master of Arts
MD	Doctor of Medicine
MP	member of parliament
MRIA	member of the Royal Irish Academy
MRSAI	member of the Royal Society of Antiquaries of Ireland
NAI	National Archives of Ireland
NCO	non-commissioned officer
NGI	National Gallery of Ireland
NHI	*A new history of Ireland* (9 vols, Oxford, 1976–2005)
NLI	National Library of Ireland

NMI	National Museum of Ireland
NUI	National University of Ireland
obit.	obituary
OC	officer commanding
ODNB	*Oxford dictionary of national biography*, ed. H. C. G. Matthew and Brian Harrison (60 vols, Oxford, 2004, and online, www.oxforddnb.com)
OFM	Order of Friars Minor (Franciscan friars)
PRO	Public Record Office
QUB	Queen's University of Belfast
QUI	Queen's University of Ireland
RCSI	Royal College of Surgeons in Ireland
RDS	Royal Dublin Society
RÉ	Radio Éireann
RHA	Royal Hibernian Academy
RIA	Royal Irish Academy
RIC	Royal Irish Constabulary
RM	resident magistrate
RTÉ	Radio Telefís Éireann
RUC	Royal Ulster Constabulary
RUI	Royal University of Ireland
TCD	Trinity College, Dublin
TD	Teachta Dála (dáil deputy)
Thom, 1844 [etc.]	*Thom's Irish almanac and official directory for the year 1844* [*etc.*] (Dublin, 1844– ; subsequent changes of title)
TNA	The National Archives of the UK
TUC	Trade Union Congress
UCC	University College, Cork
UCD	University College, Dublin
UCG	University College, Galway
UU	University of Ulster

BIBLIOGRAPHY

Archives

Br Allen papers, Christian Brothers Archive, Dublin

Belfast Central Library, newscuttings collection

Bureau of Military History

Daly archives, University of Limerick

Dublin City Archives:

   Dublin Corporation, *Diaries* (1908–16)

   Reports and printed documents of the corporation of Dublin (1913, 1914)

   Minutes of the municipal council of the city of Dublin (1912, 1913)

GRO

NAI:

   Census of Ireland 1901, www.census.nationalarchives.ie

   Building and Allied Trades Union records (file 1097)

Nathan papers, Bodleian Library, Oxford

NLI:

   Allan papers

   J. J. Doyle papers (letters from Pearse)

   Minute book of Cumann na dTeachtaire (Hanna Sheehy-Skeffington collection, MS 21,194 (47))

   MacNeill papers

   Seán T. O'Kelly papers (MSS 8469; 10,192)

   Pearse papers and letters (MS 5049)

   Redmond papers

NUI archive

Royal College of Physicians of Ireland:

   Kathleen Lynn diaries and St Ultan's papers

TCD archive:

   John Dillon papers

UCD Archives:

   Eithne Coyle papers (MS P61/4)

   MacNeill papers

Commemorative publications

Coiste Cuimhneacháin na bPiarsach. *Cuimhní na bPiarsach: memories of the brothers Pearse*. Dublin: Coiste Cuimhneacháin na bPiarsach, 1958.

Con Colbert memorial: Athea, County Limerick, 1966.

Irish Press, supplement, 9 April 1966.

Irish Times, Easter Rising supplement, 7 April 1966.

Irish Transport and General Workers' Union. *Fifty years of Liberty Hall: the golden jubilee of the Irish Transport and General Workers' Union 1909–1959*. Dublin: Three Candles, 1959.

Kiberd, Declan (ed.). *1916 rebellion handbook*. Dublin: Mourne River Press, 1998.

Lennon, Michael J. 'The Easter rising from the inside', *Irish Times* 18–23 April 1949 (six parts).

National Gallery of Ireland. *Cuimhneachán 1916: a commemorative exhibition of the Irish rebellion 1916*. Dublin: NGI, 1966.

Sinn Fein rebellion handbook, Easter 1916: a complete narrative of the rising. Dublin: Irish Times, 1917.

Reference

Breathnach, Diarmuid, agus Máire Ní Mhurchú. *Beathaisnéis 1882–1982*: iii (1992), iv (1994).

Dictionary of national biography. London, 1885–1901 and supplements.

Thom. *Irish almanac and official directory*. Dublin, 1844 and subsequent years.

Flynn, William J. *The oireachtas companion and saorstát guide*. Dublin: Hely's Ltd, 1928.

Oxford dictionary of national biography. Oxford, 2004, and online.

Walker, Brian M. *Parliamentary election results in Ireland 1918–92*. Dublin: Royal Irish Academy, 1992.

Burke. *Peerage*. London, 2000.

Who's who. London, 1936.

Who was who, iii. London, 1929–1940.

Newspapers and periodicals

Capuchin Annual	*Irish Press*
Catholic Bulletin	*Irish Times*
An Claidheamh Soluis	*Leader*
Irish Book Lover	*An Phoblacht*
Irish Independent	*Studies*

Albert, Fr, OFM. 'How Seán Heuston died', *Capuchin Annual,* 1942, 343–4.

Allen, Kieran. *The politics of James Connolly.* London: Pluto Press, 1990.

Anderson, W. K. *James Connolly and the Irish left.* Dublin: Irish Academic Press, 1994.

Anonymous. 'Events of Easter week', *Catholic Bulletin* vi, 1916, 395–6.

Anonymous. 'Fighting in the South Dublin Union area', *Catholic Bulletin* viii, 1918, 153–6, 205–20, 257–60, 309–12.

Anonymous. 'Kathleen Murphy, obituary', *Journal of the Irish Medical Association* 37, 1955, 321.

Anonymous. 'The story of Limerick and Kerry in 1916', *Capuchin Annual,* 1966, 338, 359–60.

Arthur, George. *General Sir John Maxwell.* London: John Murray, 1932.

Asquith, Lady Cynthia. *Diaries, 1915–18.* London: Hutchinson, 1968.

Barton, Brian. *From behind a closed door: secret court martial records of the 1916 Easter rising.* Belfast: Blackstaff Press, 2002.

Bell, Sam Hanna. *The theatre in Ulster: a survey of the dramatic movement in Ulster from 1902 until the present day.* Totowa, New Jersey: Rowman and Littlefield, 1972.

Bew, Paul. *Conflict and conciliation in Ireland, 1890–1910: Parnellites and radical agrarians.* Oxford: Clarendon Press, 1987.

Bew, Paul. *Ideology and the Irish question: Ulster unionism and Irish nationalism, 1912–1916.* Oxford: Clarendon Press, 1996.

Birrell, Augustine. *Things past redress.* London: Faber and Faber, 1937.

Breathnach, Turlough. 'Willie Pearse and his world', *Ireland of the Welcomes* xlviii, no.4, 1999.

Binchy, D.A. 'Eoin Mac Neill', *Dictionary of national biography 1941–1950* (editor Leopold George Wickham). London: Oxford University Press, 1976.

Bonsall, Penny. *The Irish RMs: the resident magistrates in the British administration of Ireland.* Dublin, Four Courts Press, 1997.

Booth, Eva Gore- and Esther Roper. *Prison letters of Countess Markievicz.* London and New York: Longmans, Green and Co., 1934.

Bourke, Marcus. *The O'Rahilly.* Dublin: Anvil Books, 1967.

Bourke, Marcus. 'Thomas MacDonagh's role in the plans for the 1916 rising', *Irish Sword* 8, 1967–8, 178–85.

Bowen, Elizabeth. *Bowen's Court.* London: Virago, 1942.

Boylan, Henry. *A dictionary of Irish biography* (3rd ed). New York: Roberts Rinehart, 1998.

Browne, Bernard. *County Wexford connections: a biographical data on famous and infamous Wexford connections which encompasses the whole county*. Wexford: Bernard Browne, 1985.

Browne, Bernard. *Living by the pen: a biographical dictionary of County Wexford authors*. Wexford: Bernard Browne, 1997.

Bruton, John. 'Remarks at launch' of Bryan Fanning (ed.), *An Irish century*, 21 March 2012. (Available at: www.johnbruton.com/2012/03/irish-century-studies-1912-2012.html (accessed 27 June 2012)).

Callan, Charles. 'A philosopher with a slow smile: Peadar Macken, 1878–1916', *Labour History News* v, autumn 1989, 5–9.

Callanan, Frank. *The Parnell split, 1890–91*. Cork: Cork University Press, 1992.

Callanan, Frank. *T. M. Healy*. Cork: Cork University Press, 1996.

Caulfield, Max. *The Easter rebellion*. Austin, TX: Holt, Rinehart and Winston, 1964.

Clarke, Kathleen. *Revolutionary woman: Kathleen Clarke 1878–1972, an autobiography* (edited by Helen Litton). Dublin: O'Brien Press, 1991.

Clarke, Thomas. *Glimpses of an Irish felon's prison life*. Dublin and London: Maunsel and Roberts, 1922.

Colum, Padraic. *The Land: and agrarian comedy in three acts*. Dublin: Maunsel and Co., 1905.

Colum, Padraic (ed.). Introduction, in *Poems of the Irish Revolutionary Brotherhood*, ix–xxxvi: xxv–xxxi. Boston: Small, Maynard, 1916.

Colum, Padraic. 'Thomas MacDonagh and his poetry', *Dublin Magazine* v, no. 1, spring 1966, 39–45.

Conlon, Lily. *Cumann na mBan and the women of Ireland 1913–25*. Kilkenny: The Kilkenny People, 1969.

Connolly, James. *Collected works* (2 vols). Dublin: New Books Publications, 1987–8.

Corkery, Daniel. *Fohnam the sculptor: a play in a prelude and three acts* (1939). Published Newark, Delaware: Proscenium Press, Lost Play Series, no. 11, 1973.

Coxhead, Elizabeth. *Daughters of Erin: five women of the Irish renaissance*. London: Colin Smythe, 1969.

Crookes, Gearóid. *Dublin's Eye and Ear: the making of a monument*. Dublin: Town House, 1993.

Czira, Sydney. *The years flew by: the recollections of Madame Sydney Gifford Czira*. Dublin: Gifford and Craven, 1974.

Daly, Martin [Stephen McKenna]. *Memories of the dead*. Dublin: Powell Press, 1916/17?

Daly, Mary E. (ed.). *Roger Casement in Irish and world history*. Dublin: Royal Irish Academy, 2005.

de Blacam, Aodh. *Holy Romans: a young Irishman's story*. Dublin and London: Talbot Press and Maunsel and Co., 1920.

de Paor, Liam. *On the Easter proclamation and other declarations*. Dublin: Four Courts Press, 1997.

Dillon, Geraldine Plunkett. 'Joseph Plunkett', *Dublin Magazine* v, no. 1, spring 1966, 63–5.

Dillon, Geraldine Plunkett. *All in the blood: a memoir*. Dublin: A&A Farmar, 2006.

Doerries, Reinhard R. *Prelude to the Easter rising: Roger Casement in imperial Germany*. London: Frank Cass Publishers, 2000.

Dudgeon, Jeffrey. *Roger Casement: the black diaries*. Belfast: Belfast Press, 2002.

du Maurier, Guy. *An Englishman's home: a play in three acts*. New York and London: Harper and Brothers, 1909.

Dunlevy, Pearl. 'Patriot doctor—Kathleen Lynn FRCSI', *Irish Medical Times*, 4 December 1981.

Edwards, Owen Dudley. *The mind of an activist: James Connolly*. Dublin: Gill and Macmillan, 1971.

Edwards, Owen Dudley and Fergus Pyle (ed.). *1916: the Easter rising*. London: MacGibbon and Kee, 1968.

Edwards, Owen Dudley and B. Ransom (ed.). *James Connolly: selected political writings*. London: Jonathan Cape, 1968.

Edwards, Ruth Dudley. *Patrick Pearse: the triumph of failure*. London: Victor Gollancz, 1977.

Edwards, Ruth Dudley. *James Connolly*. Dublin: Gill and Macmillan, 1981.

Eichacker, Joanne Mooney. *Irish republican women in America: lecture tours 1916–1925*. Dublin: Irish Academic Press, 2003.

Ellis, Peter Berresford (ed.). *James Connolly: selected writings*. London: Pelican, 1973.

Ellmann, Richard. *James Joyce* (rev. edn). Oxford: Oxford University Press, 1982.

Fanning, Bryan (ed.). *An Irish century: Studies 1912–2012*. Dublin: University College Dublin Press, 2012.

Fanning, Ronan. *Fatal path: British government and Irish revolution 1910–1922*. London: Faber and Faber, 2013.

Farrell, Brian. 'Markievicz and the women of the revolution', in F. X. Martin, *Leaders and men of the Easter rising: Dublin 1916*, 227–303. London: Methuen Press, 1967.

Ferreira, O. J. O. 'MacBride, John', *Dictionary of South African biography*, iii. Cape Town: Tafelberg-Uitgewers, 1977.

Finnan, Joseph P. *John Redmond and Irish unity, 1912–1918*. New York: Syracuse University Press, 2004.

Finnegan, Fr Francis. 'Obituary: Fr Francis Shaw', *Irish Province News*, 1971, 76–8.

FitzGerald, Desmond. *Memoirs of Desmond FitzGerald: 1913–1916*. London: Routledge and Kegan Paul, 1968.

Foley, Conor. *Legion of the rearguard: the IRA and the modern Irish state*. London: Pluto Press, 1992.

Foster, R. F. *W.B. Yeats: a life*, i: *The apprentice mage, 1865–1914*. Oxford: Oxford University press, 1997.

Fox, R. M. *History of the Irish Citizen Army*. Dublin: J. Duff and Co., 1943.

Fox, R. M. *James Connolly: the forerunner*. Tralee: The Kerryman, 1946.

Foy, Michael and Brian Barton. *The Easter rising*. Stroud: Sutton, 1999.

Gailey, Andrew. *Ireland and the death of kindness: the experience of constructive unionism, 1890–1905*. Cork: Cork University Press, 1987.

Gallagher, Michael. *The Irish Labour Party in transition, 1957–82*. Manchester: Manchester University Press, 1982.

Gallagher, Michael. *Political parties in the Republic of Ireland*. Manchester: Manchester University Press, 1985.

Gallagher, Michael (ed.). *Irish elections 1922–44: results and analysis*. Limerick: PSAI Press, 1993.

Gaughan, J. Anthony. *Thomas Johnson 1872–1963: first leader of the Labour Party in Dáil Éireann*. Dublin: Kingdom Books, 1980.

Gaughan, J. Anthony (ed.). *The memoirs of Senator Joseph Connolly: a maker of modern Ireland*. Dublin: Irish Academic Press, 1996.

Gibbon, Monk. *Inglorious soldier*. London: Hutchinson, 1968.

Gorham, Maurice. *Forty years of Irish broadcasting*. Dublin: RTÉ and Talbot Press, 1967.

Greaves, C. Desmond. *The life and times of James Connolly*. London: Lawrence and Wishart, 1961.

Greaves, C. Desmond. *Liam Mellows and the Irish revolution*. London: Lawrence andWishart, 1971.

Greaves, C. Desmond. *The Irish Transport and General Workers' Union: the formative years 1909–1923*. Dublin: Gill and Macmillan, 1982.

Grenan, Julia. 'Events of Easter week', *Catholic Bulletin* vii, 1917, 396–8.

Gwynn, Denis. *The life of John Redmond*. Bombay and Sydney: George G. Harrap and Co., 1932.

Gwynn, Stephen. *John Redmond's last years*. London: Edward Arnold, 1919.

Haverty, Anne. *Constance Markievicz: an independent life*. London: Pandora Press, 1988.

Hay, Marnie. 'Bulmer Hobson: the rise and fall of an Irish nationalist'. Unpublished PhD thesis, UCD, 2004.

Haydon, Anthony P. *Sir Matthew Nathan: British colonial governor and civil servant.* Brisbane: University of Queensland Press, 1976.

Hayes, Alan (ed.). 'Introduction', in *The years flew by: the recollections of Madame Sidney Gifford Czira*, ix–xx. Galway: Arlen Press, 2000 (2nd ed.; originally published 1974).

Hennessy, Thomas. *Dividing Ireland: World War I and partition.* London: Routledge, 1998.

Henry, William. *Supreme sacrifice: the story of Éamonn Ceannt 1881–1916.* Cork: Mercier Press, 2005.

Herlihy, Jim. *The Dublin Metropolitan Police; a short history and genealogical guide.* Dublin: Four Courts Press, 2001.

Heuston, John M. *Headquarters battalion, army of the Irish republic Easter week 1916.* Carlow: Nationalist Printers, 1966.

Hickey, D. J. and J. E. Doherty. *A dictionary of of Irish history since 1800.* Dublin: Gill and Macmillan, 1980.

Holohan, Paddy. 'The Four Courts area', *Capuchin Annual*, 1942, 231–7.

Hobson, Bulmer. *Ireland yesterday and tomorrow.* Dublin: Anvil Books, 1968.

Horikoshi, Tomo (ed.). *The political writings of James Connolly.* Tokyo: Gifu University, 1980.

Howard, L. G. Redmond-. *John Redmond: the man and the demand.* London: Hurst and Blackett, 1910.

Hughes, Brian. *16 lives: Michael Mallin.* Dublin: O'Brien Press, 2012.

Hunt, Hugh. *The Abbey: Ireland's national theatre 1904–1978.* Dublin: Gill and Macmillan, 1979.

Hyland, J. L. *James Connolly.* Dundalk: Historical Association of Ireland, 1997.

Inglis, Brian. *Roger Casement.* London: Hodder and Stoughton, 1973.

Jackson, Alvin. *Home rule: an Irish history, 1800–2000.* Oxford: Oxford University Press, 2003.

Jalland, Patricia. *The Liberals and Ireland: the Ulster question in British politics to 1914.* Brighton: Harvester Press, 1980.

Jeffery, Keith (ed.). *The Sinn Féin rebellion as they saw it.* Dublin: Irish Academic Press, 1999.

Johnstone, Robert Edgeworth-. *The Johnston(e)s of Magheramena and Laputa.* Privately published, 1972.

Jones, Mary. *These obstreperous lassies: a history of the Irish Women Workers' Union.* Dublin: Gill and Macmillan, 1988.

Jones, Thomas. *Whitehall diary*, iii. Oxford: Oxford University Press, 1970.

Jordan, Anthony J. *Major John MacBride, 1865–1916.* Westport, Co. Mayo: Westport Historical Society, 1991.

Jordan, Anthony J. *The Yeats–Gonne–MacBride triangle.* Dublin: Westport Books, 2000.

Keaney, Marian. *Westmeath authors: a bibliographical and biographical study*. Longford: Longford-Westmeath Joint Library Committee, 1969.

Kennelly, Brendan. 'The poetry of Joseph Plunkett', *Dublin Magazine* v, no. 1, spring 1966, 56–62.

Kiberd, Declan. *Inventing Ireland*. London: Jonathan Cape, 1995.

Kiberd, Declan. *Irish classics*. Cambridge, MA.: Harvard University Press, 2000.

Krause, David (ed.). *The letters of Sean O'Casey*, ii: *1942–54*. New York: Simon and Schuster, 1980.

Laffan, Michael. *The resurrection of Ireland: the Sinn Féin party, 1916–1923*. Cambridge: Cambridge University Press, 1999.

Laffan, Moira. *Count Plunkett and his times*. Foxrock, Dublin: Foxrock Local History Club, 1992.

Larkin, Emmet. *James Larkin: Irish labour leader, 1876–1947*. London: Pluto Press, 1989 (first published 1965).

Lee, H. W. and E. Archbold. *Social democracy in Britain*. London: Social Democratic Federation, 1935.

Lee, J. J. '"The canon of Irish history: a challenge" reconsidered', in Toner Quinn (ed.), *Desmond Fennell: his life and work*, 57–82. Dublin: Veritas, 2001.

Le Roux, Louis N. *Patrick H. Pearse*. Dublin: Talbot Press, 1932.

Le Roux, Louis N. *Tom Clarke and the Irish freedom movement*. Dublin: Talbot Press, 1936.

Levenson, Leah. *With wooden sword: a portrait of Francis Sheehy-Skeffington, militant pacifist*. Boston: Northeastern University Press, 1983.

Levenson, Samuel. *James Connolly: socialist, patriot and martyr*. London: Martin Brian and O'Keeffe, 1973.

Levitas, Ben. *The theatre of nation: Irish drama and cultural nationalism, 1890–1916*. Oxford: Oxford University Press, 2002.

Lynch, Diarmuid. *The IRB and the 1916 insurrection*. Cork: Mercier Press, 1957.

Lynch, Patrick. 'Introduction', in Desmond Ryan, *The Fenian chief: a biography of James Stephens*, xi–xxv. Dublin and Sydney: Gill and Son, 1967.

Lyons, F. S. L. *John Dillon: a biography*. Chicago: University of Chicago Press, 1969.

Lyons, J. B. *Brief lives of Irish doctors*. Dublin: Blackwater Press, 1978.

Macardle, Dorothy. *The Irish Republic* (reprinted 1968). London: Gollancz, 1937.

MacAtasney, Gerard. *Seán Mac Diarmada: the mind of the revolution*. Manorhamilton, Co. Leitrim: Drumlin Publications, 2004.

McCarthy, J. M. (ed.). *Limerick's fighting story*. Tralee: The Kerryman, 1949 (and later editions).

McCartney, Donal. *UCD: a national idea: the history of University College, Dublin.* Dublin: Gill and Macmillan, 1999.

McCoole, Sinéad. *Guns and chiffon: women revolutionaries and Kilmainham gaol: 1916–1923.* Dublin: Stationery Office, 1997.

McCoole, Sinéad. *No ordinary women: Irish female activists in the revolutionary years 1900–1923.* Dublin: O'Brien Press, 2003.

McCormack, W. J. *Roger Casement in death; or, Haunting the Free State.* Dublin: UCD Press, 2002.

McCoy, G. A. Hayes-. 'A military history of the 1916 rising', in Kevin B. Nowlan (ed.), *The making of 1916: studies in the history of the rising*, 255–338. Dublin: Stationery Office, 1969.

McCracken, Donal P. *MacBride's brigade: Irish commandos in the Anglo–Boer war.* Dublin: Four Courts Press, 1999.

Mac Curtain, Margaret. 'Women, the vote and revolution', in Margaret Mac Curtain and Donncha Ó Corráin (ed.), *Women in Irish society: the historical dimension*, 46–57. Dublin: Arlen House, 1978.

MacDonagh, Donagh. 'Thomas MacDonagh,' *An Cosantóir* v, no. 10, October 1945, 525–34.

MacDonagh, Donagh. 'Joseph Plunkett,' *An Cosantóir* v, no. 11, November 1945, 581–8.

MacDonagh, Donagh. 'Eamonn Ceannt', *An Cosantóir* vi, no. 10, October 1946, 509–16.

MacEoin, Uinseann (ed.). *Survivors: the story of Ireland's struggle.* Dublin: Argenta Publications, 1980.

MacEoin, Uinseann. *The IRA in the twilight years, 1923–1948.* Dublin: Argenta Publications, 1997.

McGarry, Milo. 'Memories of Sgoil Eanna', *Capuchin Annual*, 1930.

Mac Giolla Choille, Breandán (ed.). *Intelligence notes 1913–16.* Dublin: State Paper Office, 1966.

McHugh, Roger (ed.). *Dublin 1916: an illustrated anthology.* London: Arlington Books, 1966.

McHugh, Roger and Maurice Harmon. *A short history of Anglo-Irish literature from its origins to the present day.* Dublin: Wolfhound Press, 1982.

McKenna, Lambert. *The social teachings of James Connolly.* Dublin: Catholic Truth Society, 1920.

MacLochlainn, Piaras F. *Last words: letters and statements of the leaders executed after the rising at Easter 1916.* Dublin: Kilmainham Jail Restoration Society, 1971.

MacNeill, Eoin. *Shall Ireland be divided?* Dublin: Irish Volunteers Headquarters, 1915.

McRedmond, Louis (ed.). *Modern Irish lives: dictionary of 20th-century Irish biography.* Dublin: Gill and Macmillan, 1996.

Mansergh, Nicholas. *The unresolved question: the Anglo–Irish settlement and its undoing*. New Haven, CT: Yale University Press, 1991.

Marreco, Anne. *Rebel countess: the life and times of Countess Markievicz*. Philadelphia: Chilton Books, 1967.

Martin, F. X. (ed.). *The Irish Volunteers 1913–1915: recollections and documents*. Dublin: James Duffy, 1963.

Martin, F. X. *The Howth gun-running and the Kilcoole gun-running 1914: recollections and documents*. Dublin: Browne and Nolan, 1964.

Martin, F. X. (ed.). *The Easter rising, 1916 and University College Dublin*. Dublin: Browne and Nolan, 1966.

Martin, F. X. (ed.). *Leaders and men of the Easter rising: Dublin 1916*. London: Methuen, 1967.

Martin, F. X. '1916—myth, fact and mystery', *Studia Hibernica* vii, 1967, 72–3.

Martin, F. X. and F. J. Byrne (ed.) *The scholar revolutionary: Eoin MacNeill, 1867–1945, and the making of the new Ireland*. Shannon: Irish University Press, 1973.

Matthews, Ann. *Renegades: Irish republican women 1900–1922*. Cork: Mercier Press, 2010.

Matthews, Ann. *Dissidents: Irish republican women 1923–1941*. Cork: Mercier Press, 2012.

Maume, Patrick. *The long gestation: Irish nationalist life, 1891–1918*. Dublin: Gill and Macmillan, 1999.

Maume, Patrick. 'Anti-Machiavel: three Ulster nationalists of the age of de Valera', *Irish Political Studies* 14, no.1, 1999, 43–63.

Meenan, James (ed.). *Centenary history of the Literary and Historical Society 1855–1955*. Dublin: A&A Farmar, 2005 (revised edition, ed. Frank Callanan; originally published 1955).

Meleady, D. *Redmond: the Parnellite*. Cork: Cork University Press, 2008.

Meleady, D. *John Redmond: the national leader*. Dublin: Merrion Books, 2013.

Mitchell, Angus (ed.). *Sir Roger Casement's heart of darkness: the 1911 documents*. Dublin: Irish Manuscripts Commission, 2003.

Mitchell, Arthur. *Labour in Irish politics 1890–1930: the Irish labour movement in an age of revolution*. Dublin: Irish University Press, 1974.

Mitchell, Billy. 'Hobson's choice', *Fourthwrite* no. 2, summer 2000.

Morgan, Austen. *James Connolly: a political biography*. Manchester: Manchester University Press, 1988.

Murphy, Brian P. *Patrick Pearse and the lost republican ideal*. Dublin: James Duffy, 1991.

Murphy, Cliona. *The women's suffrage movement and Irish society in the early twentieth century*. New York and Hemel Hempstead: Harvester-Wheatsheaf, 1989.

National Graves Association. *The last post*. Dublin: National Graves Association, 1985.

Nevin, Donal. *Trade union century*. Cork: Mercier Press, 1994.

Nevin, Donal. *James Connolly: 'a full life'*. Dublin: Gill and Macmillan, 2005.

Ní Catháin, M. Proinséas. 'The academic and other writings of Rev. Professor Francis Shaw, SJ', *Studies* lx, no. 238, summer 1971, 203–7.

Ní Catháin, M. Proinséas. 'Francis Shaw S. J. (1907–1970)', *Studia Celtica* vii, 1972, 177.

Ní Éireamhoin, Eibhlín. *Two great Irish women: Maud Gonne MacBride and Countess Markievicz*. Dublin: C. J. Fallon, 1971.

Nic Shiubhlaigh, Maire. *The splendid years: recollections*. Dublin: James Duffy, 1955.

Norman, Diana. *Terrible beauty: a life of Countess Markievicz*. Dublin: Poolbeg, 1987.

Norstedt, Johann A. *Thomas MacDonagh: a critical biography*. Charlottesville, VA: University Press of Virginia, 1980.

Nowlan, Kevin B. 'Tom Clarke, MacDermott and the IRB', in F. X. Martin (ed.), *Leaders and men of the Easter rising: Dublin 1916*, 109–21. London: Methuen, 1967.

Nowlan, Kevin B. (ed.). *The making of 1916: studies in the history of the rising*. Dublin: Stationery Office, 1969.

Ó Briain, Liam. 'St Stephen's Green area', *Capuchin Annual*, 1966, 219–36.

O'Brien, Conor Cruise. *Memoir: my life and themes*. Dublin: Poolbeg Press, 1999.

O'Brien, Joseph V. *William O'Brien and the course of Irish politics, 1881–1918*. Berkeley and Los Angeles: University of California Press, 1976.

O'Brien, Nora C. *James Connolly: portrait of a rebel father*. Dublin: Talbot Press, 1935.

O'Brien, William. *Forth the banners go: reminiscences of William O'Brien*. Dublin: Three Candles Press, 1969.

O'Brien, William and Desmond Ryan (ed.). *Devoy's post bag 1871–1928, i: 1871–1880*. Dublin: C. J. Fallon, 1948.

Ó Broin, Léon. *Dublin Castle and the 1916 rising: the story of Sir Matthew Nathan*. Dublin: Helicon, 1966.

Ó Broin, Léon. *The chief secretary: Augustine Birrell in Ireland, 1907–16*. London: Chatto and Windus, 1969.

Ó Broin, Léon. *Revolutionary underground: the story of the Irish Republican Brotherhood, 1858–1924*. Totowa, NJ: Rowman and Littlefield, 1976.

Ó Broin, Léon. *W. E. Wylie and the Irish revolution, 1916–21*. Dublin: Gill and Macmillan, 1989.

Ó Buachalla, Séamas (ed.). *The letters of P. H. Pearse*, with a foreword by F. S. L. Lyons. Gerrards Cross: Colin Smythe, 1980.

Ó Buachalla, Séamas (ed.). *A significant Irish educationalist: the educational writings of P. H. Pearse*. Cork: Mercier Press, 1980.

O'Casey, Sean. *Autobiographies, i* (2nd ed.). London: Macmillan, 1992.

Ó Céirin, Kit and Cyril. *Women of Ireland: a biographic dictionary*. Kinvara, Co. Galway: Tír Eolas, 1996.

O'Connell, Thomas J. *History of the Irish National Teachers' Organisation 1868–1968.* Dublin: Irish National Teachers' Organisation, 1968.

O'Connor, Emmet. *Syndicalism in Ireland 1917–1923.* Cork: Cork University Press, 1988.

O'Donoghue, Florence. 'The Irish Volunteers in Cork, 1913–16', *Journal of the Cork Historical and Archaeological Society* lxxi, nos. 213–14, 1966, 41–8.

O'Donoghue, Florence. 'Ceannt, Devoy, O'Rahilly and the military plan', in F. X. Martin (ed.), *Leaders and men of the Easter rising: Dublin 1916*, 189–202. London: Methuen, 1967.

O Dúlaing, Donncha. *Voices of Ireland: conversations with Donncha O Dúlaing.* Dublin: O'Brien Press and RTÉ, 1984.

Ó Duibhir, Ciarán. *Sinn Féin: the first election 1908.* Manorhamilton, Co. Leitrim: Drumlin Publications, 1993.

O'Faolain, Sean. *Constance Markievicz.* London: Sphere Books, 1968 (originally published by Jonathan Cape, 1934).

O'Farrell, Elizabeth. 'Events of Easter week', *Catholic Bulletin* vii, 1917, 265–70, 329–34.

O'Farrell, Elizabeth. 'Recollections', *An Phoblacht*, 26 April, 31 May, 7 June 1926.

O'Farrell, Padraic. *Who's who in the Irish war of independence and civil war 1916–1923.* Dublin: Lilliput Press, 1997.

Ó Háinle, Cathal (eag.). *Gearrscéalta an Phiarsaigh.* Baile Átha Cliath: Helicon-Cló Thalbóid, 1979.

O'Halpin, Eunan. *The decline of the union: British government in Ireland, 1892–1920.* Dublin: Gill and Macmillan, 1987.

Ó hÓgartaigh, Margaret. *Dr Kathleen Lynn and maternal medicine.* Dublin: Rathmines, Ranelagh and Rathgar Historical Society, 2000.

Ó hÓgartaigh, Margaret. 'St Ultan's, a women's hospital for infants', *History Ireland* xiii, no. 4, July/August 2005, 36–9.

Ó hÓgartaigh, Margaret. *Kathleen Lynn, Irishwoman, patriot, doctor.* Dublin: Irish Academic Press, 2006.

O'Leary, Philip. *Gaelic prose in the Irish Free State 1922–1939.* Dublin: University College Dublin Press, 2004.

O'Mahony, Sean. *Frongoch: university of revolution.* Dublin: FDR Teoranta, 1987.

O'Neill, Marie. *Grace Gifford Plunkett and Irish freedom: tragic bride of 1916.* Dublin: Irish Academic Press, 2000.

O'Rahilly, Aodhagan. *Winding the clock: the O'Rahilly and the 1916 rising.* Dublin: Lilliput Press, 1991.

O'Rahilly, Michael Joseph. *The secret history of the Irish Volunteers.* Dublin: Irish Publicity League, 1915.

Ó Riordáin, Tomás. *Where martyred heroes rest: the story of the republican plot, Kilcrumper, Fermoy.* Fermoy, Co. Cork: Liam Lynch National Commemoration Committee, 1987.

O'Shannon, Cathal. 'Winifred Carney—a link with Easter week', *Torch* (Dublin), 27 November, 4 December, 1943.

Ó Siocháin, Seamas and Michael O'Sullivan (ed.). *The eyes of another race: Roger Casement's Congo report and 1903 diary*. Dublin: University College Dublin Press, 2003.

Ó Snodaigh, Pádraig. *Two godfathers of revisionism: 1916 in the revisionist canon*. Dublin: Fulcrum Press, 1991.

O'Sullivan, Seán. 'Portrait drawing of S. Mac Diarmada', *Capuchin Annual*, 1966, 156–7, 170–8, 302–3.

Pakenham, Thomas. *The Boer war*. London: Weidenfeld and Nicholson, 1979.

Patterson, Henry. *Class conflict and sectarianism: the Protestant working class and the Belfast labour movement, 1868–1920*. Belfast: Blackstaff Press, 1980.

Parks, Edd Winfield and Aileen Wells Parks. *Thomas MacDonagh: the man, the patriot, the writer*. Athens, GA: University of Georgia Press, 1967.

Pearse, Margaret M. 'St Enda's', *Capuchin Annual*, 1942, 227–30.

Pearse, Margaret M. 'Patrick and Willie Pearse', *Capuchin Annual*, 1943, 86–8.

Pearse, Mary Brigid. *The home life of Patrick Pearse*. Dublin: Nolan Press, 1934.

Pearse, Pádraic H. *Collected works*, i: *Plays, stories, poems*. Dublin: Talbot Press, 1917.

Pearse, Pádraic H. *Collected works*, ii: *Songs of the Irish rebels; Specimens from an Irish anthology; Some aspects of Irish literature; Three lectures on Gaelic topics*. Dublin: Maunsel and Co., 1917/18 (reprinted 1924).

Pearse, Pádraic H. *Collected works*, iii: *Political writings and speeches*. Dublin: Maunsel and Roberts, 1922 (reprinted 1966).

Perkins, Sarah Ward- (ed.). *Select guide to trade union records in Dublin*. Dublin: Irish Manuscripts Commission, 1996.

Plunkett, Geraldine (ed.). 'Foreword', in *The poems of Joseph Mary Plunkett*, vii–xvi. Dublin: Talbot Press, 1916.

Porter, Raymond J. *P. H. Pearse*. New York: Twayne Publishers, 1973.

Power, Patrick. J. 'The Kents and their fight for freedom', in *Rebel Cork's fighting story 1916–21*, 59–64. Tralee: The Kerryman, 1947 (reprinted Cork: Anvil Books, 1961, pp 33–8; and Cork: Mercier Press, 2009, pp 106–13).

Ransom, Bernard. *Connolly's Marxism*. London: Pluto Press, 1980.

Reeve, Carl and Ann Barton Reeve. *James Connolly and the United States: the road to the 1916 Irish rebellion*. Atlantic Highlands, New Jersey: Humanities Press, 1978.

Regan, John M. *The Irish counter-revolution 1921–1936: treatyite politics and settlement in independent Ireland*. Dublin: Gill and Macmillan, 1999.

Regan, Nell. 'Helena Molony (1883–1967)', in Mary Cullen and Maria Luddy (ed.), *Female activists: Irish women and change 1900–1960*, 141–68. Dublin: Woodfield Press, 2001.

Reid, B. L. *The lives of Roger Casement*. New Haven, CT: Yale University Press, 1976.

Robbins, Frank. *Under the starry plough: recollections of the Irish Citizen Army*. Dublin: Academy Press, 1977.

Robinson, Lennox. *Ireland's Abbey Theatre: a history 1899–1951*. London: Sidgwick and Jackson, 1951.

Rockett, Kevin. *The Irish filmography: fiction films 1896–1966*. Dublin: Red Mountain Press, 1996.

Ryan, Desmond. *James Connolly: his life, work and writings*. Dublin and London: Talbot Press and Labour Publishing Company Ltd, 1924.

Ryan, Desmond. *The man called Pearse*. Dublin: Maunsel and Co., 1923 (originally published 1919).

Ryan, Desmond. *Remembering Sion*. London: Arthur Blake, 1934.

Ryan, Desmond. 'Stephens, Devoy, Tom Clarke', *University Review* i, no. 12, 1937, 46–55.

Ryan, Desmond. 'Margaret Pearse', *Capuchin Annual*, 1942, 312–18.

Ryan, Desmond. *The rising: the complete story of Easter week*. Dublin: Golden Eagle Books, 1949.

Ryan, William P. *The Irish labour movement from the 'twenties to our own day*. Dublin: Talbot Press, 1919.

Sawyer, Roger. *Casement, the flawed hero*. London: Routledge and Kegan Paul, 1984.

Shannon, Martin. *Sixteen roads to Golgotha*. Dublin: Red Hand Books, 1966.

Shaw, Francis. 'MacNeill the person', in F. X. Martin and F. J. Byrne (ed.), *The scholar revolutionary: Eoin MacNeill, 1867–1945, and the making of the new Ireland*, 299–311 (note on contributor, 300). Shannon: Irish University Press, 1973.

Shaw, Francis. *Lochlann*, vi [supplement to *Norsk Tidskrift for Sprogvidenskap*, xi], 1974, 180–1.

Sheehan, Tim. *Lady hostage: Mrs Lindsey*. Dripsey, Co. Cork, 1990 (reprinted Cork: Lee Press Ltd, 2008).

Sisson, Elaine. *Pearse's patriots: St Enda's and the cult of boyhood*. Cork: Cork University Press, 2004.

Skeffington, Andrée Sheehy. *Skeff: a life of Owen Sheehy Skeffington 1909–1970*. Dublin: Lilliput Press, 1991.

Skeffington, Francis Sheehy-. *In dark and evil days*, with a biographical preface by Hanna Sheehy-Skeffington. Dublin: J. Duffy and Co., 1916.

Skinnider, Margaret. *Doing my bit for Ireland*. New York: Century Co., 1917.

Smyth, Hazel. 'Kathleen Lynn MD, FRCSI (1874–1955)', *Dublin Historical Record* xxx, no. 2, March 1977, 51–7.

Snoddy, Theo. *Dictionary of Irish artists: 20th century*. Dublin: Merlin Publishing, 2002 (originally published 1996).

Taillon, Ruth. *The women of 1916: when history was made*. Belfast: Beyond the Pale Publications, 1996.

Taylor, James W. *The 2nd Royal Irish Rifles in the great war*. Dublin: Four Courts Press, 2005.

Tierney, Michael. *Eoin MacNeill: scholar and man of action, 1867–1945*, ed. F. X. Martin. Oxford: Clarendon Press, 1980.

Townshend, Charles. *Political violence in Ireland: government and resistance since 1848*. Oxford: Clarendon Press, 1983.

Townshend, Charles. *Easter 1916: the Irish rebellion*. London: Penguin, 2005.

Tracy, Alice. 'Michael O'Hanrahan', *Carliovana* i, December 1963, 12–13, 38–9.

Travers, Charles J. 'Sean Mac Diarmada 1883–1916', *Breifne* iii, no. 9, 1966, 1–46.

Uí Chollatáin, Regina. *An Claidheamh Soluis agus Fáinne an Lae 1899–1932: anailís ar phríomhnuachtán Gaeilge ré na hAthbheochana*. Baile Átha Cliath: Cois Life, 2004.

Urquart, Diane. *Women in Ulster politics, 1890–1940*. Dublin: Irish Academic Press, 2000.

Van Voris, Jacqueline. *Constance de Markievicz: in the cause of Ireland*. Amherst: University of Massachusetts Press, 1967.

Ward, Margaret. *Unmanageable revolutionaries: women and Irish nationalism*. London: Pluto Press, 1983.

Ward, Margaret. *Maud Gonne: Ireland's Joan of Arc*. London: Pandora Press, 1990.

Ward, Margaret. *In their own voice: women and Irish nationalism*. Cork: Attic Press, 1995.

Ward, Margaret. 'The League of Women Delegates and Sinn Féin 1917', *History Ireland* iv, no. 3, autumn 1996, 37–41.

Ward, Margaret. *Hanna Sheehy-Skeffington: a life*. Cork: Attic Press, 1997.

Wheatley, Michael. *Nationalism and the Irish party: provincial Ireland 1910–1916*. Oxford: Oxford University Press, 2005.

Williams, Roche. *In and out of school: in the home of the MacDonaghs*. Nenagh, Co. Tipperary: Nenagh Guardian, 1999.

Woggon, Helga. *Silent radical, Winifred Carney 1887–1943: a reconstruction of her autobiography* (Studies in Irish Labour History, no. 6). Dublin: Irish Labour History Society, 2000.

Yeates, Pádraig. *Lockout: Dublin 1913*. Dublin: Gill and Macmillan, 2000.

INDEX

Note: page references in **bold** denote principal entries.

P

Y

Z